Praise for

ANATOMY OF THE SPIRIT

"When I had read only the first two chapters of *Anatomy of the Spirit*, I found my work and my worldview profoundly changed and brought into focus in a new way. Myss's information hits the reader right between the eyes with its powerful message about the undeniable link between our spirits and our biology and holds the key to healing our lives on all levels. Caroline Myss has distilled the wisdom of the ages into a health care system for the new millennium."   —Christiane Northrup, M.D., author of
Women's Bodies, Women's Wisdom

"There is much here that makes sense . . . everyone interested in holistic health will want to read what Myss has to say."   —*Booklist*

"One of the hottest new voices in the alternative health/spirituality scene . . . There's wisdom here, in words that eschew New Age jargon and that make otherwise esoteric material accessible to a general readership. This book has breakout potential."   —*Publishers Weekly*

"An exceptionally brilliant and practical model of personal power."
—*The Macon Telegraph*

"A thorough and intriguing contribution to the literature of holistic healing."
—*Body, Mind, Spirit*

"Caroline Myss is a brilliant teacher, and I am honored to endorse her new book, *Anatomy of the Spirit*. It will further clarify your mind/body connection."   —Louise L. Hay, author of *You Can Heal Your Life*

"A vision most often can be brought to life only if lived as deeply and as truly as one is able, and over many years' time. The work of Caroline Myss derives from the latter. Through decades of strong focus and strong living, she has brought forth a deeply insightful work that offers meaning on many levels, each one intense, spirited, and useful. *Anatomy of the Spirit* is a rare undertaking by a completely original thinker."
—Clarissa Pinkola Estés, Ph.D., author of
Women Who Run with the Wolves; The Gift of Story;
and *The Faithful Gardener*

Anatomy of the Spirit

The Seven Stages
of Power and Healing

Caroline Myss, Ph.D.

THREE RIVERS PRESS • NEW YORK

Copyright © 1996 by Caroline Myss
Foreword copyright © 1996 by Crown Publishers, Inc.
All rights reserved. No part of this book may be reproduced or transmitted in any form or by any means, electronic or mechanical, including photocopying, recording, or by any information storage and retrieval system, without permission in writing from the publisher.

Grateful acknowledgment is made to Princeton University Press for permission to reprint "Seven Power Centers or Chakras of the Kundalini System" from *Mythic Image* by Joseph Campbell. Copyright © 1974 by Princeton University Press. Reprinted by permission of Princeton University Press.

Published by Three Rivers Press, New York, New York.
Member of the Crown Publishing Group.

Random House, Inc. New York, Toronto, London, Sydney, Auckland

www.randomhouse.com

THREE RIVERS PRESS is a registered trademark and the Three Rivers Press colophon is a trademark of Random House, Inc.

Originally published in hardcover by Harmony Books, a division of Crown Publishers, in 1996.

Printed in the United States of America

Library of Congress Catalog Card Number 96-220328

ISBN 0-609-80014-0

35 34 33 32

*This book is dedicated with boundless love and gratitude to
my three personal angels,
without whom I could never have survived
the darkest times of my life:
my mother, who is my constant source of strength;
my brother, Edward,
who is my continual source of humor and optimism;
and my sister-in-law, Amy,
who has become a family treasure.*

Contents

Foreword

On rare occasions, you may meet a unique person who dramatically alters your perceptions of the world and of yourself. You are about to meet just such an extraordinary individual. Author and medical intuitive Caroline Myss will intrigue, provoke, and inspire you with her views on spirituality and your personal responsibility for your own health. Some aspects of Caroline's work will seem so commonsensical to you that you will wonder why you hadn't thought of them that way before. Other ideas of hers will push your emotional and psychological buttons and cause you to reevaluate your spiritual path.

I was introduced to Caroline's philosophy a dozen years ago. Her simple, powerful message is that each of us is born with an inherent spiritual task, a sacred contract to learn to use our personal power responsibly, wisely, and lovingly. For thousands of years, the concept that power corrupts and absolute power corrupts absolutely has dominated society. Authority and control, money and sex have provided the artificial trappings of power. A recent magazine article featuring John F. Kennedy, Jr., for instance, emphasized that he had had more than adequate money and sexual security but no power. The article then trivialized power by extending the popular illusion that JFK Jr. could somehow buy power by publishing a jet-set magazine. If this is your own idea of power, be prepared to be shaken deeply by

Anatomy of the Spirit, for Caroline offers a much deeper vision of true power—the power of the human spirit.

There have been, throughout the ages, talented intuitives and mystics who have sensed the power centers of the human body. Alice Bailey, Charles W. Leadbetter, and Rudolf Steiner have all written in this field, but no one has captured the breadth and depth of our electromagnetic spiritual framework as well as Caroline. Never before has the anatomy of the spirit been so powerfully revealed. Herein lies the foundation for medicine of the twenty-first century.

The single most important question that people have asked throughout history has been "What is my purpose in life?" Caroline answers this question simply and profoundly. One's purpose is to live in a manner that is consistent with one's spiritual ideals, to live the Golden Rule every moment of one's life, and to live every thought as a sacred prayer. It is simple—but far from easy!

Imagine for one moment that you have entered a room filled with people, and that you know instantly how uncomfortable you feel. Imagine further that you can tune in to the chatter inside each person's subconscious, that you "know" the energy and health of each individual in the room. Even more important, imagine that you know in detail about your own energy and about every factor that is draining your intellectual, physical, and emotional power. The basic wisdom transmitted in this book gives you the tools to begin to see your own and others' energy.

Quantum physicists have confirmed the reality of the basic vibratory essence of life, which is what intuitives sense. Human DNA vibrates at a rate of 52 to 78 gigahertz (billions of cycles per second). Although scientific instruments cannot yet evaluate any one person's specific frequency or the blocks to the flow of such energy, two basic facts cannot be denied. First, life energy is not static; it is kinetic; it moves around. And second, talented intuitives such as Caroline can evaluate it, even though neither the human mind nor the energy system can yet be accurately physically measured. Indeed, in my twenty-five years of work with intuitives throughout the world, none has been as clear or accurate as Caroline.

Caroline tunes in to the subtle energy of our systems and reads the language of our electromagnetic being. Her diagnoses repeatedly document the effects of emotional energy, past and present, on physical health; she senses deep and traumatic experiences, beliefs, and attitudes that alter the frequencies of cells and the integrity of our energy system. She reads our spirits, which are ultimately our true power.

In this book you will find detailed information on the seven power centers of your body. These centers are critical regulators of the flow of life energy. They represent the major biological batteries of your emotional biography. "Your biography becomes your biology"—if you learn nothing else from this work, this fact alone will be useful to you. You will also learn how to avoid being sapped or zapped by your own attachments or by other people's negative energy; how to secure your sense of self and honor so that your personal power base is not eroded by the false symbols of power—money, sex, and external authority; and how to develop your own intuitive abilities.

The Anatomy of the Spirit presents an exciting new ecumenical way to understand the seven energy centers of the body. It integrates Judaic, Christian, Hindu, and Buddhist concepts of power into seven universal spiritual truths. As Caroline writes, "The universal jewel within the four major religions is that the Divine is locked into our biological system in seven stages of power that lead us to become more refined and transcendent in our personal power."

You will be transformed forever by the power of this merging of the metaphysical meaning of the Christian sacraments, the Kabbalah, and the chakras. Knowledge is power, and the knowledge presented in this book is the key to personal power.

This book presents the essence of alternative medicine, with a clarity that will inspire you to live your spiritual ideals and that will awaken you to the miracles of self-healing. I am delighted to have been present during the long gestation of this seminal work. My life has been enriched by this knowledge beyond my dreams. May yours be equally graced by Caroline's wisdom.

C. Norman Shealy, M.D., Ph.D.
Founder, Shealy Institute for Comprehensive Health Care
Founding President, American Holistic Medical Association
Research and Clinical Professor of Psychology,
Forest Institute of Professional Psychology
Author of *Miracles Do Happen*

God be in my head and in my understanding
God be in my eyes and in my looking
God be in my mouth and in my speaking
God be in my tongue and in my tasting
God be in my lips and in my greeting

God be in my nose and in my smelling/inhaling
God be in my ears and in my hearing
God be in my neck and in my humbling
God be in my shoulders and in my bearing
God be in my back and in my standing

God be in my arms and in my reaching/receiving
God be in my hands and in my working
God be in my legs and in my walking
God be in my feet and in my grounding
God be in my joints and in my relating

God be in my guts and in my feeling
God be in my bowels and in my forgiving
God be in my loins and in my swiving
God be in my lungs and in my breathing
God be in my heart and in my loving

God be in my skin and in my touching
God be in my flesh and in my paining/pining
God be in my blood and in my living
God be in my bones and in my dying
God be at my end and at my reviving

Extended from the traditional prayer by Reverend Jim Cotter
and printed in his book *Prayer at Night*, Cairns Publications,
Sheffield, England, 1988.

Preface:
Becoming Medically Intuitive

In the autumn of 1982, after ending my career as a newspaper journalist and obtaining a master's degree in theology, I joined forces with two partners to start a book publishing company called Stillpoint. We published books about healing methods that were alternatives to establishment medicine. Despite my business interest in alternative therapies, however, I wasn't the least bit interested in becoming personally involved in them. I had no desire to meet any healers myself. I refused to meditate. I developed an absolute aversion to wind chimes, New Age music, and conversations on the benefits of organic gardening. I smoked while drinking coffee by the gallon, still fashioning myself after an image of a hard-boiled newspaper reporter. I was not at all primed for a mystical experience.

Nonetheless, that same autumn, I gradually recognized that my perceptual abilities had expanded considerably. For instance, a friend would mention that someone he knew was not feeling well, and an insight into the cause of the problem would pop into my head. I was uncannily accurate, and word of it spread through the local community. Soon people were phoning the publishing company to make appointments for an intuitive assessment of their health. By the spring of 1983 I was doing readings for people who were in health crises and life crises of various kinds, from depression to cancer.

To say I was in a fog would be a gross understatement. I was confused and a little scared. I could not figure out how I was getting these impressions. They were, and still are, like impersonal daydreams that start to flow as soon as I receive a person's permission, name, and age. Their impersonality, the nonfeeling sensation of the impressions, is extremely significant because it is my indicator that I am not manufacturing or projecting these impressions. It's like the difference between looking through a stranger's photograph album, in which you have emotional attachments to no one, and looking through your own family's photo album. The impressions are clear but completely unemotional.

Because I also didn't know how accurate my impressions were, after a couple months of consultations I found myself dreading each appointment intensely, feeling each was a high-risk experience. I got through the first six months only by telling myself that using my medical intuition was a bit of a game. I got excited when I made an accurate "hit" because, if nothing else, an accurate hit meant my sanity was intact. Even so, each time I wondered: "Will 'it' work this time? What if no impressions show up? What if I'm wrong about something? What if someone asks me something I can't answer? What if I tell someone she's healthy, only to learn later that she's had a terminal diagnosis? And above all, what's a journalist-theological-student-turned-publisher doing in this borderline occupation in the first place?"

I felt as if I were suddenly responsible for explaining the will of God to dozens of sad, frightened people, without any training. Ironically, the more these folks wanted insight into what God was doing to them, the more I wanted insight into what God was doing to me. The pressure I felt finally resulted in years of migraine headaches.

I wanted to carry on as if my emerging skill were no different from a talent for baking, but I knew better. Having grown up Catholic and studied theology, I was keenly aware that transpersonal abilities lead one inevitably to the monastery—or to the madhouse. Deep in my soul, I knew that I was connecting with something that was essentially sacred, and that knowledge was splitting me in two. On the one hand, I feared that I would become incapacitated, like mystics of old; on the other, I felt destined for a life in which I would be evaluated and judged by believers and skeptics. No matter how I envisioned my future, however, I felt I was headed for misery.

But I was fascinated by my newfound perceptual ability, nonetheless, and was compelled to keep on evaluating people's health. In these early days the impressions I received were mainly of a person's immediate physical health and the related emotional or psychological stress. But I could also *see* the energy surrounding that person's body. I saw it filled with information about that person's history. And I saw that energy as an extension of that person's spirit. I began to realize something I had never been taught in school: that our spirit is very much a part of our daily lives; it embodies our thoughts and emotions, and it records every one of them, from the most mundane to the visionary. Although I had been taught, more or less, that our spirit goes either "up" or "down" after death, depending upon how virtuously we have lived, I now saw that our spirit is more than that. It participates in every second of our lives. It is the conscious force that is life itself.

I carried on with my health readings on a sort of automatic pilot, until one day my ambivalence toward my skill was resolved. I was in the middle of a session with a woman who had cancer. The day was hot, and I was tired. The woman and I sat facing each other in my small office at Stillpoint. I had completed her evaluation and was hesitating for a moment before sharing it with her. I dreaded telling her that the cancer had spread throughout her body. I knew she was going to ask me why this catastrophe had happened to her, and I felt irritated by my responsibility of answering her. Sure enough, as I opened my mouth to speak, she reached over, put her hand on my leg, and asked, "Caroline, I know I have a serious cancer. Can't you tell me why this is happening to me?"

My indignation rose to meet the hated question, and I almost snapped, "How would I know?"—when suddenly I was flushed with an energy I had never felt before. It moved through my body, as if it were pushing me aside in order to make use of my vocal cords. I could no longer see the woman in front of me. I felt as if I had been shrunk down to the size of a dime and ordered to "stand watch" from inside my head.

A voice spoke through me to this woman. "Let me walk you back through your life and through each of the relationships of your life," it said. "Let me walk with you through all the fears you've had, and let me show you how those fears controlled you for so long that the energy of life could no longer nurture you."

This "presence" escorted this woman through every detail of her life, and I mean *every detail*. It recalled the smallest of conversations for her; it recounted moments of great loneliness in which she had wept by herself; it remembered every relationship that had held any meaning for her. This "presence" left the impression that every second of our lives—and every mental, emotional, creative, physical, and even resting activity with which we fill those seconds—is somehow known and recorded. Every judgment we make is noted. Every attitude we hold is a source of positive or negative power for which we are accountable.

I was awestruck by this experience. From the sidelines I began to pray, half out of fear and half out of humility in facing the intimate and ultimate design of the universe. I had always assumed that our prayers are "heard," but I had never been quite sure how. Nor had I figured with my simple human reasoning how any system, even a Divine one, could keep track of everyone's needs, giving requests for healing priority over, say, requests for financial assistance. I was unprepared for this sacred spectacle in which every second of life is lovingly held to be of great value.

As I prayed, still only an observer, I asked that this woman remain completely unaware that it was not I who was speaking to her. Since I couldn't have answered her question "Why do I have cancer?" I also couldn't have explained how I knew details about her past. As soon as I released that prayer, I was again looking directly into her face.

I found that my hand was on her knee, mirroring her reaching out to me, although I had no recollection of having put it there.

My entire body was trembling, and I removed my hand. All she said was, "Thank you so much. I can live with everything now." She paused, then continued, "Even my death doesn't scare me. Everything is just fine."

She left my office, and a moment later so did I, in a profoundly shaken state. I walked into a beautiful open field that surrounded Stillpoint, and I agreed to cooperate with this intuitive ability, no matter the outcome.

Since that autumn day in 1983, I have worked wholeheartedly as a medical intuitive. This means that I use my intuitive ability to help people understand the emotional, psychological, and spiritual energy that lies at the root of their illness, dis-ease, or life crisis. I can sense the type of illness that has developed, often before the individual is even aware of having an illness at all. The people I work with usually are aware, however, that their lives are not in balance and that something is wrong.

No dramatic "first event" ushered my intuitive abilities into my life. They simply woke up inside me, easily, naturally, as if they had always been there, awaiting the appropriate time to emerge. When I was growing up, I had always been alert intuitively, reacting continually to my gut instincts, as most people do. You, too, instinctively and sometimes consciously evaluate other people's energies, but usually you know that person or have had at least some contact with them before. What's unusual about my intuition is that I can evaluate people with whom I've had no contact whatsoever. In fact, I prefer to have had no previous contact, because looking directly into a frightened face interferes enormously with my ability to "see" clearly.

The more I have used my intuition, the more accurate it has become. Now it feels almost ordinary to me, although its workings will always remain a little mysterious. While I can teach you up to a certain point about how to become intuitive, I'm actually not quite sure how I learned it myself. I suspect that I became extremely intuitive as a consequence of my curiosity about spiritual matters, combined with a deep frustration I felt when my life didn't unfold according to plan. On the other hand, it's equally possible that my medical intuition was simply the result of something I ate. Knowing how the gods work, I would not find it surprising in the least.

It was not easy, even after pledging to cooperate with it, to perfect my intuitions. I had no models and no teacher, although eventually I had the support and guidance of medical colleagues. Now, however, after fourteen years of continuous work, the skill feels like a sixth sense to me. This means to me that it's time for me to teach others about the language of energy and medical intuition.

By working with my intuitions, I have identified the emotional and psychological causes of illness. Unquestionably, a strong link exists between physical and emotional stresses and specific illnesses. This connection has been well documented, for instance, with regard to heart disease and hypertension and the so-called type A personality. My particular insights, however, have shown me that emotional *and spiritual* stresses or dis-eases are the root causes of *all* physical illnesses. Moreover, certain emotional and spiritual crises correspond quite specifically to problems in certain parts of the body. For instance, people who come to me with heart disease have had life experiences that led them to block out intimacy or love from their lives. People with low back pain have had persistent financial worries; people with cancer often have unresolved connections with the past, unfinished business and emotional issues; people with blood disorders frequently have deep-seated conflicts with their families of origin. The more I studied the human energy system, the more I realized that very little is created "randomly" in our bodies or, for that matter, in our lives. The links between our emotional and spiritual stresses and specific illnesses are best understood in the context of the anatomy of the human energy system—the anatomy of our own spirits—which is the nucleus of the material that I now teach throughout the United States and in many other countries, and the focus of this book.

Being medically intuitive has helped me learn not only about the energy causes of disease but about the challenges we face in healing ourselves. Of great significance to me was the realization that "healing" does not always mean that the physical body recovers from an illness. Healing can also mean that one's spirit has released long-held fears and negative thoughts toward oneself or others. This kind of spiritual release and healing can occur even though one's body may be dying physically.

Learning the language of the human energy system is a means to self-understanding, a way through your spiritual challenges. By studying energy anatomy, you will identify the patterns of your life and the deep interworkings of your mind, body, and spirit. This self-knowledge can bring you pleasure and peace of mind and lead to emotional and physical healing, along the way.

This introduction to medical intuition is the summation of my fourteen years of research into anatomy and intuition, body and mind, spirit and power. In its pages I teach you the language of energy with which I work. By gaining a fluent knowledge of energy anatomy, you will also become aware of your body as the manifestation of your own spirit. You will be able to read your own body like a scripture. Understanding the language of energy enables you to see your own spirit in your body and to understand what generates it and makes it—and you—strong. The language of energy will give you a new view of your personal power. You will also learn what weakens your spirit and personal power so that you can stop further loss of energy. Using the language of energy and understanding the human energy system will help you have clearer intuitive impressions by giving you body-based, concrete referents that take the edge off the sensation that you are looking blindly into empty air for information.

In this book, I draw on the deep, abiding, ancient wisdom of several spiritual traditions—the Hindu chakras, the Christian sacra-

ments, and the Kabbalah's Tree of Life—to present a new view of
how body and spirit work together. Please note that I have deliberately not included the rich teachings of Islam, not because I do not
honor its truths, but because I have not lived with the tradition as I
have with Judeo-Christian, Hindu, and Buddhist teachings. Therefore, I do not feel that I can write about Islam with any integrity. By
learning to see your body and spirit in a way that draws on old truths,
you can begin to develop your own intuition and to understand and
manage your own spirit.

While I had originally intended to focus this book "simply" on
the human energy system, on the philosophy and practices of energy
diagnosis, and on medical intuition, I realized as I began writing that
I could not accurately portray these energy concepts without this
spiritual framework. I believe we are meant to understand our body-
minds as individual spiritual powers expressive of a greater Divine
energy. We are meant to discover both our personal power and our
shared purpose for being alive within a spiritual context.

We all share a type of physical body that becomes ill or heals for
the same reasons. We also share emotional and psychological crises
common to the human experience. Everyone fears abandonment,
loss, and betrayal; anger is as toxic within a Jewish body as it is
within a Christian or Hindu body; and we are all drawn to love.
When it comes to the health of our spirits and our bodies, we have
no differences.

Thus the mind-body focus of this book is infused with the spiritual language of *symbolic sight*. Symbolic sight is a way of seeing and
understanding yourself, other people, and life events in terms of universal archetypal patterns. Developing symbolic sight will enhance
your intuitive ability because it will teach you a healthy objectivity
that brings out the symbolic meaning of events, people, and challenges, most especially perhaps the painful challenge of illness. Symbolic sight lets you see into your spirit and your limitless potential for
healing and wholeness.

The people who attend my lectures and workshops are diverse:

they are health professionals, or people seeking assistance with their own health, or people who wish to become medically intuitive. Yet they all share in common a desire to understand the power of their spirits. They want to develop an internal clarity, their own intuitive voice. The physicians who fill my workshops share with me their frustrations that when they get a hunch that an emotional or even spiritual cause underlies a patient's illness, they are not at liberty to make a spiritual diagnosis because spiritual ideas have no authority within conventional science. Many physicians withhold their intuitive impressions because, as one put it, "hunch and proof are not yet compatible with the requirements of health insurance companies." Another physician told me, "I don't need medical intuition. I have enough of that. I want to learn about the family patterns and the deeper spiritual issues of my patients, because I know that's the information they need to heal. They need more than drugs, which only temporarily mask their symptoms." The desire for a spiritual context and interpretation of life is universal. I believe that the language of energy and the practice of symbolic sight can help bridge the gap between conventional medical and spiritual views of health and healing.

Nonetheless, when I first began intuiting the presence of illness, as I mentioned earlier, I was frightened and disturbed by my own lack of medical and spiritual context. So for the first two years, I held back much of the information that I sensed. I limited my assistance to helping people interpret the emotional, psychological, and spiritual stresses and factors underlying the development of their illness. I did not discuss specific medical treatments or surgical procedures but instead referred clients to physicians. In 1984, however, I met C. Norman Shealy, M.D., Ph.D. I began intensive training with him in the physical anatomy of the human body. By speaking to and through Norm to patients about their lives and illness, I was able to refine my understanding of the impressions I received. This gave me the comfort zone I needed to permit my skill to mature, although I still do not treat clients and only try to

help them interpret the spiritual issues at the root of their emotional or physical crisis.

Through my years of working with Norm, who became my medical colleague and dear friend, I learned that my skill is of most value
in the stages before a physical illness actually develops. Before the
body produces a physical illness, energy indicators, such as prolonged lethargy and depression, tell us we are losing our vitality. People in such stages seek the advice of their physicians because they
know they aren't feeling well—they are picking up signals that their
bodies are losing energy. Frequently, however, medical tests indicate
that nothing is wrong because they cannot yet identify anything happening at the physical level. Conventional medical tests have no way
of measuring energy loss, and most physicians do not give credence
to the idea of energy dysfunction. Yet new, perplexing diseases that
do not respond to conventional medical treatments are emerging
continually. Some of them, like AIDS, can be diagnosed through
conventional medical methodology, while others seem to develop as
a result of the high-voltage pace of our lives and our constant exposure to electromagnetic energy from computers, satellite dishes, cellular phones, and the many other devices with which we are
overloading our environment. Illnesses such as chronic fatigue syn-
drome and environmental disorders, at present, are "unofficial" illnesses; according to conventional medical standards, they lack an
identifiable microbial cause. Yet they are most certainly official illnesses within the energy definition of a health dysfunction, because
their symptoms indicate that the patient is experiencing a loss of
power in the energy field.

Medical intuition can help physicians who understand the human
body to be both a physical system and an energy system, who have a
spiritual context for the human experience, to identify the energy
state of a physical illness and treat the underlying cause as well as the
symptoms. Treatment in the energy field can include an array of
therapies, such as psychological counseling, acupuncture, massage,

and homeopathy. The essential ingredient for energy healing remains, however, the active involvement of the patient. No matter how urgently a medical intuitive warns of the probability of an illness, warnings do not heal. Action does.

Nothing would please me more than to transmit my own intuitive skill to you immediately through my books and workshops. But it is only through years of practice that you will fully develop your own intuitions. The "intuitive residency" I did with Norm, a Harvard-educated neurosurgeon and founder of the American Holistic Medical Association, gave me my ability to work as a professional. Anyone can benefit from following the teachings in this book and improve one's intuitive clarity, but because a residency program is so essential to developing intuition fully, in the near future Norm and I intend to help medically intuitive students do their residency programs at holistic health centers throughout the country. Norm and I hold a program on the science of intuition at his farm in Springfield, Missouri, which is aimed at teaching people to use intuition as a normal part of their perceptual skills.

The idea of a medical intuitive residency program would have seemed fairly outrageous a decade ago, yet as a society we have since become more and more open to medical treatments that use the ancient knowledge of energy flow in and around the human body, including acupuncture, acupressure, and chi kung, among others. As Larry Dossey, M.D., writes in *Meaning and Medicine*, we need to practice "Era III Medicine"—therapies that combine spiritual and physical, holistic and allopathic approaches to physical and emotional healing. I cannot help feeling that medical intuitives will eventually become essential members of health care teams, both in this country and around the world.

The conventional medical world is on the brink of recognizing the link between energy or spiritual dysfunction and illness. It is inevitable that it will someday cross the divide between body and spirit, but in the meantime we can help ourselves by building our own bridges to our spirit by learning the language of energy and the skill of symbolic sight. Through this book I hope that you will learn to think of yourself in the language of energy as vividly as you now see your physical body, and that you will begin to care for your spirit as consciously as you now care for your physical body.

Introduction:
A Brief Personal History

As I say to people attending my workshops and my lectures: I am taking you into the world that exists "behind my eyes." But if I first tell you about the series of wake-up calls that led to my own perspective, if I first introduce you to the many different people and events that over the years directed me toward becoming a medical intuitive, you may become more aware of the inner guidance at work in your own life.

Turning Points

Everything that has professional, personal, and spiritual value for me, I have learned through my work as a medical intuitive. As a college student, however, I was headed in a very different direction. Overloaded with ambition, I studied journalism, and in my junior year I decided that I would win the Pulitzer prize before I turned thirty. The problem with this plan, I discovered while working at my first newspaper job, was that I lacked the talent required for successful newspaper reporting.

I quit the paper, but I could not accept that my only dream career—being a writer—would not come true. Having no backup dream, I descended into a poisonous, gluey depression, a classic "dark night of the soul." During the worst months I would sleep late into the morning, then sit on the floor of my home office staring at half-written magazine articles.

One morning, just as I was coming out of a deep sleep, still in that state between wakefulness and sleep, I was overwhelmed with the sensation that I had died and was only remembering this lifetime. I felt grateful that my life was over. When I finally opened my eyes and realized I was still very much alive, nausea overtook me and I spent the morning vomiting my disappointment. Exhausted, I returned to bed to try to evaluate where I had miscalculated in planning my life. At that point a memory of a homework assignment in a journalism class exploded into my mind.

My journalism professor had spent a fair amount of time emphasizing the importance of objectivity in accurate newspaper reporting. Objectivity, she said, meant keeping yourself emotionally detached from the subject on which you are reporting, and seeking out only the "facts" that describe a situation. She asked us to imagine that a building was on fire, and that four reporters, each standing on a different corner, were covering the story. Each reporter would have a different view of the same event. Each would interview the people on his or her corner. The question the teacher posed to us was: Which reporter had the real facts and the accurate viewpoint? That is, which reporter saw the truth?

Suddenly, that simple assignment from years ago took on immense symbolic meaning for me. Perhaps "truth" and "reality" are actually only matters of perception, I thought. Perhaps I had been looking at life with only one eye, seeing the building from only one corner and sharing it with others who also lacked depth perception. I realized that I had to open my other eye and get out of that corner.

My exhausted, frustrated mind then made another leap backward. The year after I graduated from college, I had left my hometown, Chicago, to go to work for a summer in Alaska. I traveled cross-country with good friends to Seattle, where we boarded a ferry and headed up the inland passage for a three-day trip to Haines. None of us slept the whole time, so that by the time we arrived in Haines, we were practically seeing double.

We were met at the dock by a man who drove us in a van from the ferry to the local hotel. We went to our room and collapsed on the beds, everyone but me falling into a deep sleep. I was too wound up, so I left the hotel and started wandering around the town. The van driver spotted me, stopped his vehicle, and asked me where I was going. I told him I was out for a walk. He told me to jump in his van, which I did, and he dropped me off in front of an old two-story wooden building. "Go on up to the second floor," he said. "The name of the woman who lives there is Rachel. Go talk to her for a while, and I'll come back for you."

Today, back in Chicago, such behavior would be considered fairly dangerous. But at the time my reasoning ability was eclipsed by my exhaustion and by my fascination with Alaska. So I did just what he suggested—I walked up the stairs and knocked on the door. A Native American woman in her early eighties—Rachel—opened the door and said, "Well, come on in. I'll make you some tea." This was Alaskan etiquette—gracious, trusting, warm hospitality. She did not seem surprised to see me; nor did she act as if I were an imposition. For her, this was just an ordinary experience of someone dropping in for tea and conversation.

As I sat dreamily in Rachel's home, I felt as if I were between two different worlds. Half the apartment was decorated with objects from Russian culture—icons of the Black Madonna, a samovar in which Rachel was making the tea, Russian lace window curtains. The other half was pure Athabascan Indian, including a small totem pole and an Indian blanket that hung on the wall.

Looking up from the samovar, Rachel noticed that I was looking at the totem pole. "Do you know how to read a totem pole?" she asked.

"No," I replied. "I didn't realize you could read one."

"Oh my, yes. Totem poles are spiritual statements about the guardians of the tribe," Rachel said. "Look at that one. The animal on the top is the bear. That means that the spirit of the bear—strong, clever at stalking his prey but never killing just to kill, only for protection, and needing long periods of sleep to recover his strength—this spirit guides our tribe. We must imitate that spirit."

Hearing those words, I woke up. I was in the presence of a good teacher, and a good teacher brings me to attention instantly.

Rachel told me that she was half Russian and half Athabascan and had lived in Alaska long before it became a state. As she shared, albeit briefly, her background and Athabascan spiritual traditions with me, she changed my life forever.

"See that blanket on the wall? That blanket is very special. In the Athabascan culture, being a blanket-maker or a songwriter or having any occupation is a matter of great honor. You have to have permission from a songwriter to sing his songs because his songs contain his spirit. And when you are a blanket-maker, you are forbidden to begin weaving a blanket unless you know you will live long enough to finish it. If you find out that you need to die"—mind you, she said *"need to die"*—"you must perform a ceremony with someone who will agree to finish the task for you, because you cannot leave one part of your work unfinished before you die. Otherwise, you leave a part of your spirit behind.

"That blanket was almost finished, when the Great Spirit came in a dream to the woman who was making it and told her to prepare to leave the earth. She asked the Spirit if she could live long enough to finish the blanket, and the Spirit said yes, she would be given that much more time. She died two days after finishing that blanket. Her spirit is in that blanket in a good and powerful way, and it gives me strength."

Life is simple, Rachel said. "You are born into life to care for each other and for the earth. And then you receive word that your time is coming to an end, and you must make the proper arrangements to depart, leaving behind no 'unfinished business.' You must make your apologies, pass on your tribal responsibilities, and accept from the tribe its gratitude and love for your time with them. Simple as that."

Rachel paused to pour our tea, then began again.

"Tomorrow night I go to a ceremony, a potlatch ceremony. A man is preparing to leave the earth, and he will give to the tribe all of his belongings. He will lay his clothes and his tools in a long dish. The tribe will symbolically accept his belongings, meaning that he will be released from any tribal responsibilities so that he can complete the work of his spirit. Then he will leave us," said Rachel.

I was dumbstruck by Rachel's serenity and matter-of-fact attitude, especially her calmness about death. Where was all the fear about death to which I was so accustomed in my own culture? Rachel had just blown up my entire world as I understood it—in particular, my concept of the spiritual dimension of life, or God—yet she was as casual as a summer rain. I wanted to dismiss the truths she offered over tea as nothing more than primitive beliefs, but my gut feeling told me she knew a God that was far more real than my own.

"How does this man know he is going to die? Is he sick?" I asked.

"Oh," she said, "he went to the medicine man. The medicine man looked at his energy. His energy told the medicine man what was happening to him."

"How does the medicine man know these things?"

She seemed shocked at my ignorance. "Tell me," Rachel said, looking directly into my eyes. "How is it that you do *not* know such things? How can you live without knowing what your spirit is doing and what your spirit is saying to you?"

She added, "Everyone goes to the medicine man to learn what his spirit is saying. Years ago the medicine man said to me, 'You will have a broken leg soon if you do not walk better.' I knew he did not mean my physical walk. He meant that I was not honest because I wanted another woman's man. I needed to not see that man anymore. It was hard for me because I loved this man. But my spirit was becoming sick from dishonesty. I left this place for a while, and when I returned, I walked straight."

I desperately wanted to stay with Rachel for a while and learn more from her. I offered to clean her home, run errands, anything. But when the van driver came to collect me, she sent me away, and I never saw her again. As I climbed into the van, the driver said, "She's something, isn't she?"

When I returned home from Alaska that fall, my body arrived without my spirit. It took me months to unite them again. Before meeting Rachel, I had not considered the power of our spirits as she had described it. I had never considered that we weave our spirits into everything we do and everyone we meet. Nor had I thought that my life choices expressed my spirit or affected my health.

I see now that Rachel's story of emotional and physical healing is a good example of how using symbolic sight can change our lives. Although I did not know it at the time, my afternoon with her was my introduction to medical intuition. While I wasn't to begin my own work in this field for another eight years, the memory of her drew me out of my post-newspaper depression and set me on a different course. I decided to study theology in graduate school, which I hoped would give me a greater perspective, akin to Rachel's, and help me finally break free of my street corner, my preconceptions and mental limitations. Perhaps the God I thought I knew was not the God that actually existed, since he was certainly not answering my prayer to be a writer. Perhaps the God I did not yet know would prove more responsive.

I arrived in graduate school in a state of crisis, feeling powerless for the first time in my life. Still, I completed a master's degree in the study of mysticism and schizophrenia—the madness encountered on the path toward spiritual sanity. Later, I would come to see that my very feeling of powerlessness had led me to study power, for the lives of mystics are lessons in physical, emotional, and spiritual bereavement and disempowerment, followed by rebirth into a new relationship to power. Behind closed doors, through anguish and ecstasy, mystics gain access to the spirit, access so profound that they become capable of breathing an energy, like Divine electricity, into ordinary words and acts. They become able to heal others through acts of genuine love, forgiveness, and faith.

Some of the best-known mystics of the Christian culture, Saint Francis of Assisi, Saint Clare of Assisi, Julian of Norwich, Saint Teresa of Avila, Saint Catherine of Siena, and the more contemporary Padre Pío, are said to be in a continuous intimate dialogue with God, living in clarity well beyond ordinary consciousness. The world "behind their eyes" is infinitely more real to them than the world before their eyes. Mystics' perceptions about reality and power are different from those of ordinary people. In the language of Christianity, mystics are "in the world, but not of the world." In the language of Buddhism and Hinduism, they are detached from the illusions of the physical world; they can see symbolically, clearly, because they are awake. (The word *buddha* means "one who is awake.") Although the spiritual path to attaining this degree of consciousness and clarity can be arduous, no matter how much physical misery these mystics encountered along the way, none of them ever asked to return to ordinary consciousness.

In my own use of intuition and symbolic sight to help people see why they have become ill, I often ponder the lives of mystics, especially the theme of the individual's relationship to power. When I was still new to intuition, I had not yet made the connection between disease, healing, and personal power, but I now believe that power is the foundation of health. My own objectivity—my symbolic perspective on life—helps me to evaluate people's relationships to power and how power influences their bodies and spirits.

These days I use Rachel's language to tell people that they have woven their spirits into negative things and that to recover their health they need to retreat for a while, pull their spirits back, and learn to walk straight again. Would that we could follow such simple instructions, because our spirits do contain our lives and our life choices. We do indeed weave our spirits into the events and relationships of our lives. Life *is* as simple as that.

An Intuitive Apprenticeship

As I look back at the past fourteen years, I see now that a schedule had been arranged for my education, one directed toward teaching me to interpret the language of energy for intuitive diagnosis. From 1983 to 1989, when I was an apprentice intuitive, extraordinary synchronicities helped teach me what I needed to know.

First, I noticed that I was meeting "clusters" of people who were all coping with the same disorder. In one week three people would contact me with the same type of cancer. A few weeks later, I would have calls from three other people, all of whom suffered from migraine headaches. Eventually I met clusters of people with diabetes, breast cancer, colon problems, prostate cancer, mitral valve prolapse, depression, and numerous other health problems. Before my decision to accept my intuitions, the people who contacted me had not shown up in any particular pattern.

Simultaneously, the quality of information I was receiving increased. It showed me how the emotional, psychological, and physical stress in the subjects' lives had contributed to the development of their illness. At first I simply noted the impression I received of each person, not thinking to compare one person's stress patterns with another's. Eventually, though, I began to see that no illness develops randomly, and I reviewed my previous cases to look for any emotional and psychological patterns that preceded a particular illness. By 1988 I was able to identify the emotional, psychological, and physical stress patterns of nearly a hundred different illnesses. These patterns have since proven valid and useful to many physicians and other health professionals whom I have taught.

Meeting Norm Shealy was another extraordinary event. Besides being a neurosurgeon, Norm is the founder of the American Holistic Medical Association and the leading American expert on the management of pain. Since 1972 he has also been interested in metaphysical subjects.

In the spring of 1984 I was invited to attend a fairly exclusive midwestern conference—not because of my intuitive abilities but as a publisher at Stillpoint, which was still my main occupation. During the conference I met a psychologist who pointed out Norm Shealy to me. For no apparent reason he said, "See that man over there? He's a physician who has an interest in medical intuitives." I became incredibly nervous, but I decided to approach Dr. Shealy and tell him that I was medically intuitive.

Over lunch one day, when I was seated next to him, I told him that I was able to diagnose people at a distance. He didn't seem the least impressed. Rather, he peeled an apple and asked me, "How good are you?" I told him that I wasn't sure. Then he asked, "Can you identify a brain tumor in someone? Can you see a disease forming in a person's body? I don't need anyone to tell me that someone's 'energy' is low; I can see that for myself. I need someone who can scan a person like an X-ray machine."

I told Dr. Shealy that I was uncertain of my accuracy since I was relatively new at this. He said he would give me a call sometime, when he had a patient he thought might benefit from my skill.

The next month—May 1984—he phoned me at Stillpoint. He had a patient in his office, he told me, then gave me the patient's name and age and waited for my response. I recall the evaluation I gave vividly because I was so nervous; I spoke of my impressions in images rather than in physiological terms. I told Dr. Shealy that I felt as if his patient had concrete running down his throat. I then commented on the emotional issues that, from my point of view, preceded the development of his physical condition. The patient, an addict, was so terrified to admit his condition that he was physically unable to speak the truth about it. The words froze in his throat.

When I was finished, Dr. Shealy said thanks and hung up. I had no idea whether I had done an adequate job, but later he told me that the man had cancer of the esophagus.

That was the beginning of my work with Norm Shealy. His non-emotional responses to my evaluations turned out to be an enormous blessing. Had he carried on about my skill in those days, I would have become self-conscious and probably would have tried to impress him, which no doubt would have interfered with my accuracy. As it was, his detachment kept me objective and clear. So as I learned from my journalism teacher and as I now teach others, detachment is essential to accomplishing an accurate evaluation. Nothing causes more interference than the need to be "right" or to prove that you can do an intuitive evaluation.

Over the next year Norm helped me study human anatomy, and he called me several more times for evaluations on his patients. With each patient my evaluations became more and more technically accurate. Instead of receiving vague images of body organs, I could soon recognize and distinguish the exact vibrations of a specific disease and its location in a person's physiology. Each illness and each body organ, I learned, has its own "frequency" or vibrational pattern.

It never occurred to me back then that Norm and I would one day become a working team. While I had already committed myself to understanding my skill, I was still investing most of my energy in Stillpoint's success. Then in March 1985 I encountered a young man whose courage in confronting and healing his illness gave me the courage to open myself to my intuitions in a new way.

While working with Norm, I had become more confident in my ability to identify by name the illnesses that I sensed, as well as their energy stresses and precursors. I avoided directing clients into a specific course of healing, however, leaving that to Norm. What little I knew about healing was limited to the manuscripts I read and to conversations with my associates.

On a Saturday morning in March 1985, I received a telephone

call from a man named Joe, whom I had met casually after a lecture I gave in Kansas City. He told me that he had a feeling that something was wrong with his son, Peter, and asked if I would do an evaluation. Because Peter was already an adult, I asked Joe to contact him and get his permission for me to evaluate him. Within ten minutes the father called me back to say that Peter was open to any help I could give him. I asked for Peter's age—and when he told me, I instantly was overwhelmed with the feeling that he had leukemia. I did not mention this to Joe, but I asked for Peter's phone number, saying I would like to speak directly to him.

As I made notes on the intuitive impressions I was receiving, I realized that the vibration I was sensing was not the one for leukemia after all. But I couldn't identify the frequency, since I hadn't encountered it before. Then suddenly I realized that Peter was HIV positive. My conversation with him remains vivid in my memory, because I knew I would feel strange if some strange woman across the country telephoned me and said, "Hi, I've just checked out your energy system, and not only are you HIV positive, but you've already begun to develop AIDS." Peter's body was, in fact, beginning to manifest the symptoms of *Pneumocystis carinii* pneumonia (PCP), the most common lung disorder associated with the HIV virus.

What I actually said to Peter that morning was, "Peter, I'm a friend of your father's. I'm a medical intuitive," and I tried to explain what I did. Finally I said, "Peter, I've evaluated your energy, and you have AIDS." His reply was, "Jesus, Caroline, I'm so scared. I've had two tests, and they've both come out HIV positive."

The sound of his voice, his instant trust, caused a rush of emotion to flow through me, and we talked about what he should do next. Peter told me that his father did not even know he was homosexual, much less that he had AIDS. I said I would not tell his father anything, but I encouraged him to be honest about his life and health. We spoke for about a half hour. As soon as I hung up, his father called and asked about my conclusions. I told Joe that Peter needed to speak with him, and that I did not feel it was appropriate for me to share the contents of Peter's and my conversation. He said, "I know what's wrong with my son. He wants to drop out of law school, and he's afraid to tell me." I did not reply, and we concluded our conversation.

Twenty minutes later, Joe phoned me back. "I've been thinking about the worst possible thing that could be wrong with my son," he said. "And if my son called me and said, 'Dad, I have AIDS,' I realized that I would still love him." I responded, "I hope you mean that, because that is exactly what you're going to hear."

Another thirty minutes passed, and Joe called again to tell me Peter was on his way home and that by noon the next day, they would both be in my living room in New Hampshire. I was stunned and immediately called Norm.

Norm and I created a healing program for Peter, which included adopting a healthy, near-vegetarian diet, doing aerobic exercise, quitting smoking, using castor-oil packs across his abdomen for forty-five minutes a day, and psychotherapy, to help him liberate himself from his secrecy about being gay. Peter did what he needed to do to heal, without complaining or feeling that healing was an effort. In fact, he had an "Is that all?" attitude.

Many people, I might note here, enter their healing programs as if they were being punished. Norm and I have since worked with countless individuals, including a woman who suffered from obesity, diabetes, and chronic pain. We spoke with her about how she could improve her condition immediately by changing to a healthy nutritional program and exercising moderately. Her response was, "Absolutely not. I could never do those things. I don't have any will power. What other suggestions do you have for me?" Peter, in contrast, accepted his personal responsibility for healing with gratitude and treated all the demands of his healing program as effortless. Six weeks later, his blood test was HIV negative. Peter is now a practicing attorney, and he remains HIV negative to this day.

Afterward, Norm and I wrote up this case study in our first book,

AIDS: Passageway to Transformation (Stillpoint, 1987). As a consequence of working with Peter, Norm and I began to hold workshops
for people who were either HIV positive or who had developed
AIDS, believing deeply that if one person could heal himself, others
could as well.

From Hobby to Profession

Peter's dramatic healing from an illness considered terminal brought
me the first of several invitations I got to lecture abroad on the subject of AIDS and on healing in general. His case was a turning point
for me and led me to begin to contemplate the origins of illness—
specifically, how and why an illness develops; what it takes to heal an
illness; and why some people heal and others don't. I particularly
began to wonder what might predispose an entire culture to be susceptible to an epidemic. What emotional and physical stress triggers
a group's chemistry to lead to illness?

Thinking symbolically, I could almost see the manifestations
of AIDS as a global illness. The lung disease *Pneumocystis carinii*
pneumonia may be symbolic of the destruction of the rain forests,
from which the earth draws the greatest proportion of its oxygen
supply. Similarly, Kaposi's sarcoma, the cancerous skin lesions that
form in many AIDS patients, is symbolic of the destruction of the
earth's natural surface, perhaps most dramatically by the testing of
nuclear weapons, but also by toxic wastes and other forms of pollu-
tion. And finally, the human immune system could symbolize the
earth's ozone layer, which is now as fragile as the immune system in
a very ill patient.

Some people referred to Peter's case as a "miracle," implying that
he had received a special grace from God that assisted his healing and
that without that grace he would never have gotten well. While that
might be the case, one must still ask, "What does it take to make a
miracle happen?" I believe that our cell tissues hold the vibrational

patterns of our attitudes, our belief systems, and the presence or absence of an exquisite energy frequency or "grace" that we can activate by calling back our spirits from negative attachments.

As *A Course in Miracles* says, "Miracles are natural. Something is wrong when they don't happen." Peter's healing induced me to discover what we do that interferes with the energy that makes miracles happen. For instance, you can be a vegetarian and run six miles a day, but if you are in an abusive relationship, or hate your job, or have daily fights with your parents, you are losing energy—or power—in a pattern of behavior that can lead to illness or prevent your healing from an illness. On the other hand, if you are spiritually centered and call back your energy from negative beliefs, you can eat cat food and still stay healthy.

Please understand that I am not advocating that you eat an unhealthy diet and avoid exercise—it's just that these factors *alone* will not keep you healthy. Nor am I saying that a commitment toward becoming spiritually conscious *guarantees* your health. It will, however, enhance your life and self-understanding and set the stage for maximizing healing, be it spontaneous or gradual, physical and spiritual.

The more I have come to understand the relationship between our interior dynamics and the quality of our health—and our lives in general—the more I have felt committed to my work as an intuitive. Norm and I have continued our research together and in 1988 published our findings on the emotional and psychological issues that precede the development of illnesses in *The Creation of Health* (Stillpoint, 1988).

The Final Turn in the Road

Shortly after completing that book, I suffered an accident in which I nearly bled to death. The trauma turned a nosebleed into a massive hemorrhage. In the ambulance on my way to the hospital, I was sitting on the stretcher, bleeding into an enormous bowl on my lap since I would have choked if I had lain back when suddenly my head fell forward and I was instantly on the outside of the ambulance, floating down the highway while observing through the ambulance window my body and the frantic activity of the rescue workers to save me.

Suddenly I was euphoric, completely light and vibrationally alive in a way I had never been before. It occurred to me that I was out of my body, perhaps even dead. I awaited the "tunnel" I had heard so much about, but none appeared. Instead, I felt myself drifting away from the earth. I entered into a state of calm so intense that remembering it even now has a powerful effect on me. Then I saw an image of Norm. He was standing on a stage, preparing to give a lecture, holding up a copy of *The Creation of Health*. I heard him say, "I thought this was going to be the beginning of our work together, but it has sadly turned out to be the end."

I got an urgent desire to return to my body, to regain physical life, and immediately I felt myself racing toward and into my body. After this experience I asked myself only one question: "Why didn't I see my publishing company from that state?" I knew then that I would leave the company and pursue medical intuition for the rest of my life.

As a professional medical intuitive, I have worked with as many as fifteen physicians around the country, including Christiane Northrup, M.D., an OB/GYN who is one of the founders of a women's health clinic called Women to Women in Yarmouth, Maine, and author of *Women's Bodies, Women's Wisdom* (Bantam, 1994). Chris phoned me for a personal health evaluation in the autumn of 1990, and after our session she called me for intuitive evaluations of many of her patients. The opportunity to work with Chris and other physicians signaled my own coming of age as a medical intuitive. It showed that my work with the human energy system could be used to help physicians help others.

From 1990 through 1992 in addition to expanding my practice

with physicians, I conducted an overwhelming number of work-shops, both alone and with Norm, in the United States, Australia, Europe, Mexico, and Canada. In those early workshops I would lecture on the human energy system, then perform an intuitive health evaluation on every one of the workshop participants. Sometimes this meant that I did as many as 120 health evaluations over the course of one weekend. Often I would end a workshop bathed in sweat. At the end of a working day, I was exhausted. After two years of this work, I was burning out.

As has always happened for me, just when I came to the end of my strength, a new door opened. In February 1992 I was teaching a workshop in upstate New Hampshire. The group had just returned from lunch, and I began the afternoon session by sitting down next to a woman and asking her, "What can I do for you today?" I assumed she would mention a health problem, as the other participants had, and then I would be off and running, so to speak. Instead, she crossed her arms over her chest, looked at me as if I were a con artist, and said, "I don't know. You tell me. I paid my money."

To say I filled up with rage is like saying it gets a bit cool in a Montana winter. I wanted so much to pick up this woman and escort her to the door that I actually began to hyperventilate. I took a deep breath and said, "You know, I'm going to sit here next to you until I can think of a reason to thank you for that comment. And we might be here for a very long time." The atmosphere in the workshop grew tense. No one moved.

And then it hit me. I jumped out of my seat and announced, "I will no longer do any personal health evaluations on anyone. Instead, I will teach you to evaluate yourselves. There is only one of me, and if I keep this up, I'm not going to live very long. If any of you want your money back, ask for it now. Otherwise, take out your notebooks because we're going to work, and you're going to learn to see your bodies as I see them. I'll help you a great deal more if I can teach you to locate a problem in your own body without needing me to do it for you."

I looked at this now-shaken woman and said, "I think you just might have saved my life. I am grateful to you." No one asked for a refund, and that day I began to teach others "self-diagnosis."

By the autumn of 1992, Norm and I were discussing developing a training program in the science of intuition. We met with an entrepreneur from the Netherlands who agreed to finance the first stages of our training program, and in 1993 we began our intensive workshops on teaching medical intuition, which led eventually to my writing this book. Teaching this system in workshops has given me the privilege of hearing the life stories of many participants, some of whose case histories I describe in this book. Among them are patients who healed themselves in energy terms, avoiding the development of an actual physical illness, and in physical terms, reversing or healing an illness that had already appeared.

In organizing this book, I have followed the sequence that has worked successfully for me in teaching the technical aspects of medical intuition and intuitive health evaluations. Chapter 1 in Part I introduces the principles of medical intuition as I have come to know them and offers instructions on how to apply them yourself.

Chapter 2 in Part I introduces a complementary and, I believe, new model of the human energy system based upon the synthesis of three spiritual traditions: the Hindu teachings regarding the chakras, the symbolic meaning of the seven Christian sacraments, and the mystical interpretation of the ten sefirot—or Tree of Life—presented in the Zohar, which is the major text of the Kabbalah, the mystical teachings of Judaism. The seven chakras, the seven Christian sacraments, and the Tree of Life symbolize the seven levels of the human energy system and the seven stages of human development, or the seven essential lessons of the universal spiritual path, or the hero's journey, as Joseph Campbell would have described it.

Chapter 2 is, in many ways, the heart of the book because it presents a spiritual-biological profile of the human energy system.

Chapter 2 concludes with an extensive interpretation of the spiritual and energy perceptions that I now use to guide me in my work. These perceptions will provide the foundation for your learning the language of energy and symbolic sight. They may help you gain insights into the energy patterns of your own and your loved ones' physical and spiritual health.

In Part II, Chapters 1 through 7 give the anatomy of the seven power centers of the human body, with basic information and real-life case studies that illustrate how we use energy data in our spiritual development.

The Afterword, "A Guide for the Contemporary Mystic," suggests how you can apply symbolic sight to your personal development and health.

As I tell my students at the beginning of each workshop, take with you only what feels accurate and truthful to your own heart.

PART I

A New Language of the Spirit

CHAPTER I

Energy Medicine and Intuition

I disappoint some people when I discuss intuition because I firmly believe that intuitive or symbolic sight is not a gift but a skill—a skill based in self-esteem. Developing this skill—and a healthy sense of self—becomes easier when you can think in the words, concepts, and principles of energy medicine. So as you read this chapter, think of learning to use intuition as learning to interpret the language of energy.

The Human Energy Field

Everything that is alive pulsates with energy and all of this energy contains information. While it is not surprising that practitioners of alternative or complementary medicine accept this concept, even some quantum physicists acknowledge the existence of an electromagnetic field generated by the body's biological processes. Scientists accept that the human body generates electricity because living tissue generates energy.

Your physical body is surrounded by an energy field that extends as far out as your outstretched arms and the full length of your body. It is both an information center and a highly sensitive perceptual system. We are constantly "in communication" with everything around us through this system, which is a kind of conscious electricity that transmits and receives messages to and from other people's bodies. These messages from and within the energy field are what intuitives perceive.

Practitioners of energy medicine believe that the human energy field contains and reflects each individual's energy. It surrounds us and carries with us the emotional energy created by our internal and external experiences—both positive and negative. This emotional force influences the physical tissue within our bodies. In this way your biography—that is, the experiences that make up your life—becomes your biology.

Experiences that carry emotional energy in our energy systems include: past and present relationships, both personal and professional; profound or traumatic experiences and memories; and belief patterns and attitudes, including all spiritual and superstitious beliefs. The emotions from these experiences become encoded in our biological systems and contribute to the formation of our cell tissue, which then generates a quality of energy that reflects those emotions. These energy impressions form an energy language, which carries literal and symbolic information that a medical intuitive can read.

Here is an example of the kind of message the energy field may communicate. Let's say you had some trouble with math when you were in elementary school. Knowing the fact that twelve makes a dozen would not ordinarily carry an emotional charge such as would alter the health of cell tissues. On the other hand, if you were humiliated by the teacher because you didn't know that fact, the experience would carry an emotional charge that would create cellular damage, especially if you were to dwell on that memory through adulthood or use it as a touchstone for determining how to deal with criticism, or authority figures, or education, or failure. An intuitive might pick up the literal image of your exchange with the teacher or any other negative symbol linked to that experience.

Positive images and the energy of positive experiences are also held in the energy field. Think of a time when someone praised you for a job well done, or a kind act, or for some help you gave someone. You feel a positive energy—a surge of personal power within your body. Positive and negative experiences register a memory in cell tissue as well as in the energy field. As neurobiologist Dr. Candace Pert has proven, neuropeptides—the chemicals triggered by emotions—are thoughts converted into matter. Our emotions reside physically in our bodies and interact with our cells and tissues. In fact, Dr. Pert can no longer separate the mind from the body, she says, because the same kinds of cells that manufacture and receive emotional chemistry in the brain are present throughout the body. Sometimes the body responds emotionally and manufactures emotional chemicals even *before* the brain has registered a problem. Remember, for instance, how quickly your body reacts to a loud noise before you've had time to think.

As Dr. Pert said on Bill Moyers's *Healing and the Mind*, "Clearly, there's another form of energy that we have not yet understood. For example, there's a form of energy that appears to leave the body when the body dies. . . . Your mind is in every cell of your body." Moyers: ". . . You're saying that my emotions are stored in my body?" Pert: "Absolutely. You didn't realize that? . . . There are many phenomena that we can't explain without going into energy."

Reading the Field

In addition to reading specific dramatic childhood experiences, sometimes an intuitive can even pick up on superstitions, personal habits, behavior patterns, moral beliefs, and preferences in music and literature. At other times the energy impressions are more symbolic. For instance, from one patient who was suffering from tightness of breath, I kept receiving the symbolic impression of him being shot in the heart before a firing squad. Obviously this had not literally happened to him, but he had undergone extensive medical tests, which could locate no known physical cause for his condition. After I shared my impression with him, he told me that his wife had betrayed him several times with other men, and being shot through the heart was exactly how he felt about her actions. By admitting these emotions, which he had previously tried to ignore, he was able to address the problems both in his marriage and in his health.

Our emotional energy converts into biological matter through a highly complex process. Just as radio stations operate according to specific energy wavelengths, each organ and system in the body is calibrated to absorb and process specific emotional and psychological energies. That is, each area of the body transmits energy on a specific, detailed frequency, and when we are healthy, all are "in tune." An area of the body that is not transmitting at its normal frequency indicates the location of a problem. A change in intensity of the frequency indicates a change in the nature and seriousness of the illness and reveals the stress pattern that has contributed to the development of the illness.

This way of interpreting the body's energy is sometimes called "vibrational medicine." It resembles the most ancient medical practices and beliefs, from Chinese medicine to indigenous shamanic practices to virtually every folk or alternative therapy. The truth is that energy medicine is not new; but I believe my interpretation of it and of how you can use it to heal spiritually in conjunction with contemporary medical treatments is unique. If a person is able to sense intuitively that he or she is losing energy because of a stressful situation—and then acts to correct that loss of energy—then the likelihood of that stress developing into a physical crisis is reduced, if not eliminated completely.

While I can parse the language of energy for you so that you can begin to see and feel the human energy field, begin to understand its corresponding spiritual anatomy, begin to know the sources of your personal power, and begin to develop your own intuition, I have some trouble explaining exactly how I personally acquire energy information. Other intuitives appear to have the same difficulty, but we all pick up on information that has the strongest impulse—the most intensity. These impulses usually relate directly to the part of the body that is becoming weakened or diseased. As a rule, a person's energy system transmits only the information that is essential to bring the conscious mind to an awareness of the imbalance or disease. Like the "shot in the heart" image, symbolic information can sometimes be disturbing. But this intensity is necessary in order that the body's message can break through the habitual mental or emotional patterns that caused the disease to form in the first place. Medical intuitions cooperate with the body's intention to promote its own health and life; that is, our energy will always seek health, in spite of what we may do to ourselves physically. If, for example, we tell a lie, our energy field will often communicate to the other person the "energy fact" that we are not telling the truth. Energy does not and cannot lie.

Stay with Your First Impression

When you receive an intuitive impression about yourself or the person you are reading, pay attention to whatever image comes up. Most people are looking for safe intuitions, not healthy ones, and safe insights, not healthy insights, because they usually want a safe passage into the future, into the unknown. So you may be tempted to dismiss a disturbing image that you receive, or one that is not congruent with your own desires or those of the person you are reading. Most people who come to me for an evaluation have already intuited themselves that something is wrong, but they are hoping that I will give that feeling some other meaning, such as "You're merely going through a natural body change, but nothing is wrong with you physically." But it is important to tell people the truth, not what they want to hear. Again and again I have had to confirm the negative intuitive impressions of people seeking my help. Their abilities are as accurate as mine; these people *know* they are ill. But since I do not share their

fear, my intuitions can interpret their data better than they themselves can.

People must face that which they fear. For instance, in the case
of the man "shot through the heart," it seemed on the surface safer
to him to avoid confronting his adulterous wife with his suspicions
that she was cheating on him. Instead of acting on his intuitions, he
directed his hurt and anger "underground," into his body, which
manifested eventually as chest pains. His body and spirit were striving to wake him up to the need to deal with his wife's cheating, but
as so many people do, he had hoped that by not confronting the
problem, it would go away. His body, however, revealed that the
true cost of this "safe" approach was a challenge to his health. This
man's story illustrates how powerful intuitions really are and how
they can break through the most determined mindset to lead us
toward healing.

Life is painful at times, and spiritually, we are meant to face the
pains that life presents. In the Western world, however, we often
misrepresent God's plan for us and expect life to be comfortable and
free of trouble. We measure God's presence in our lives by our level
of personal comfort; we believe God is here if our prayers are
answered. But neither God nor Buddha nor any other spiritual leader
or tradition guarantees or encourages a pain-free life. Spiritual teachings encourage us to grow past and through painful experiences, each
of which is a spiritual lesson. Developing intuitive ability will help us
learn the lessons inherent in our experiences.

Have a Reflective State of Mind

There is no one formula by which you can develop your intuition.
Some people develop it through meditation, or as a result of mastering a certain talent or sport. I have often heard people say that intuitive ability is the result of a spiritual lifestyle, but that is not accurate.
Intuitive ability is present in everyone because it is a survival skill, not
a spiritual intention. Maintaining a reflective or meditative attitude,

however, facilitates your reception of intuitions. Objectivity will help you interpret the impressions you receive and put them into a symbolic spiritual context.

Objectivity Is Key

I learned through experience to discern the difference between personal and impersonal impressions; my indicator of an accurate intuition is a *lack* of emotion. For me, a clear impression has *no* emotional energy connected to it whatsoever. If I feel an emotional connection to an impression, then I consider that impression to be contaminated. The person you are reading, however, will often feel some emotional charge from the impression you receive.

For me, impressions are neither auditory nor visual. Rather, they are like quick mental images that contain a very subtle electrical current. As I scan someone's body, I focus on each energy center and wait for an image. After about five seconds the imagery process starts, and it continues to unfold until it stops on its own. The duration varies from person to person; reading some people requires almost an hour, while others take less than ten minutes.

Every now and again I encounter a person whom I cannot read or help. I can only speculate on why this is so. A few times I was left with the feeling that nothing I said would make any sense to them, and at other times I had the impression that the person was looking for only a very specific type of answer that I could not provide, such as why their marriage had failed. Also, I am virtually useless to anyone if I am exhausted or if something intensely personal is on my mind.

As you learn to read the human energy system, your first step is to study the principles underlying the practice, and the next is to gain some practical experience. This book provides you with the theoretical concepts and some pointers in exploring your own intuitive abilities. In developing your skill and trying it out in your own life, however, you *must* trust your gut responses—a fact I cannot emphasize enough.

The First Principle:
Biography Becomes Biology

According to energy medicine, we are all living history books. Our bodies contain our histories—every chapter, line, and verse of every event and relationship in our lives. As our lives unfold, our biological health becomes a living, breathing biographical statement that conveys our strengths, weaknesses, hopes, and fears.

Every thought you have had has traveled through your biological system and activated a physiological response. Some thoughts are like depth charges, causing a reaction throughout the body. A fear, for instance, activates every system of your body: your stomach tightens, your heart rate increases, and you may break into a sweat. A loving thought can relax your entire body. Some thoughts are more subtle, and still others are unconscious. Many are meaningless and pass through the body like wind through a screen, requiring no conscious attention, and their influence upon our health is minimal. Yet each conscious thought—and many unconscious ones—does generate a physiological response.

All our thoughts, regardless of their content, first enter our systems as energy. Those that carry emotional, mental, psychological, or spiritual energy produce biological responses that are then stored in our cellular memory. In this way our biographies are woven into our biological systems, gradually, slowly, every day.

The story of a young patient of Norm's is a good example of how this process works. Norm called me for a phone consultation on this patient, a dentist, who was not feeling well in general and was becoming increasingly exhausted. He had an acute pain around the right side of his abdomen, and he was also seriously depressed.

Increasing and continual exhaustion that takes the edge off mental and emotional clarity is an energy symptom that indicates something is wrong in the body. Most people do not consider it a symptom because it is not actually painful. But when exhaustion continues, even when the person is getting more sleep, the body is trying to communicate that the person is "energetically ill." Responding to this message at the energy stage can often prevent the development of an illness.

Depression is another symptom that all is not well. Within the clinical world, depression is generally considered an emotional and mental disorder. But prolonged depression often precedes the development of a physical illness. In energy terms, depression literally is a release of energy—or life-force, if you will—without consciousness. If energy is like money, depression is like opening your wallet and announcing, "I don't care who takes my money or how it is spent." Prolonged depression inevitably creates chronic exhaustion. If you don't care who spends your money or how much, inevitably you will end up broke. Just so, without energy you cannot support your health.

As Norm examined his dentist-patient, he had the feeling that the man was developing an illness. Because of the man's abdominal pain, Norm ran tests for pancreatic cancer, but they came back negative. So he called me for a consultation. As is our habit, he gave me only the patient's name and age and said nothing about the pain or his own suspicions. In my evaluation I saw that the right side of this patient's body, around the pancreas, was generating toxic energy. I told Norm that this man was burdened by an enormous feeling of responsibility and that it had become a constant source of anguish for him. He felt intensely that he was unable to live as he wanted to, and he dwelled on this feeling almost to the exclusion of any other emotion. (Obviously, we all have negative feelings, but not all negativity produces a serious physical illness. To create disease, negativity has to become the dominant emotion, as it did with this young dentist.)

After I'd shared this evaluation with Norm, I told him that the patient had pancreatic cancer. Norm admitted he had already suspected that disease but the tests had come back "all clear." He said good-bye and returned to his patient. He recommended to the dentist that he evaluate how well his life's work was serving him. More than likely, Norm said, he would have to make some changes to get what he wanted. The patient admitted that he wanted to leave dentistry, but he felt he couldn't go into something else because of the impact his decision would have on his dependents. Norm didn't tell him that he had the energy frequency of pancreatic cancer, but he talked with him about his career frustrations and tried to help him shift his negative attitude. Unfortunately, the man was unable to act on Norm's advice. He defined responsibility as an obligation to care for others to the exclusion of himself, and he was unable to reconceptualize a life that included self-care and self-fulfillment as well.

Two weeks later, this young man's primary physician repeated the tests for pancreatic cancer. This time they proved positive. The man was operated on immediately, but he died within four months of his surgery.

It sometimes takes a concerted effort to shift your mind to allow yourself to heal. While the dentist could not accept that his professional sadness and feeling of entrapment were changing his body chemistry and health, it was easier for others to recognize these patterns in him. Accepting the idea that every part of your life—from your physical history to your relationships to every attitude, opinion, and belief you carry inside yourself—affects your biological makeup is only part of the healing process, however. You also have to get that acceptance to move from the mental level into the physical level, into your body, to feel the truth viscerally and cellularly and believe it wholly.

It is very easy to learn something new and apply that knowledge only casually. The idea that biography becomes biology implies that we participate to some degree in the creation of illness. But—and this is a crucial point—we must not abuse this truth by blaming ourselves or any patients for becoming ill. People rarely choose consciously to create an illness. Rather, illnesses develop as a consequence of behavioral patterns and attitudes that we do not realize are biologically toxic until they have already become so. Only when illness forces us to review our attitudes do we come close to comprehending that our day-to-day fearful or bitter attitudes are, in fact, biologically negative substances.

Again, we all have negative feelings, but not all negativity produces disease. To create disease, negative emotions have to be dominant, and what accelerates the process is *knowing* the negative thought to be toxic but giving it permission to thrive in your consciousness anyway. For instance, you may know you need to forgive someone, yet you decide that remaining angry gives you more power. Remaining obsessively angry makes you more likely to develop a disease because the energy consequence of a negative obsession is powerlessness. Energy is power, and transmitting energy into the past by dwelling on painful events drains power from your present-day body and can lead to illness.

Power is essential for healing and for maintaining health. Attitudes that generate a feeling of powerlessness not only lead to low self-esteem, but also deplete the physical body of energy and weaken overall health. Thus, the next principle to explore is the primary significance of power for health.

The Second Principle: Personal Power Is Necessary for Health

One day Norm called me to do an evaluation of a woman who was suffering from depression and chronic pain in her neck and lower back. Norm asked me if I felt that she would benefit from various electromagnetic treatments. I said, "Absolutely not. She hasn't enough power in her system to benefit from those devices."

This was the first time I had ever commented on a person's power in relation to healing. Norm asked me to elaborate, and only then did

I realize what I had just said. Suddenly I had an entirely different sense of the human energy system as an expression of personal power.

I explained to Norm that this woman's attitudes had caused her to lose power in her life. She felt inadequate, I said, was always looking for approval, and had a tremendous fear of being alone. Her self-esteem was based only on her ability to control others, primarily her children. Her fears and inadequacies were like a black hole, magnetically drawing everyone, particularly her children, toward it, only to crush them eventually. She continually criticized her children in an attempt to keep them dependent upon her, since weak children find it difficult to leave the nest. She found flaws in their every accomplishment, whether scholastic or sports related, because she could not risk empowering them with emotional support. Because controlling others requires a tremendous investment of energy, and because she never actually felt in control, she was continually exhausted. Her chronic pain was also the result of her inability to control others. By the time she arrived in Norm's office, she looked defeated.

This woman could not cope with the inevitability of her children leaving home, yet she denied that she acted in anything but her children's best interests. In her own view she was a supportive mother because she provided her children with a clean home, healthy food, and decent clothing. Yet she systematically strove to undermine their emotional development, a fact that she could not admit.

Since conventional medical treatments had not helped her, Norm was considering an alternative approach that included psychotherapy, cranial stimulation through an electrical device, and color and light therapy. If she had used these techniques, I realized, she might have benefited for a week or maybe a month, but she would not heal completely until she gave up her pathological struggle for control.

That afternoon I saw that for an alternative therapy to succeed, the patient must have an *internal* concept of power—an ability to generate internal energy and emotional resources, such as a belief in his or her self-sufficiency. This woman had only an *external* concept of power, which she drew from an external source—her children. This patient could certainly go to psychotherapy sessions. But unless she confronted the truth about herself, she would only be chronicling her complaints for an hour each week. No actual healing would take place. As M. Scott Peck has pointed out in *People of the Lie* and *The Road Less Traveled*, seeing and admitting the truth about ourselves, about our role in creating our own problems, and about how we relate to others is vital for healing.

Evaluating this woman gave me insight into the role of power in our lives and our energy systems. Power is at the root of the human experience. Our attitudes and belief patterns, whether positive or negative, are all extensions of how we define, use, or do not use power. Not one of us is free from power issues. We may be trying to cope with feelings of inadequacy or powerlessness, or we may be trying to maintain control over people or situations that we believe empower us, or we may be trying to maintain a sense of security (a synonym for power) in personal relationships. Many people who lose something that represents power to them—money, or a job, or a game—or who lose someone in whom their sense of self or power is vested—a spouse or lover, a parent or child—develop a disease. Our relationship to power is at the core of our health.

Consider the first principle—that biography becomes biology—together with this second principle—that personal power is necessary for health. Power mediates between our internal and external worlds, and as it does so, it communicates in a language of myth and symbol. Consider, for example, the most common symbol of power—money. When a person internalizes money as a symbol of power, its acquisition and control become symbolic of that person's health: when she acquires money, her biological system receives the signals that power is coming into her body. Her mind transmits the unconscious message "I have money. Therefore, I'm safe, I'm secure. I have power, and all is well." This positive message transmitted in the biological system generates health.

Of course, making lots of money doesn't guarantee health, but poverty, powerlessness, and illness are undeniably linked. When you have trouble making money or you suddenly lose money, your biological system may weaken. I recall one man who during the mid-1980s seemed to have the Midas touch. His company was increasingly successful, and he had the energy of ten people. He worked late hours, socialized into the early morning, then showed up for work before everyone else, always alert, cheerful, and on top of things. Then in October 1987 the stock market crashed—and his company collapsed along with it. Within months his health deteriorated. He developed migraines, then lower back pain, and finally a fairly serious bowel disorder. He could no longer tolerate his late hours or his social schedule, and he withdrew from all activities besides maneuvering the survival of his financial empire.

This man was unaware that he had "calibrated" his health to money-making. But when he became ill, he saw the connection immediately. He realized that for him, money represented freedom and the ability to lead a lifestyle that he had always dreamed about. When he lost his fortune, he lost his power, and in only a matter of weeks his biology crashed too. Certainly the stress of recovering a business would weaken anyone, but this man had undergone just as much stress when his company was on the rise, and that type of stress had empowered him.

Each of us has numerous power symbols, and each such symbol has a biological counterpart. The dentist with pancreatic cancer had a symbol of power—his job. But since he had grown to despise his job, he was losing power each day. The power drain created a biological response that continued until it had created a terminal disease.

Our lives are structured around power symbols: money, authority, title, beauty, security. The people who fill our lives and the choices we make each moment are expressions and symbols of our personal power. We often hesitate to challenge a person who we believe holds more power than we do, and we frequently agree to things because we believe we haven't the power to refuse. In countless situations and relationships, the underlying dynamic at work is the negotiation of power: who has it, and how we can maintain our share of it.

Learning the symbolic language of energy means learning to evaluate the dynamics of power in yourself and others. Energy information is always truthful. Although a person may verbally agree to something in public, his energy will state how he really feels, and his real feelings will find their way into some symbolic statement. Our biological and spiritual systems always seek to express truth, and they will always find a way to do so.

You need to become conscious of what gives you power. Healing from any illness is facilitated by identifying your power symbols and your symbolic and physical relationship to those symbols, and heeding any messages your body and intuitions are sending you about them.

The Third Principle: You Alone Can Help Yourself Heal

Energy medicine is a holistic philosophy that teaches, "I am responsible for the creation of my health. I therefore participated, at some level, in the creation of this illness. I can participate in the healing of this illness by healing myself, which means simultaneously healing my emotional, psychological, physical and spiritual being."

Healing and curing are not the same thing. A "cure" occurs when one has successfully controlled or abated the physical progression of an illness. Curing a physical illness, however, does not necessarily mean that the emotional and psychological stresses that were a part of the illness were also alleviated. In this case it is highly possible, and often probable, that an illness will recur.

The process of curing is passive; that is, the patient is inclined to give his or her authority over to the physician and prescribed treatment instead of actively challenging the illness and reclaiming health. Healing, on the other hand, is an active and internal process that includes investigating one's attitudes, memories, and beliefs with the desire to release all negative patterns that prevent one's full emotional and spiritual recovery. This internal review inevitably leads one to review one's external circumstances in an effort to recreate one's life in a way that serves activation of will—the will to see and accept truths about one's life and how one has used one's energies; and the will to begin to use energy for the creation of love, self-esteem, and health.

The language of conventional medicine sounds more military than that of energy medicine: "The patient was attacked by a virus," or "A substance contaminated the cell tissue, resulting in a malignancy." Conventional medical philosophy considers the patient an innocent—or virtually powerless—victim who has suffered an unprovoked attack.

In a conventional medical treatment, the patient follows a program prescribed by the physician, so that the responsibility for healing lies with the doctor. Whether the patient cooperates with his health provider is certainly noted during such a treatment, but his attitude is considered unimportant to the process—drugs and surgery are to do most of the work. By contrast, in holistic therapies the patient's willingness to participate fully in his own healing is necessary for its success.

Holistic and conventional medicine take two different attitudes toward power: active and passive. The chemical treatments of conventional medicine require no conscious participation on the part of the patient, but a holistic technique like visualization is enhanced by an active, involved patient. An energy connection occurs, in other words, between the consciousness of the patient and the healing capacity of the therapy and sometimes even of the therapist. When a person is passive—with an attitude of "just do it to me"—he does not fully heal; he may recover, but he may never deal fully with the source of his illness.

Acquisitioners

The mother with depression and chronic neck and back pain is an example of someone with only passive power. This kind of dependent person feels she must acquire power from her external environment and from or through someone else. She thinks, consciously or unconsciously, "Alone, I am nothing." Such a person seeks to acquire power through money; social status; political, social, military, or religious authority; and relationships with influential people. She does not directly express her own needs but becomes skilled at tolerating or manipulating unsatisfactory situations.

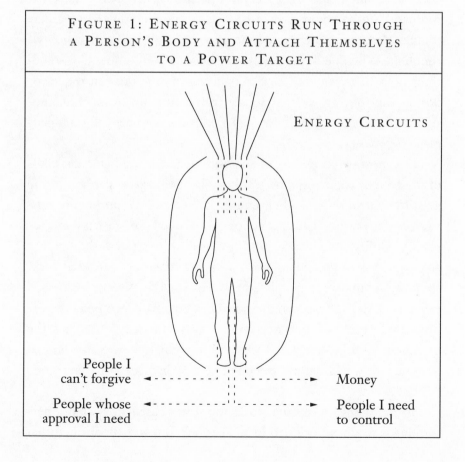

FIGURE 1: ENERGY CIRCUITS RUN THROUGH A PERSON'S BODY AND ATTACH THEMSELVES TO A POWER TARGET

ENERGY CIRCUITS

People I can't forgive ◄ - - - - - - - - - ► Money

People whose approval I need ◄ - - - - - - - - - ► People I need to control

In the human energy system, our individual interactions with our environment can be thought of symbolically as electromagnetic circuits. These circuits run through our bodies and connect us to external objects and other people. We are drawn to power objects or people, or "power targets," so that we can draw their power into our system. Our connection with a power target, however, draws some power away from our own field and into the target.

At first I thought of these energy circuits as symbolic, but I have come to believe that they are actually real pathways of energy. So often I hear people comment that they feel "hooked" on a person or an experience from their past. Some people remark that they feel "drained" after being with a certain person or in a particular environment. These common words, in fact, come closer than we may think to describing the interaction of our energy field with our environment. When people say they are "hooked" on someone or something in a negative way, or are overidentifying with an object or possession, they are unconsciously conducting an intuitive diagnosis—they are identifying how they are losing power. I call such people *acquisitioners*.

The most extreme type of acquisitioner is the addict. Regardless of the type of addiction a person has—be it to drugs, alcohol, or the need to control others—their energy circuits are so thoroughly connected to the target that they no longer have the use of their own reasoning ability. One case that tragically illustrates the energy consequences of an addiction came to my attention during a workshop in Denmark for people who were either HIV positive or had developed AIDS. A woman there named Anna had become HIV positive as a result of her occupation, prostitution. Anna had the demeanor of a little girl and was extremely petite. She also limped because four weeks before, several of her ribs had been broken by one of her "clients."

At one point during the workshop, I was discussing what a person needs to do in order to heal a serious illness. I mentioned that addictions, such as tobacco, drugs, and alcohol, detract from a person's healing process. During a break Anna came up to me and said, "But, Caroline, how bad could it be to smoke only two cigarettes per day?" As I looked at her, I realized that if I were holding the cure for AIDS in my left hand and a cigarette in my right and I said to her, "Pick the one you want," her mind would have chosen the cure for AIDS, but all her energy circuits would have gone directly to that one cigarette.

I cannot emphasize this point strongly enough: the targets to which acquisitioners connect their energy circuits are people or objects to which they have surrendered their power—specifically, the power to control them. Anna's addiction to cigarettes maintained more authority over her than her desire to heal. Unaccustomed to making empowering choices for herself, she was tied into a pattern of releasing her energy into the hands of others—most often her pimp and her cigarettes, the two power targets that controlled her entirely. Healing was beyond her reach because her power now existed *outside* the boundaries of her physical body.

Our minds cannot easily compete with our emotional needs. Anna knew very well that both her occupation and her addiction to cigarettes were hazardous to her health. But she still craved tobacco emotionally because she believed it relaxed her, and she remained involved with her pimp because she believed that he took care of her. Anna's mind had rationalized her emotional attachment, and it was trying to negotiate her healing process by proposing that two cigarettes could not possibly harm her health. Unable to pull away from her addictions, Anna was unable to regain her power to heal.

It is not the mind but our emotional needs that control our attachment to our power targets. The famous adage "The heart has reasons that reason knows naught of" captures perfectly this dynamic. Acquisitioners inevitably find using their intuition extremely difficult. So attached is their self-esteem to the opinion of their power target that they automatically negate any information that their own intuition transmits to them. Clear intuition requires the ability to respect your own impressions. If you need another person to validate your own impressions, you interfere tremendously with your ability to intuit.

Since healing is nonnegotiable, acquisitioners find healing a more formidable challenge than people who have a sense of active power. Healing is, above all, a solo task. No one can heal on behalf of another person. We can assist others, to be sure, but no one can, for instance, forgive someone on behalf of someone else. Nor can any of us cause someone to release the painful memories or experiences that he needs to release in order to heal. Because the very nature of passive power is "power through attachments," it runs contrary to an acquisitioner's entire biology to release or detach himself from targets that are draining his energy. Acquisitioners are almost programmed for conventional medical treatment. This is not necessarily always negative; conventional treatment is the most appropriate form of healing for them as long as they remain passive.

Redirecting Power

Most people who attend my workshops come because they realize they need to change their lives. Some are afraid to leave their partner or their job, while others are trying to find a way to live with a situation that is incompatible with their emotional needs. I can't begin to calculate the number of times people have said, "I think I was better off before I realized how unhappy I was."

Once we make conscious our emotional needs, however, it's impossible to forget them. Once we become aware of the source of any unhappiness, we cannot expunge that awareness. We have to make choices. The ability to choose is an active power—and the sensation of having active power is both thrilling and threatening, because it makes us *want* to change those parts of our lives that are no longer appropriate. And changing those parts inspires us to challenge other aspects of our lives that are not satisfactory.

Changing our lives is often difficult because of our existing loyalties. Usually we learn about loyalty within our family structure and as a connection toward our family. Loyalty to oneself, however, is an entirely different virtue, and adhering to it can cause tremendous upheaval in a family. Becoming loyal to herself may, for instance, cause a woman to recognize that she can no longer remain within her marriage. Upon sharing this information with her husband, she will be told, "Think of the children." Her case is an extremely common example of group loyalty conflicting with loyalty to oneself. While living in an unsatisfactory situation, we may try for a while to honor the demands of group loyalty, and we may avoid thinking about our personal emotional needs. At some point, however, our emotional body becomes sufficiently "empowered" that the mind can no longer fool the heart. The unhappy wife will either end up in unceasing personal turmoil by remaining in the marriage, or she will pursue a divorce while filled with guilt that she has been disloyal to the group, her family. In truth, there are not many ways to successfully introduce your personal needs into a circumstance that was created before you realized what your personal needs were.

Julie attended one of my workshops because she was suffering from serious ovarian and breast cancer. Her marriage was dysfunctional, as it had been for several years. She wanted to heal her cancer, but she lived with a man who treated her with total contempt, a pattern that had begun two years after they married. He frequently told Julie that he was repulsed by the very sight of her, in spite of the fact that she was an extremely attractive woman. To try to gain his approval, she starved herself and exercised constantly. She described herself as a master of manipulation, which she used to cope with her marriage, although her manipulations did not get her what she wanted. When Julie wanted attention from her husband, she would invent interesting stories about people she said she had met while shopping. One time she telephoned him at his office with a made-up story that a man had tried to rape her while she was jogging. No matter what story she fabricated, however, nothing seemed to ignite either his concern or his respect.

Money was another issue between them. Although Julie's husband earned a very high salary, he kept her on a tight allowance, demanding that she account for every cent. In spite of this humiliation, Julie never considered getting a job to supplement her personal income, believing she had no marketable skills.

Sexual activity had ceased after two years of marriage. Julie's efforts to keep this part of her marriage alive caused her further humiliation. After her diagnosis of cancer, her husband refused to sleep in the same bed with her. Her response to that rejection was to sleep on the floor of the doorway into their bedroom. Every morning he would literally step over her on his way to the bathroom, occasionally spitting on her when she looked up at him and asked for help.

When asked why she did not leave him, Julie replied that she had never been able to take care of herself emotionally or financially, and now more than ever, she needed someone to take care of her. Ironically, whenever she spoke about her husband, a sort of drifty look would come over her face, almost as if she were under a spell, and she would say he was a genuinely caring man who was simply under a great deal of pressure from his business. He really loved her, she added; it was just that he had a difficult time showing affection.

When I suggested to Julie that she see a psychotherapist, she said that her husband believed therapists did no one any good, so she could not go to one. I also suggested that some measure of strength might return to her body if she ate foods that were good for her, including an intense vitamin regimen with a healthy diet. Again, Julie replied that if her husband approved of these suggestions, she would act on them.

In energy terms it is significant that Julie developed cancer in her female system—first in her ovaries, then her breast. Her illness was a symbolic statement of her feelings of rejection as a woman. As you'll read in the next chapter, our sexual organs contain our biographical energy, specifically that of our relationships to people as well as our way of being in our external environments. Julie could not see herself as having any personal power because she saw her husband as the source of her security; her biology was constantly receiving "powerlessness signals." Julie died within a year.

Active power types are quite different from acquisitioners like Julie. They are "self-motivators"—they believe self-care is a priority,

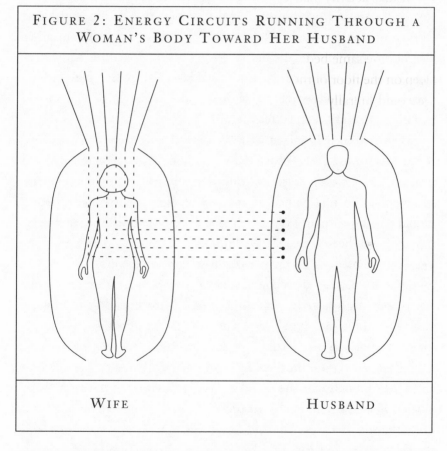

FIGURE 2: ENERGY CIRCUITS RUNNING THROUGH A
WOMAN'S BODY TOWARD HER HUSBAND

WIFE   HUSBAND

NOTE: *Because this woman is totally dependent upon her husband, all her energy circuits are attached to his energy field. This imbalance results in the woman having no energy to keep her own body healthy and simultaneously generates in her husband a feeling of being "smothered."*

and their energy circuits are attached to awareness, strength, and emotional stamina. A self-motivator is able to do whatever is required to maintain the balance of body, mind, and soul.

Like Julie, Joanna had a dysfunctional marriage and developed breast cancer. Although Joanna's marriage was not quite the emotional horror story Julie's was, it had its problems. Joanna's husband, Neal, kept company with several other women. Joanna knew about it but tried to overlook it. In her attempt to live with his adultery, she started to attend workshops for empowering women. Through these workshops she eventually saw that Neal's behavior was violating her emotional boundaries. Prior to the workshops Joanna had never thought in terms of personal emotional boundaries. She had entered marriage, as many people do, with the idea that two people should become one emotional system.

Joanna soon recognized that her breast cancer—which appeared in the area of the body associated with giving and nurturing—would heal only if she took steps to honor herself, to develop self-esteem. Increasingly Joanna gained an internal image of herself as a strong individual. By thinking of herself as an *individual*, she began a relationship with herself that she had not previously considered possible, since her concept of identity had always *required* a spouse.

As Joanna came to recognize her own needs, she exercised her new inner authority by standing up to Neal and demanding he adhere to their marriage vows. He promised to change his behavior—but that promise lasted less than a month. Joanna finally realized that she could not change him—and that she herself had changed so much that she could no longer accept his emotional violations. If she were to heal her cancer, she had to remove herself from the situation that was ruining her health. She divorced Neal and recovered from her cancer.

Support groups for people with illnesses often bring their members to a new self-definition. By acknowledging their own needs and evaluating their lives accordingly, they admit that their present circumstances are neither acceptable to the person they are becoming nor conducive to their healing. They realize that they have to take steps to change. In the process of healing, they learn to detach themselves from objects or people who are drawing the strength right out of their bodies.

The necessity of change makes healing a terrifying experience for many people. These individuals know, consciously or unconsciously, that unplugging their energy circuits from a power target is the same as saying good-bye to it. They enter into an unsettling limbo where they want simultaneously to unplug from their power target and to hang on to it. Some people end up trying to live in the two worlds simultaneously, not entirely inhabiting the one that no longer suits them, yet never quite moving on to the next either. Thus it is that many people journey to the well of healing but find, once they get there, that they cannot actually drink.

Healing requires taking action. It is not a passive event. We are meant to draw on our inner resources, to find the material strength to leave behind our outmoded beliefs and behaviors, and to see ourselves in new healthy ways—to take up our beds and walk.

Learning Symbolic Sight

In Part II, as I describe the power issues that are woven into our psyches and our biology, try to diagnose your own relationship with each of the seven power centers of your body. Make yourself the subject of your first intuitive evaluation. In the process, you will find yourself becoming more aware of the extraordinary world that lies behind your eyes. Ultimately, you will learn *symbolic sight*, the ability to use your intuition to interpret the power symbols in your life.

I offer the following guidelines as a beginning point. When a person seeks to see more, healing is inevitable. But you need an internal method of absorbing this information to make it *real* for you.

First and foremost, focus your attention on learning to interpret your life's challenges symbolically. Find a meaning in them. Think and feel how they connect to your health. Bring attention every day to the challenges you face and to how your mind and spirit respond to them. Observe what causes you to lose power, and where you feel the loss. Evaluate the spiritual and biological activity that occurs as a consequence.

Second, think of yourself at all times as an *energy being* as well as a physical one. The energy part of yourself is the transmitter and recorder of all your thoughts and interactions. Keep in mind at all times that your biography becomes your biology. Develop the habit of evaluating the people, experiences, and information you allow into your life. Developing symbolic sight begins with intention: consciously and regularly evaluate your interactions and their influence on your emotional and physical power. And remember that if you have a private agenda—that is, if you want to see things in a certain way—you will interfere with your reception of energy information.

Third, conduct energy self-evaluations on a daily basis. After you become skilled at it, self-scanning will take only a few moments. To practice, use the model of the human energy system presented in Chapter 2 as a reference. Reflect on each power center for a minute or two in a quiet, objective way. Don't wait to become ill before you attend to the health of your energy system. Learn to sense the stress accumulating in your energy field, and take the steps to heal yourself at the energy level. Make self-evaluation a habit.

Fourth, when you discover an energy leak, focus on only the essentials that can help you recover your energy. Always address the question "Why am I losing power?" In healing any imbalance, whether it is energetic or physical, you must always involve both your mind and your heart. Always strive to see beyond the physical components of a crisis. Refer to each of the seven sacred truths of energy (as introduced in Chapter 2). One or more of those truths will be involved in your stressful situation. Ask yourself which of those truths are symbolically represented there.

For example, if you are in a crisis at work, you may want to refer to the sacred truth *Honor Oneself*. It may well speak to the issues that are being played out in your life. By grabbing hold of that one perception, you lift yourself out of the quicksand of illusion—you get the spiritual or symbolic height you need to interpret your situation impersonally and to learn the power lesson that the situation holds for you.

Spiritual instruction teaches us to keep our focus on ourselves—not in an egocentric way but as a way of consciously managing our energy and power. So, your fifth task is to learn *what* rather than *who* draws power from you. Understand that the person who seems to be drawing your energy is actually only a reflection of some part of yourself. For instance, if you are jealous of someone, the important issue for you is not that specific person but the shadow side of your nature as it is reflected in that person. In effect, that person serves as your teacher. Concentrating on the person of whom you are jealous will not heal you. You will only be sent more and more teachers, each more intense than the previous one. Your task is to learn the lesson that the teacher has for you rather than to resent the teacher.

When you erroneously conclude that a specific person is the cause of your feeling depleted, you are slipping into fear and blame. You need to refocus on your power center until you get an impression of what kind of power that person has in relation to you. Once you set your sights on the lesson rather than the teacher, you have achieved a significant benefit of symbolic sight: you see that truth being delivered to you through the challenge.

Sixth, simplify your requirements for healing. The requirements to heal any illness are essentially the same. Think of the illness as a power disorder—almost like a technical malfunction. Once you identify which sacred truth applies to your situation, organize your internal healing process around learning from that truth. Combine your internal healing with any conventional medical treatment that is essential, and stick to your program. Reach out for any support that you require, and use that support appropriately. Remember that the task is to move through your wounds, not to live in them. Don't waste time by thinking, acting, or praying like a victim. Feeling victimized only adds to your illness, and should it become a full-time state of mind, it would qualify as an illness in itself.

Do all that is necessary to support your physical body, such as taking the appropriate medicine, maintaining a daily exercise program, and eating properly. Simultaneously, do all that is necessary to support your energy body, such as releasing unfinished business and forgiving injuries from the past. Make whatever personal changes are necessary for healing to take place—leave that stressful job or marriage; take up a meditation practice; or learn cross-country skiing. The specific changes you make are not the important point here. The point is to actually make the changes that healing requires.

Talking does not heal; taking action does. While it is essential to work at maintaining a positive attitude whatever your illness, healing requires dedication and commitment. Visualization will not work if you practice it only once a week, and no one's body becomes fit from only one trip to the gym. Healing one's body or one's life challenges—or developing symbolic sight—requires daily practice and attention. Healing illness in particular may be a full-time occupation, although you can simplify the steps required to accomplish the task.

If you are using a complex healing "package"—that is, several different therapies and therapists, several physicians, several herbal and vitamin programs—but are making little or no progress, you may actually be blocking your own healing. Perhaps becoming healthy in some way threatens you more than you realize. Perhaps you are unable to let go of something from the past, or perhaps becoming healthy would alter the balance of power between you and another person. Use your head in thinking about this, because obviously, some illnesses are genuinely more serious than others, and the lack of healing does not always signal that you are blocking your healing process. But if ten different therapies and therapists are not enough to bring some degree of healing into your life, then you need to consider the possibility of conscious or unconscious interference or the very real possibility that your healing may include preparation to leave this physical life.

Seventh, simplify your spirituality. All my earthly studies of heaven have led me to the conclusion that heaven is not a complicated realm. Therefore one's personal theology should not be complicated. Seek to believe only what heaven has issued as essential. For example:

- All circumstances can be changed in a moment, and all illness can be healed. The Divine is not limited by human time, space, or physical concerns.
- Be consistent: live what you believe.
- Change is constant. Every life goes through phases of difficult change as well as peace. Learn to go with the flow of change rather than try to stop change from occurring.
- Never look to another person to make you happy—happiness is an internal, personal attitude and responsibility.
- Life is essentially a learning experience. Every situation, challenge, and relationship contains some message worth learning or teaching to others.
- Positive energy works more effectively than negative energy in each and every situation.
- Live in the present moment, and practice forgiveness of others.

We gain nothing by believing that heaven "thinks and acts" in complex ways. It is far better, and more effective, to learn to think the way heaven does—in simple and eternal truths.

In all likelihood we have made our lives far more complex than they have to be. Achieving health, happiness, and an energy balance comes down to deciding to focus more on the positive than on the negative and to live in a manner spiritually congruent with what we know is the truth. Making those two commitments alone is sufficient to allow the power contained within our Divine biological system to influence the content and direction of our lives.

We are all meant to learn the same truths and to allow our Divinity to work within and through us; this is a simple task, though hardly an easy one. The settings and people in our lives are different, but the challenges they represent to us are identical, as are the influences that these challenges have upon our bodies and our spirits. The more we are able to learn this truth, the more we can develop symbolic sight—the ability to see through physical illusions and recognize the lesson being offered to us by life's challenges.

CHAPTER 2

Made in the Image of God

Ever since I got my first medical intuitions, I have been aware that they are basically about the human spirit, even though they describe physical problems and even though I use energy terms to explain them to others. *Energy* is a neutral word that evokes no religious associations or deeply held fears about one's relationship to God. It is much easier for someone to be told "Your energy is depleted" than "Your spirit is toxic." Yet most of the people who come to me have, in fact, been in spiritual crises. I have described their crises to them as energy disorders, but doing so was not as helpful as discussing them in spiritual terms, too, would have been.

I ultimately did incorporate spiritual language into my energy descriptions after I realized the congruencies between the Eastern chakras and Western religious sacraments. It happened suddenly, during one of my workshops on energy anatomy. As I was giving the opening lecture, I drew seven circles on the blackboard, lined up vertically to represent the power centers of the human energy system. As I turned to face the empty circles, I was struck by the fact that there are not only seven chakras but also seven Christian sacraments. In that moment I understood that their spiritual messages are the same. Later, as I researched and explored their similarities more deeply, I learned that the Kabbalah, too, has seven corresponding teachings. These three traditions' congruencies led me to see that spirituality is far more than a psychological and emotional need: it is an inherent biological need. Our spirits, our energy, and our personal power are all one and the same force.

The seven sacred truths that these traditions share lie at the core of our spiritual power. They instruct us in how to direct the power—or life-force—that runs through our systems. In effect, we embody these truths in our seven power centers. They are part of our internal physical and spiritual guidance system, and at the same time they are a universal, external guidance system for our spiritual behavior and for the creation of health. Our spiritual task in this lifetime is to learn to balance the energies of body and soul, of thought and action, of physical and mental power. Our bodies contain an immanent blueprint for healing.

The Book of Genesis describes Adam's body as created "in the image of God." The message in this phrase is both literal and symbolic. It means that people are energy duplicates of a Divine power—a system of seven primary energies whose truths we are meant to explore and develop through this experience called life.

When I realized that the human energy system embodies these seven truths, I could no longer limit myself to an energy vocabulary, and I began incorporating spiritual ideas in my intuitive diagnoses. Because our biological design is also a spiritual design, the language of energy and spirit used together crosses a variety of belief systems. It opens avenues of communication between faiths and even allows people to return to religious cultures they formerly rejected, unburdened by religious dogma. People in my workshops have readily adopted this energy-spirit language to address the challenges inherent in their physical illnesses, stress disorders, or emotional suffering. Seeing their problem within a spiritual framework accelerates their healing process because it adds a dimension of meaning and purpose to their crisis. They are able to help themselves heal; they co-create their health and re-create their lives. Because all human stress corresponds to a spiritual crisis and is an opportunity for spiritual learning, you can gain insight into the use, misuse, or misdirection of your spirit, your personal power, in almost any illness.

The source of human consciousness, spirit, or power is considered Divine in most religious and cultural traditions, from the ancient Greek and Hindu teachings to the Chinese and Mayan. Most every culture's myths recount Divine interaction with humanity in stories of the gods mating with human beings to produce godlike and half-godlike offspring. These offspring embody the full spectrum of human behavior—from great acts of creation, destruction, and vengeance to petty acts of jealousy, rivalry, and pique, to transcendental acts of metamorphosis, sex, and sensuality. The early cultures that created these divine mythologies were exploring their emotional and psychological natures and the powers inherent in the human spirit. Each culture expressed its own view of the transformations and passages of the universal spiritual journey—the hero's journey, in Joseph Campbell's parlance.

Among God stories, however, the Jewish tradition is unique, because Yahweh is never depicted as being sexual. God is referred to as having a right and left hand, but the description never continues "below the waist." Unlike other spiritual traditions, the Jews transferred only limited human qualities to Yahweh, maintaining a more distant relationship with their inaccessible Divine.

When Christianity appeared on the scene, however, its then-still-Jewish followers gave their God a human body, calling him Jesus, the son of God. The Christians' great heresy, for other Jews, was to cross the biological divide and begin their new theology with a biospiritual event—the Annunciation. In the Annunciation the angel Gabriel announces to the Virgin Mary that she has shown great favor with the Lord and is to bear a son and call him Jesus. The implication is that God is the biological father of this child. Suddenly the abstract Divine principle in Judaism called Yahweh was mating with a human woman.

Christians made Jesus' birth into a "biological theology" and used Jesus' life as evidence that humanity is made in the "image and likeness of God." Jews and Christians alike believed our physical bodies, particularly male physical bodies, to be like God's. More contemporary theological writings have challenged that biological likeness, revising it into a spiritual likeness, but the original notion that we are biologically made in the image of God remains, nonetheless, a major literal and archetypal aspect of the Judeo-Christian tradition.

The thread common to all spiritual myths is that human beings are compelled to merge our bodies with the essence of God, that we want to have the Divine in our bones and blood and in our mental and emotional makeup. In belief systems around the world, conceptions of the Divine's spiritual nature reflect the best human qualities and characteristics. Since at our best we are compassionate, then God must be all-compassionate; since we are capable of forgiveness, then God must be all-forgiving; since we are capable of love, then God must be only love; since we try to be just, Divine justice must rule over our efforts to balance right and wrong. In Eastern traditions Divine justice is the law of karma; in the Christian world it underlies the Golden Rule. We have woven the Divine, one way or another, into all aspects of our lives, our thoughts, and our actions.

Today many spiritual seekers are trying to infuse their daily lives with a heightened consciousness of the sacred, striving to act as if each of their attitudes expressed their spiritual essence. Such conscious living is an invocation, a request for personal spiritual authority. It represents a dismantling of the old religions' classic parent-child relationship to God and a move into spiritual adulthood. Spiritual maturation includes not only developing the ability to interpret the deeper messages of sacred texts, but learning to read the spiritual language of the body. As we become more conscious and recognize the impact of our thoughts and attitudes—our internal life—upon our physical bodies and external lives, we no longer need to conceive of an external parent-God that creates for us and on whom we are fully dependent. As spiritual adults we accept responsibility for co-creating our lives and our health. Co-creation is in fact the essence of spiritual adulthood: it is the exercise of choice and the acceptance of our responsibility for those choices.

Managing our power of choice is the Divine challenge, the sacred contract that we are here to fulfill. It begins with choosing what our thoughts and attitudes will be. Whereas choice once meant our ability to respond to that which God has created for us, it now means that we are participants in what we experience—that we co-create our physical bodies through the creative strength of our thoughts and emotions. The seven sacred truths of the Kabbalah, the Christian sacraments, and the Hindu chakras support our gradual transformation into conscious spiritual adults. These literal and symbolic teachings redefine spiritual and biological health and help us understand what keeps us healthy, what makes us ill, and what helps us heal.

The seven sacred truths transcend cultural boundaries, and at the symbolic level they constitute a road map for our life journey—a road map imprinted in our biological design. Again and again the sacred texts tell us that our life's purpose is to understand and develop the power of our spirit, power that is vital to our mental and physical well-being. Abusing this power depletes our spirit and siphons the life-force itself out of our physical bodies.

Because Divine energy is inherent in our biological system, every thought that crosses our minds, every belief we nurture, every memory to which we cling translates into a positive or negative command to our bodies and spirits. It is magnificent to see ourselves through this lens, but it is also intimidating, because no part of our lives or thoughts is powerless or even private. We are biological creations of Divine design. Once this truth becomes a part of your conscious mind, you can never again live an ordinary life.

The Symbolic Power
of the Seven Chakras

Eastern religions teach that the human body contains seven energy centers. Each of these energy centers contains a universal spiritual life-lesson that we must learn as we evolve into higher consciousness. Only after I had been conducting regular intuitive evaluations for many years did I realize that I had been instinctively focusing on these seven energy centers. This sacred, ancient imagery is remarkably accurate in its depiction of the human energy system, its habits, and its tendencies.

The chakra system is an archetypal depiction of individual maturation through seven distinct stages. The chakras are vertically aligned, running from the base of the spine to the crown of the head, suggesting that we ascend toward the Divine by gradually mastering the seductive pull of the physical world. At each stage we gain a more refined understanding of personal and spiritual power, since each chakra represents a spiritual life-lesson or challenge common to all human beings. As a person masters each chakra, he gains power and self-knowledge that become integrated into his spirit, advancing him along the path toward spiritual consciousness in the classic hero's journey.

The following is a very brief summary of the spiritual life-lessons represented by the seven chakras (see figure 3):

The first chakra: lessons related to the material world
The second chakra: lessons related to sexuality, work, and physical desire
The third chakra: lessons related to the ego, personality, and self-esteem
The fourth chakra: lessons related to love, forgiveness, and compassion

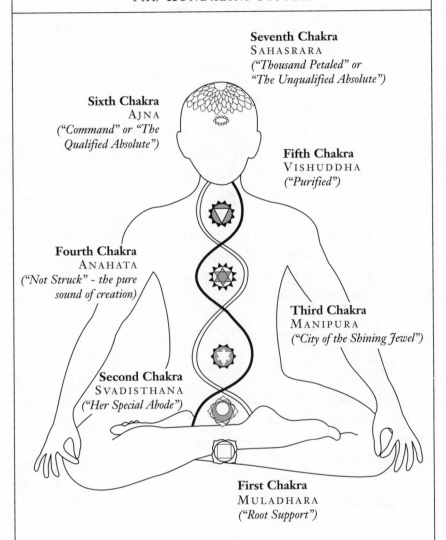

FIGURE 3: SEVEN POWER CENTERS OR CHAKRAS OF THE KUNDALINI SYSTEM

Seventh Chakra
SAHASRARA
("Thousand Petaled" or
"The Unqualified Absolute")

Sixth Chakra
AJNA
("Command" or "The
Qualified Absolute")

Fifth Chakra
VISHUDDHA
("Purified")

Fourth Chakra
ANAHATA
("Not Struck" - the pure
sound of creation)

Third Chakra
MANIPURA
("City of the Shining Jewel")

Second Chakra
SVADISTHANA
("Her Special Abode")

First Chakra
MULADHARA
("Root Support")

The chakras are depicted as lotuses. The spirals indicate the contrasting energies of psyche and spirit: the fiery energies or darker helix contrast with the lighter, spiritual energies and lighter helix, all of which must be brought together in balance.

Source: Joseph Campbell, *The Mythic Image* (Princeton, N.J.: Princeton University Press, 1974)

The fifth chakra: lessons related to will and self-expression
The sixth chakra: lessons related to mind, intuition, insight, and wisdom
The seventh chakra: lessons related to spirituality

These seven spiritual life-lessons direct us toward greater consciousness. If we ignore our responsibility and need to address consciously these seven spiritual lessons, however, their energy can manifest itself in illness. Indeed, the many Eastern spiritual traditions understand illness to be a depletion of one's internal power, or spirit. The congruencies among major spiritual traditions underscore the universal human experience of the connection between the spirit and the body, illness and healing.

Seen symbolically rather than literally, the seven Christian sacraments clearly parallel the seven chakras in meaning.

The Symbolic Power of the Christian Sacraments

The early Christian church identified seven sacraments, or officially recognized rituals, that were to be conducted by the ordained leaders of the church. These seven sacraments were, and still are, sacred ceremonies that imprint the individual with—to use Christian language—specific qualities of "grace or Divine energy." Each quality of grace is unique to its sacrament. While the seven Christian sacraments are now associated primarily with the Roman Catholic Church, other Christian traditions have maintained many of them, such as Baptism, Marriage, and Ordination.

Symbolically, each sacrament also represents a stage of empowerment that invites the Divine directly into a person's spirit. The term *sacrament* itself means a ritual invoking the power of the sacred into the soul of the individual. The symbolic significance of the sacraments transcends their religious significance, and my references to them should not be misconstrued to suggest that people need literally to receive the sacraments from a Christian institution.

The sacraments provide symbolic tasks for growth into spiritual maturity and for healing. But they are also concrete in their depiction of what we must do at major stages in our lives to accept the personal responsibility that comes with spiritual maturity. The sacraments also are acts that we are meant to perform besides rituals that are performed on us. They represent powers we are meant to bestow on others as well as to receive from others. Consider the sacrament of Baptism, for instance, in which a family accepts physical and spiritual responsibility for a child they have brought into the world. Our challenge as spiritual adults is to accept symbolically, fully, and gratefully the family into which we were born. Symbolically, Baptism also means honoring your family and yourself by forgiving family members for any pain they caused you during your childhood. The power contained in such forgiveness is precisely the power that heals the body.

The seven sacraments and their symbolic purposes are as follows:

Baptism: to receive or bestow an expression of grace representing gratitude for one's life in the physical world

Communion: to receive or bestow an expression of grace —in the form of a "host"—that represents holy union with God and with the people in one's life

Confirmation: to receive or bestow an expression of grace that enhances one's individuality and self-esteem

Marriage: to receive or bestow a blessing making sacred a union with oneself, symbolic of recognizing and honoring the essential need to love and care for oneself in order that one can fully love another

Confession: to receive or bestow the grace to cleanse one's spirit of negative acts of will

Ordination: to receive or bestow the grace to make sacred
one's path of service

Extreme Unction: to receive or bestow the grace to finish
one's unfinished business not just before death, but
as a daily part of one's life, thus allowing a person to
love in "present time"

These seven stages of personal initiation represent inherent
powers that we are meant to actualize, powers that we need consciously to utilize and employ through meeting the challenges that
life presents.

The Symbolic Power of the Ten Sefirot

The ten sefirot, or Tree of Life of the Kabbalah, comprise a complex
teaching that evolved over many centuries, one strikingly comparable
to that of the chakras and sacraments. In the medieval Kabbalah the
ten sefirot describe the ten qualities of the Divine nature. Since three
of the ten qualities are partnered with another three, the ten qualities
can actually be grouped in *seven* levels, often portrayed as an upside-
down mythical Tree of Life with its roots in the heavens above. The
ten sefirot are considered the Divine blueprint of the teaching that
"the human being is created in the image of God" (Genesis 1:27),
according to Daniel Chanan Matt in *The Zohar: The Book of Enlightenment* (Paulist Press, 1983). The Divine shares these ten qualities
with human beings—they are spiritual powers that we are mandated
to develop and refine in our life journey.

Although Judaism maintains the most abstract face of God, the
ten sefirot come as close to describing the personality of Yahweh as
is permissible. Unlike the other religious traditions, Judaism never
considered its prophets to be direct incarnations of the Divine itself.
In contrast, even Buddhism began with a man, Siddhartha, who was
anointed to carry the message of enlightenment among the people of

FIGURE 4: THE TEN SEFIROT: THE TREE OF LIFE

 KETER

The energy of the Divine that flows into physical manifestation

The energy of the Divine mother, symbolic of understanding and the intelligence of God

 BINAH

 HOKHMAH

The energy of wisdom and the contact point between the Divine mind and human thought

The energy of the power of judgment

 GEVURAH

 HESED

The energy of the love and mercy of God

 TIF'ERET

The energy of compassion, harmony, and beauty

The energy of the majesty of God

 HOD

 NEZAH

The energy of the endurance of God

 YESOD

The energy of the procreative force of God

The energy of the mystical community of Israel—symbolic of the mystical community of humanity

 SHEKHINAH

the earth. Buddhism does not describe a humanlike God force, but Hinduism has many gods who came to earth, and Christianity has the "son of God," who lived for thirty-three years among humankind.

The ten sefirot are the qualities of the Divine that also form the archetypal human being. These qualities are interpreted both as the essence of God and as paths by which we can return to God. Each quality represents a progression toward a more powerful revelation of the "names" or "faces" of God. Often, the ten qualities are described as the garments of the King—garments that allow us to look directly at the King, the source of Divine light, without being blinded. The other image, the upside-down tree, symbolizes that the roots of these ten qualities rest deeply within a Divine nature that draws us back to the heavens through prayer, contemplation, and action. Our task is to ascend to our Divine source by evolving these ten qualities within ourselves.

The qualities in the ten sefirot, the Christian sacraments, and the chakra system are virtually identical. The only difference is in how the powers are numbered. Whereas the sacraments and the chakras begin with the base as the number one and count upward, the ten sefirot begin with the number one at the top (the roots of the tree) and count downward. Other than that, the qualities attributed to each of the seven levels are virtually identical.

The acceptable order of the ten sefirot, the names most commonly used, and their symbolic meaning (see figure 4) are as follows:

1. **Keter** (sometimes spelled Kether Elyon)—the supreme crown of God, representing the part of the Divine that inspires physical manifestation. This sefirah is the most undefined, therefore the most inclusive. There is no identity, no specificity in this point of beginning between heaven and earth.

2. **Hokhmah**—wisdom. This sefirah represents the contact point between the Divine mind and human

thought. Through this energy physical manifestation begins to form; form precedes actual expression. This sefirah could, in contemporary Jungian language, be associated with the unconscious energy called the animus, because it has a male tone to it. It is partnered with the third sefirah, Binah.

3. **Binah**—understanding and the intelligence of God. Binah is also the Divine mother, the womb where all is made ready for birth. This is the anima counterpart to Hokhmah.

4. **Hesed**—the love or mercy of God; also greatness. This sefirah is partnered with the fifth sefirah, Gevurah.

5. **Gevurah** (also known as Din)—power, judgment, and punishment. Hesed and Gevurah are considered the right and left arms of God. The two qualities balance each other.

6. **Tif'eret** (also known as Rahamin)—compassion, harmony, and beauty. This sefirah is considered the trunk of the tree or, to use a comparable symbol, the heart of the tree.

7. **Nezah** (also known as Netsah)—the endurance of God. This sefirah is partnered with the eighth, Hod, and together they represent the legs of the body.

8. **Hod**—the majesty of God. Together, Nezah and Hod form the right and left legs of God. They are also the source of prophecy.

9. **Yesod**—the phallus, the procreative force of God, merging energy into physical form. This sefirah is also known as the Righteous One, which, in Proverbs 10:25, was referred to as the "foundation of the world."

10. **Shekhinah** (also known as Keneset Yisra'el and

Malkhut or Malkhuth)—the feminine, the mystical
community of Israel. All of Israel is her limbs (Zohar
3:23 lb). Balancing the male energy of Yesod, Shekhinah is female and has many female names: Earth,
Moon, Rose, Garden of Eden. This is the grounded
life-force, feeding all that is alive.

When Tif'eret (compassion) and Shekhinah (the feminine) are
merged, the human soul awakens and the mystical journey begins. At
that moment the sefirot cease to be merely abstract and become as
well a detailed road map of spiritual development, directing the individual on her path of ascent.

Even at a casual glance, the archetypal meanings of the chakras,
the sacraments, and the sefirot are identical. If you can feel and
understand the symbolic power contained in all of these traditions,
you have begun to use the power of symbolic sight. You can understand theology as a science of healing for the body, mind, and spirit.

Combining the wisdom of the chakra system with the sacred
power inherent in the Christian sacraments and the Divine characteristics articulated in the ten sefirot gives us insight into the needs
of our spirits and our bodies. That which serves our spirits enhances
our bodies. That which diminishes our spirits diminishes our bodies.

How the Chakras, Sacraments, and Sefirot Work Together

Each of the seven levels of power in our biological system contains
a single sacred truth. This truth continually pulsates within us,
directing us to live according to the right use of its power. We are
born with an inherent knowledge of these seven truths woven into
our energy system. Violating these truths weakens both our spirit
and our physical body, while honoring them enhances the strength
of our spirit and our physical body.

Energy is power, and our bodies require energy; therefore, our bodies require power. The chakras, the sefirot, and the sacraments all speak of interacting with power and of taking control of our own power in gradually more intense processes. At the first level, for example, we learn to handle having a group identity and the power that comes within the family; at later levels we individualize and manage power as adults. Gradually, we learn to manage our minds, our thoughts, and our spirits. Every choice we make, motivated by either faith or fear, directs our spirit. If a person's spirit is impelled by fear, then fear returns to her energy field and to her body. If she directs her spirit in faith, however, then grace returns to her energy field, and her biological system thrives.

All three traditions hold that releasing one's spirit into the physical world through fear or negativity is a faithless act of choosing personal will over the will of the heavens. In Eastern spiritual terms, every action creates karma. Acts of awareness create good karma; acts of fear or negativity create bad karma, in which case one must "retrieve" one's spirit from the fear that motivated the negative action. In the Christian tradition the sacrament of Confession is the act of retrieving one's spirit from negative places in order to enter heaven "complete." In the language of Judaism, a fear that holds such power over a human being is a "false god." In the words of my Athabascan teacher, Rachel, one calls back one's spirit from its misdirections so that one can walk straight.

We are simultaneously matter and spirit. In order to understand ourselves and be healthy in both body and spirit, we have to understand how matter and spirit interact, what draws the spirit or lifeforce out of our bodies, and how we can retrieve our spirits from the false gods of fear, anger, and attachments to the past. Every attachment we hold on to out of fear commands a circuit of our spirit to leave our energy field and, to use a biblical phrase, "breathe life onto earth"—earth that costs us health. What drains your spirit drains your body. What fuels your spirit fuels your body. The power that fuels our bodies, our minds, and our hearts does not originate in our DNA. Rather, it has roots in Divinity itself. The truth is as simple and eternal as that.

Three truths are common to these spiritual traditions and to the principles of medical intuition.

1. Misdirecting the power of one's spirit will generate consequences to one's body and life.

2. Every human being will encounter a series of challenges that tests his allegiance to heaven. These tests will come in the form of the disintegration of one's physical power base: the inevitable loss of wealth, family, health, or worldly power. The loss will activate a crisis of faith, forcing one to ask, "What is it, or who is it, that I have faith in?" Or "Into whose hands have I commended my spirit?"

   Apart from such major losses, the trigger that causes people to seek deeper meaning and psychological and spiritual "ascension" is usually a physical disorder that creates a personal or professional earthquake. We all tend to look upward when the ground beneath our feet shifts out of control.

3. To heal from the misdirection of one's spirit, one has to be willing to act to release the past, cleanse one's spirit, and return to the present moment. "Believe as if it were true now" is a spiritual command from the Book of Daniel to visualize or pray in present time.

In all three of our spiritual traditions, the physical world serves the learning of our spirits, and the "tests" we encounter there follow a well-ordained pattern.

In the chakra system (see figure 5) each energy center warehouses a particular power. These powers ascend from the densest physical power to the most etheric or spiritual power. Remarkably, the challenges we face in our lives tend to follow this alignment as well. Chakras one, two, and three are calibrated to the issues that engage us with physical or external power. Chakras four, five, six, and seven are calibrated to nonphysical or internal power. When we align them with the sacraments and the sefirot, we have not only the script for the development of our consciousness but a spiritual language of healing as well as a symbolic life map of the inevitable challenges in our healing process.

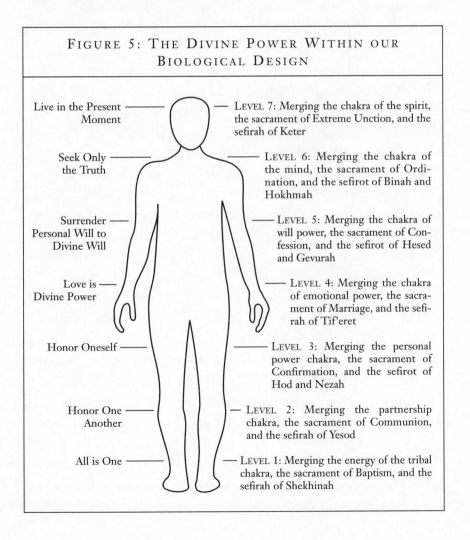

FIGURE 5: THE DIVINE POWER WITHIN OUR BIOLOGICAL DESIGN

Live in the Present Moment — LEVEL 7: Merging the chakra of the spirit, the sacrament of Extreme Unction, and the sefirah of Keter

Seek Only the Truth — LEVEL 6: Merging the chakra of the mind, the sacrament of Ordination, and the sefirot of Binah and Hokhmah

Surrender Personal Will to Divine Will — LEVEL 5: Merging the chakra of will power, the sacrament of Confession, and the sefirot of Hesed and Gevurah

Love is Divine Power — LEVEL 4: Merging the chakra of emotional power, the sacrament of Marriage, and the sefirah of Tif'eret

Honor Oneself — LEVEL 3: Merging the personal power chakra, the sacrament of Confirmation, and the sefirot of Hod and Nezah

Honor One Another — LEVEL 2: Merging the partnership chakra, the sacrament of Communion, and the sefirah of Yesod

All is One — LEVEL 1: Merging the energy of the tribal chakra, the sacrament of Baptism, and the sefirah of Shekhinah

The Seven Sacred Truths

External Power

Level One: The merging of the first or Tribal chakra (Muladhara), the sacrament of Baptism, and the sefirah of Shekhinah.

The power created by these three archetypal forces transmits into our energy and biological systems the sacred truth *All Is One.* We are interconnected with all of life and to one another. Each of us must learn to honor this truth. By connecting to the energy of any of these three archetypal forces we can connect to this truth. The Tribal chakra resonates to our need to honor familial bonds and to have a code of honor within ourselves. You first encounter the truth *All Is One* within your biological family, learning to respect the "blood bond." Your family may also teach you, "We are all part of one Divine family. All is one," in your church or synagogue. Your bond to your biological family is symbolic of your connection to everyone and all that is life. As Thich Nhat Hanh says, we "inter-are." Violating this energy bond by, for instance, considering those who are different from us to be less than us creates conflict within our spirit and therefore within our physical body. Accepting and acting according to the basic truth *All Is One* is a universal spiritual challenge.

In the actual Christian sacrament of Baptism, a family makes a twofold commitment. First, it accepts its physical responsibility for the new life that has been born into it, and second, all members accept their responsibility to teach the child spiritual principles. Fulfilling these responsibilities creates a strong foundation of faith and truth upon which one can rely throughout life.

For a spiritual adult the sacrament of Baptism as a symbol carries two other commitments. First, we have a spiritual need to accept fully our family of origin as having been "Divinely chosen" for teaching us the lessons we need to learn in this lifetime. Second, we commit ourselves to accepting personal responsibility for living honorably as a member of the human tribe, for doing unto others as we would have them do unto us, and for respecting all life on this earth. By fulfilling these two commitments, we are, in essence, baptizing ourselves and honoring our own lives. Reneging on this commitment by, for instance, viewing our family of origin in negative terms depletes a great deal of power from our energy system because it opposes the higher truth within the energy system.

The sefirah of Shekhinah, whose name means "divine presence," is the Divine consciousness that creates and protects the mystical community of Israel. In a more symbolic and universal perspective, the Divine consciousness creates and protects all tribes of the human race. Shekhinah is also the doorway into the Divine: "One who enters must enter through this gate" (Zohar 1:7b)—a most appropriate description, as Shekhinah resonates to the first or Tribal chakra of the human energy system. In order to ascend in spiritual truth, it suggests, we must first honor our families and all human communities.

Level Two: The merging of the Partnership chakra (Svadisthana), the sacrament of Communion, and the sefirah of Yesod.

The power created by these three archetypal forces transmits into our systems the sacred truth *Honor One Another.* From the Partnership chakra we receive the power to act with integrity and honor within all our relationships, from marriage to friendship to professional bonds. This energy is particularly active because it resonates in all financial and creative activity. Integrity and honor are necessary for health. When we violate our honor or compromise it in any way, we contaminate our spirits and our physical bodies.

Symbolically, the sacrament of Communion radiates into our system the truth that each person "with whom we share a union" is a part of our lives by Divine design. When we "break bread" with someone, we are symbolically acknowledging that we are all part of one spiritual family, that everyone we know is there by Divine design, and that we all need one another to enrich our lives. That some of these "unions" are painful is a necessity. Everyone in your life plays a role essential to your development. Your challenge is to become mature enough to recognize and live by this truth. It is unnatural, from a spiritual perspective, to view people as enemies, or to be an enemy yourself. Negative relationships generate negative energy, which blocks symbolic sight. We cannot see the Divine purpose in a union that we choose to interpret negatively.

The sefirah of Yesod embodies second chakra or communal energy. Yesod is the phallus, the procreative need to sow seeds of life, to create matter out of energy, form out of potentiality. Within this sefirah creation is a mutual act, a natural dualism from which life springs. Symbolically, Yesod represents our energy need to form sacred unions with other human beings, unions from which the continuation of life comes. We are spiritually driven to connect with the sacred within other people, to merge souls with a partner. Intimacy is itself a form of sacred union, and the sefirah of Yesod naturally draws us to those with whom a sacred union is possible. We violate our own spirits when we fail to honor our vows to others within a sacred union or when we dishonorably break those vows. Life does sometimes require us to reconsider our covenants, and divorces in marriage as well as in other unions do occur. The act of divorce in itself is not dishonorable; but we are meant to be conscious about the manner in which we conduct ourselves during the process of recanting a vow.

Level Three: The merging of the Personal Power chakra (Manipura), the sacrament of Confirmation, and the sefirot of Hod and Nezah.

The power created by these four archetypal forces transmits into our systems the sacred truth *Honor Oneself.* All four of the archetypal forces at this level direct us to develop self-esteem and self-respect. The chakra contains our "survival intuition," our sense that protects us when we are in physical danger and alerts us to the negative energy and actions of other people. We violate this energy when we disregard our gut instincts.

The symbolic meaning of the sacrament of Confirmation is the acceptance of responsibility for the *quality* of person we become. Part of the process of becoming conscious of ourselves is an "initiation" experience or a "coming of age" ceremony. The spirit requires such an experience or ceremony as a marker for emergence into adulthood; when this marker is absent, a conscious or unconscious negative impression or void manifests itself in psychological weaknesses. Some of these manifestations are: a continual need for the approval of other people, which can give rise to unhealthy identifications with gangs, cults, or other inappropriate groups; an inability to appreciate oneself; and an inability to develop a healthy sense of oneself as an individual. The ability to glean intuitive guidance from one's own spirit rests on a strong sense of self and on respect for that self.

Equally significant is the role of self-esteem in healing and in maintaining a healthy body. When we lack self-respect, our relationships with others are temporary and fragile states of intimacy. We continually fear abandonment because the terror of being alone drives our actions. To confirm oneself—to consciously develop and acknowledge a personal code of honor—is crucial to the creation of a healthy body. There is no health without honor.

The symbolic meaning of the sefirah of Nezah is endurance—the power to maintain strength and stamina beyond the capacity of the physical body alone. This power awakens when we accept our life as it is. We lose this power when we focus on what is missing from life, or when we see life as empty and meaningless and need to learn to accept our personal responsibility for having created it. The symbolic meaning of the sefirah of Hod is majesty or integrity, an energy that allows us to transcend the limitations of self and awaken our spiritual connection with Divine authority. The energy of Hod is enhanced by developing an attitude of appreciation and gratitude for all one has, and for the gift of life itself.

Together, Nezah and Hod are the symbolic legs of the human body. Together with the feminine and masculine energies of the third chakra, they suggest the need to create spiritual union out of internal duality—and that without self-esteem and personal honor, we will never be able to stand on our own, either literally or symbolically.

Internal Power

Level Four: The merging of the Emotional Power chakra (Anahata), the sacrament of Marriage, and the sefirah of Tif'eret.

The power created by these three archetypal forces transmits into our systems the sacred truth *Love Is Divine Power.* This energy center is the central power point within the human energy system, the symbolic doorway into our internal world.

The energy of this chakra communicates to us the knowledge that love is the only authentic power. Not only our minds and spirits but our physical bodies require love to survive and thrive. We violate this energy when we act toward others in unloving ways. When we harbor negative emotions toward others or toward ourselves, or when we intentionally create pain for others, we poison our own physical and spiritual systems. By far the strongest poison to the human spirit is the inability to forgive oneself or another person. It disables a person's emotional resources. The challenge inherent within this chakra is to refine our capacity to love others as well as ourselves and to develop the power of forgiveness.

Symbolically, the sacrament of Marriage brings into our lives the need and responsibility to explore love. First we must love ourselves, and our first marriage must be a symbolic one: a commitment to attend consciously to our own emotional needs, in order to be able to love and accept others unconditionally. Learning to love ourselves is a challenge to all of us; none of us is born loving ourselves. We have to work toward it. When we neglect ourselves emotionally, we not only become emotionally toxic, we bring that toxin into all of our relationships, particularly into an actual marriage.

The sefirah of Tif'eret, symbolic of the heart and sun within the human body, pulsates into each of us the energies of compassion, harmony, and beauty—the tranquil qualities of love. The energy radiated by Tif'eret balances all the Divine qualities in the ten sefirot. We are, by nature, compassionate beings who thrive in an atmosphere of tranquillity and harmony. These energies are essential to physical health as well as to emotional development and "acts of the heart." When the heart is not filled with the vital energies of love and harmony, no amount of money and power can keep it tranquil. An empty heart creates an empty life, often resulting in illness—a concrete expression of disharmony that hopefully will get the mind's attention. Violations of the heart must be rectified, or healing will be impossible.

Level Five: The merging of the chakra of Willpower (Vishuddha), the sacrament of Confession, and the sefirot of Hesed and Gevurah.

The power created by these four archetypal forces transmits into our systems the sacred truth *Surrender Personal Will to Divine Will.* This surrender is the greatest act we can perform to bring spiritual stability into our lives. Every one of us has some awareness that we were born for a specific purpose, that life contains a Divine plan. The fifth chakra is the center for that awareness and for our desire to make contact with the Divine plan.

As we mature, we all try to build our lives according to our own will. First we separate from our parents; we establish our independence, and we seek a career. Then, inevitably, some event or crisis occurs. Perhaps an occupation does not unfold according to plan; or a marriage does not work out; or an illness develops. Regardless of the specific crisis, we find ourselves in a situation that forces us to confront the limitations of our own inner resources that prevent us from successfully completing our plans. Once we are in that inevitable situation, we ponder some questions: "What am I meant to do with my life? What was my purpose in being born?" These questions set the stage for aligning our will to the Divine plan—the most profound choice we can make.

That one choice, made in faith and trust, allows Divine authority to enter our lives and reorder our struggles into successes and our wounds into strengths. While we may or may not consciously desire to surrender our personal will to Divine authority, we are sure to encounter numerous opportunities to do so. An incentive to make that choice lies in the life stories—and life struggles—of people who experienced nothing but pain and failure until they said to God, "You take over." Extraordinary acts of synchronicity then filled their lives, and new relationships their hearts. I have yet to meet the person who ever regretted saying to the Divine, "All yours."

Symbolically, the sacrament of Confession communicates to our systems the knowledge that it is against our natural design to distort truth. Lying is a violation of both body and spirit because the human energy system identifies lies as poison. Spirit and body alike require honesty and integrity to thrive. For that reason we inherently need to rid ourselves of all distortions we have created. Confession is symbolic of purging all that is not honorable within us. It heals the damage we create by the misuse of our will power. Cleansing the spirit is the most essential step in the healing process. In psychological-spiritual healing programs such as the twelve-step programs, confession and the surrender of personal will to "a power greater than oneself" are the very basis of success. Psychotherapy, too, is a contemporary, secular form of confession. Confession retrieves the spirit from the authority of the physical world and redirects it into the Divine world.

From the sefirah of Hesed, meaning "greatness" and "love," we receive the natural instinct and the spiritual directive to speak in ways that do not harm others. Communication using this quality of energy is effortless; we violate it and poison ourselves when we do not speak the truth. Indeed, we must not confess our wrongdoings to others if doing so will hurt them further. We are meant to confess so that we can redirect our energy into positive actions and behavior, and release ourselves from the burden of negative and guilt-inducing emotions. We are not designed to be critical of others or ourselves; we think ill of others only out of fear. To release words that hurt others contaminates both that person and ourselves, and our physical body holds us responsible for this form of destruction. (In Buddhism this is the precept of Right Speech.) Our inborn knowledge of responsibility generates the guilt we often feel from our negative acts, which is why we are compelled to seek confession in order to heal.

The sefirah of Gevurah, meaning "judgment" and "power," transmits into our energy systems the awareness that we should never intentionally judge another person or ourselves negatively. Negative judgments create negative consequences, both in the body and in the external environment.

Level Six: The merging of the chakra of the Mind (Ajna), the sacrament of Ordination, and the sefirot of Binah and Hokhmah.

The power created by these four archetypal forces transmits into our systems the sacred teaching *Seek Only the Truth.* From the Mind chakra we receive the energy to search for answers to the mysteries we encounter. It is by Divine design that we ask "Why?" and want to know more today than we did yesterday. The energy pulsating from this chakra continually directs us to evaluate the truth and integrity of our beliefs. As we instinctively know from birth, to have faith in anything or in anyone that lacks integrity contaminates our spirits and bodies.

We will all encounter circumstances that cause us to change our beliefs and thereby come closer to truth. We mature in our beliefs, step by step, experience after experience. The energy from the sixth chakra is relentlessly pushing us to let go of perceptions that are untrue. When we act against this energy, consciously blocking deeper truths from entering our mental field, our perceptual system clouds over.

The sacrament of Ordination, in the literal sense, is the act of being made a priest and officially taking up the life task of channeling the sacred. We all want our contributions to other people's lives to be valuable and meaningful, feel that what we do is sacred. (In Buddhism this is called Right Livelihood.) No matter our life's task—healer, parent, scientist, farmer, good friend—we can become vessels for Divine energy. Symbolically, we attain ordination when those with whom we live or work recognize that the contributions we make are beneficial to their personal or spiritual growth. Striving to become supportive and nonjudgmental of the people with whom we live or work also creates a channel within us for Divine energy. People who radiate this supportiveness and love are rightly recognized as possessing ordained energy. They are vessels of Divine intervention. Each one of us has the potential to become such a Divine channel, to be of service to others by reflecting sacred energy, which is a contemporary definition of priesthood.

To help us become this kind of vessel of divine energy and action, the sefirah of Hokhmah transfer into our systems the impulse to invoke the assistance of Divine wisdom into our reasoning abilities, particularly at times when human logic seems to lead nowhere. Hokhmah helps us learn to balance reason and judgment, to keep us aligned with truth, and to make decisions that create the best consquences for ourselves and those with whom we interact.

Supporting the energy of Hokhmah is the sefirah of Binah, pulsating into the often hard-edged energy of human reasoning the softer, more emotionally linked power of Divine understanding. The combination of Hokhmah and Binah is meant to serve as an internal guidance system, inspiring us to transcend the limitations of human thought and reach, like the Biblical figure of Soloman, a mental clarity that allows Divine reasoning to merge with our own thought process.

The more we can release our learned tendency to judge, the more we open our minds to a quality of understanding that is Divine in origin. Human reasoning can never answer the mysteries of our lives. It can never explain the complexity of why things happen as they do. We can achieve a genuine sense of peace about life only by releasing our need to know why things happen in terms of human reasoning and by embracing Divine reasoning: "Let me know what I am able to know and trust that behind all events, no matter how painful, there is a reason from which good can come."

Level Seven: The merging of the chakra of the Spirit (Sahasrara), the sacrament of Extreme Unction, and the sefirah of Keter.

The power created by these three archetypal forces transmits into our systems the sacred truth *Live in the Present Moment.* Because we are essentially spiritual creatures, our spiritual needs are as crucial to our well-being as our physical needs, maybe even more so.

The Spirit chakra tells us that our spirits are eternal. We are more than our physical bodies, a truth that can comfort us during the many closures of life that are part of the human experience. Our bodies' apparent relation to chronological time is only an illusion, one that our spirits are tasked with revealing. It is unnatural to our Divine design to let our thoughts live for too long in the past; such an imbalance creates time warps that interfere with our ability to live in the present and receive spiritual guidance each day. That guidance will make no sense to us if we focus only on unraveling the mysteries of yesterday. If we live fully in the present moment, the mysteries of yesterday will gradually be unraveled for us.

Our spirits are drawn instinctively to this sacred truth. From it we can receive inspiration that lifts us into ecstasy. We thrive—and we heal—in ecstatic moments, when our spirits become stronger than our bodies and our bodies can respond to the commands of our spirits.

The need to live in the present moment is supported by the sacrament of Extreme Unction. This sacrament was created to help people release their spirit prior to death. Symbolically, this sacrament recognizes our need to call back our spirit, to finish our unfinished business, at various points in life. The energy of this sacrament gives us the ability to release our past experiences in order not to "carry the dead with us." The power and symbolism of this sacrament is therefore not limited merely to the end of life. Biologically and spiritually we need to bring all things to closure, and we can call on this sacramental energy to help us do so. After any painful and traumatic experience, we always receive internal guidance that can help us release the past and move on with our lives. When we choose to keep the past more alive than the present, we interfere with the flow of the life force. We distort the "present" because we begin to view everything happening "today" through the past, thereby weakening our bodies and spirits. We become diseased from "carrying the dead" with us for too long.

From the sefirah of Keter, symbolic of our connection to the world of the infinite, we receive the knowledge that there is no death; there is only life. No one has gone before us whom we will not meet again—that is a Divine promise. We are meant to rest in the comfort and power of that sacred truth.

We are born knowing these seven sacred truths. Indeed, each of us essentially is a "biological edition" of them. We are taught variations of these truths again as children through our tribes' religious practices. And even if we are not consciously taught these truths, they awaken in us automatically—in our guts, in our minds, in our sense of the natural order of life. As we mature, we come to understand the content of these truths with ever more clarity and depth, and we are increasingly able to respond to their messages, to interpret their information symbolically and see their archetypal messages.

The truths contained in the scriptural teachings of the different religious traditions are meant to unite us, not separate us. Literal interpretation creates separation, whereas symbolic interpretation—seeing that all of them address the identical design of our spiritual natures—brings us together. As we shift our attention away from the external world and into the internal one, we learn symbolic sight. Within, we are all the same, and the spiritual challenges we face are all the same. Our external differences are illusory and temporary, mere physical props. The more we seek what is the same in all of us, the more our symbolic sight gains authority to direct us.

Merging Hindu, Buddhist, Christian, and Jewish spiritual traditions into one system with common sacred truths constitutes a powerful system of guidance that can enhance our minds and bodies and show us how to manage our spirits within the world

In Part II the seven chakras will be described in detail in terms of their inherent power, with special emphasis on the fears that cause us to lose that power. As you study this material, study yourself with the intention of identifying "into whose hands have you commended your spirit."

PART II

The Seven Sacred Truths

My understanding of the chakra system developed out of my work as a medical intuitive.* Sharing my work with readers of this book is like taking you into my mind and laboratory. For yourself, take with you only what feels right to your heart and spirit, and leave the rest behind.

In Part II I discuss each chakra separately so that you can familiarize yourself with its specific characteristics, significance, and content. When I analyze an illness in terms of energy medicine, however, I also evaluate the entire patient, including physical symptoms and mental habits, relationships and diet, spiritual practice and career. Keep this same rule in mind as you study the human energy system. A complete energy evaluation has to include all seven chakras, regardless of the location of a physical illness, as well as all aspects of the patient's life.

As you read about the chakras, you will see that the issues involved in chakras one, two, and three are the ones where most people spend their energy. Not coincidentally, most illnesses result from a loss of energy from these three chakras. Even when an illness, like a heart condition or breast cancer, develops in the upper region of the body, its *energy* origin can usually be traced to stress patterns in issues of the lower three chakras, such as in marriage or partnership, family, or occupation. Emotions such as rage and anger hit us physically below the belt, while an emotion like unexpressed sadness is associated with disease above the belt. For instance, the major emotion behind breast lumps and breast cancer is hurt, sorrow, and unfinished emotional business generally related to nurturance.

---

*There are a number of different interpretations of the chakra system, some of whose perspectives I share. Joseph Campbell's *The Mythic Image* (Princeton, N.J.: Princeton University Press, 1974) is one of the most widely accepted. Transpersonal philosopher W. Brugh Joy, M.D., also deals with the chakras in *A Map for the Transformational Journey* (New York: Tarcher/Putnam, 1979). Barbara Ann Brennan uses them in her practice of energetic healing in *Hands of Light: A Guide to Healing Through the Human Energy Field* (Bantam, 1987); and Harish Johari gives a deeply spiritual interpretation in *Chakras: Energy Centers of Transformation* (Destiny Books, 1987).

Nurturance also has to do with the health of relationships, however, and relationships are primarily a first and second chakra issue. Thus, several—if not all—the chakras have to be used to understand completely why a person has become ill.

For all of the many complex energies that run through our systems, the first chakra is by far the most complex, because it is the beginning or root energy center of your body.

Please note that the issues and illnesses listed here are to be understood as follows: negative extremes of any listed emotional issue can serve as a major influence in the development of any of the noted dysfunctions in each of the specified chakra descriptions.

Energy Anatomy

CHAKRA	ORGANS
1	Physical body support Base of spine Legs, bones Feet Rectum Immune system
2	Sexual organs Large intestine Lower vertebrae Pelvis Appendix Bladder Hip area
3	Abdomen Stomach Upper intestines Liver, gallbladder Kidney, pancreas Adrenal glands Spleen Middle spine

MENTAL, EMOTIONAL ISSUES	PHYSICAL DYSFUNCTIONS	
Physical family and group safety and security	Chronic lower back pain	**1**
Ability to provide for life's necessities	Sciatica	
Ability to stand up for self	Varicose veins	
Feeling at home	Rectal tumors/cancer	
Social and familial law and order	Depression	
	Immune-related disorders	
Blame and guilt	Chronic lower back pain	**2**
Money and sex	Sciatica	
Power and control	Ob/gyn problems	
Creativity	Pelvic/low back pain	
Ethics and honor in relationships	Sexual potency	
	Urinary problems	
Trust	Arthritis	**3**
Fear and intimidation	Gastric or duodenal ulcers	
Self-esteem, self-confidence, and self-respect	Colon/intestinal problems	
	Pancreatitis/diabetes	
Care of oneself and others	Indigestion, chronic or acute	
Responsibility for making decisions	Anorexia or bulimia	
Sensitivity to criticism	Liver dysfunction	
Personal honor	Hepatitis	
	Adrenal dysfunction	

Energy Anatomy (cont'd)

CHAKRA	ORGANS
4	Heart and circulatory system
	Lungs
	Shoulders and arms
	Ribs/breasts
	Diaphragm
	Thymus gland
5	Throat
	Thyroid
	Trachea
	Neck vertebrae
	Mouth
	Teeth and gums
	Esophagus
	Parathyroid
	Hypothalamus
6	Brain
	Nervous system
	Eyes, ears
	Nose
	Pineal gland
	Pituitary gland

MENTAL, EMOTIONAL ISSUES	PHYSICAL DYSFUNCTIONS	
Love and hatred	Congestive heart failure	**4**
Resentment and bitterness	Myocardial infarction (heart	
Grief and anger	attack)	
Self-centeredness	Mitral valve prolapse	
Loneliness and commitment	Cardiomegaly	
Forgiveness and compassion	Asthma/allergy	
Hope and trust	Lung cancer	
	Bronchial pneumonia	
	Upper back, shoulder	
	Breast cancer	
Choice and strength of will	Raspy throat	**5**
Personal expression	Chronic sore throat	
Following one's dream	Mouth ulcers	
Using personal power to create	Gum difficulties	
Addiction	Temporomandibular joint	
Judgment and criticism	problems	
Faith and knowledge	Scoliosis	
Capacity to make decisions	Laryngitis	
	Swollen glands	
	Thyroid problems	
Self-evaluation	Brain tumor/hemorrhage/	**6**
Truth	stroke	
Intellectual abilities	Neurological disturbances	
Feelings of adequacy	Blindness/deafness	
Openness to the ideas of others	Full spinal difficulties	
Ability to learn from experience	Learning disabilities	
Emotional intelligence	Seizures	

Energy Anatomy (cont'd)

CHAKRA	ORGANS
7	Muscular system
	Skeletal system
	Skin

MENTAL, EMOTIONAL ISSUES	PHYSICAL DYSFUNCTIONS	
Ability to trust life	Energetic disorders	**7**
Values, ethics, and courage	Mystical depression	
Humanitarianism	Chronic exhaustion that is not	
Selflessness	linked to a physical disorder	
Ability to see the larger pattern	Extreme sensitivities to light,	
Faith and inspiration	sound, and other	
Spirituality and devotion	environmental factors	

CHAPTER I

The First Chakra: Tribal Power

The energy content of the first or Tribal chakra is *tribal power*. The word *tribe* is not only a synonym for family but an archetype, and as such it has connotations beyond its more conventional definition. Archetypally the word *tribal* connotes group identity, group force, group willpower, and group belief patterns. All of these meanings make up the energy content of our first chakra. The first chakra grounds us. It is our connection to traditional familial beliefs that support the formation of identity and a sense of belonging to a group of people in a geographic location.

To connect to the energy of your first chakra, focus your attention for a few moments on something tribal that triggers an emotional response in you.

- listening to the national anthem
- observing a military spectacle
- watching an athlete receive a gold medal at the Olympics
- witnessing the marriage of someone you care about
- learning that a child has been named after you

As you focus on the experience you choose, be aware that the area of your body generating the response is your Tribal chakra.

Location: Base of the spine (at the coccyx).

Energy connection to the physical body: Spinal column, rectum, legs, bones, feet, and immune system.

Energy connection to the emotional/mental body: The first chakra is the foundation of emotional and mental health. Emotional and psychological stability originate in the family unit and early social environment. Various mental illnesses are generated out of family dysfunctions, including multiple personalities, obsessive-compulsive disorder, depression, and destructive patterns like alcoholism.

Symbolic/perceptual connection: First chakra energy manifests in our need for logic, order, and structure. This energy orients us in time and space and to our five senses. As children, we perceive and learn about the physical world through our five senses. First chakra energy has trouble interpreting our lives symbolically, for our five senses give us literal perceptions and cause us to take things at face value. Not until we are older are we able to seek out the symbolic meaning of events and relationships.

Sefirot/Sacrament connection: The sefirah of Shekhinah, literally meaning the mystical community of Israel, is symbolic of the spiritual community of all humanity and to the feminine spirit of the earth known as Gaia. The symbolic meaning of the sacrament of Baptism is to honor one's biological family as sacred and divinely chosen as the appropriate tribe from which to begin one's life journey.

Primary fears: Fears of physical survival, abandonment by the group, and loss of physical order.

Primary strengths: Tribal/family identity, bonding, and the tribal honor code; the support and loyalty that give one a sense of safety and connection to the physical world.

Sacred truth: The sacred truth inherent in the first chakra is that *All Is One.* We learn this truth and explore its creative power through experiences connected to tribal or group dynamics. It carries the message that we are connected to all of life and that every choice we make and every belief we hold exerts influence upon the whole of life. The symbolic meaning of the sefirah of Shekhinah is that we are all part of one spiritual community. As a part of our spiritual development and our biological health, this sacred truth has physical expressions in honor, loyalty, justice, family and group bonds, groundedness, our need for a spiritual foundation, and the ability to manage physical power for survival.

We begin to discover that *All Is One* as we start life within our tribe or family. To be a part of a tribe is a primal need, since we are completely dependent upon our tribe for basic survival needs: food, shelter, and clothing. As tribal beings, we are energetically designed to live together, to create together, to learn together, to be together, to need one another. Each of our tribal environments—from our biological tribe, to the tribes we form with co-workers, to our tribal bonds with friends—provides the essential physical settings within which we can explore the creative power of this truth.

Tribal Culture

No one begins life as a conscious "individual" with conscious willpower. That identity comes much later and develops in stages from childhood through adulthood. Beginning life as a part of a tribe, we become connected to our tribal consciousness and collective willpower by absorbing its strengths and weaknesses, beliefs, superstitions, and fears.

Through our interactions with family and other groups, we learn the power of sharing a belief with other people. We also learn how painful it can be to be excluded from a group and its energy. We learn as well the power of sharing a moral and ethical code handed down from generation to generation. This code of behavior guides children of the tribe during their developmental years, providing a sense of dignity and belonging.

If tribal experiences energetically interconnect us, so do tribal attitudes, be they sophisticated perceptions such as "We are all brothers and sisters" or superstitions such as "The number 13 is bad luck."

Tribal power, and all the issues related to it, are energetically connected to the health of our immune system, as well as to our legs,
bones, feet, and rectum. Symbolically, the immune system does for
the physical body exactly what tribal power does for the group: it
protects the entire body from potentially damaging external influences. Immune-related disorders, chronic pain, and other difficulties
with the skeleton are energetically activated by weaknesses in personal tribal issues. Difficult tribal challenges cause us to lose power
primarily from our first chakra, making us susceptible—should a
challenge become an extreme stress—to immune-related diseases,
from the common cold to lupus.

The Tribal chakra represents our connection to both positive and
negative group experiences. Epidemics are a negative group experience to which we can become energetically susceptible if our own
personal first chakra fears and attitudes are similar to those held by
the culture's overall "first chakra." Viral and other epidemics are very
much a reflection of both the current social issues of the cultural
tribe and the health of the social tribe's "immune system." This point
is essential to note because each of us is connected through our first
chakra attitudes to our culture and its attitudes.

A dramatic example of a social tribe's energy capacity to manifest
an illness is the polio epidemic of the 1930s and 1940s. In October
1929, the American economy crashed and the Great Depression
began, affecting the entire nation. In describing how the American
people felt, journalists and politicians, business executives and workers, men and women all described themselves as having been "crippled" by the economic disaster.

In the early 1930s the polio epidemic surfaced—symbolically
representing the crippled spirit of the nation as a community. Those
who felt most economically crippled, either by actual experience or
by the fear of it, were energetically the most susceptible to the polio
virus. Because children absorb their tribe's energy, American children
were as susceptible to the viral disease as to the economic dis-ease.

All Is One: when an entire tribe becomes infected with fear, that energy extends to its children.

This sense of being crippled was so quickly woven into the tribal psyche that American voters even elected a president crippled by the polio virus, Franklin D. Roosevelt, a living symbol both of physical weakness and of indomitable resilience. It took a physical tribal event and experience of physical strength, World War II, to heal the American tribal spirit. The sense of heroism and tribal unity, supported by the sudden increase in jobs, restored pride, power, and honor to each tribal member.

By the end of the war, the American nation had assumed a global leadership role again. In fact, the United States became *the* leader of the free world because it developed nuclear weapons—a position that brought enormous pride and power into the culture's Tribal chakra. Once again, this recovery was reflected in the language of the tribal spokespeople who described their newly healed culture as economically "on its feet again." With that shift in consciousness, reflecting a healed tribal spirit, the polio virus could be defeated. The spirit and attitude of the tribe was ultimately stronger than the virus. Not coincidentally Jonas Salk discovered the vaccine for polio in the early 1950s.

A more contemporary example of this same dynamic is the HIV virus. In the United States this virus is most prevalent among drug users, prostitutes, and the gay population. In other countries, such as Russia and numerous African nations, it thrives among those whose quality of life barely allows for survival. In Latin America the virus thrives among middle-class women who are married to philandering men. These men are not gay but have sex with other men as a "macho" exercise. Those who contract this virus, regardless of the means, share a common sense of being victimized by their tribal culture.

While everyone has been victimized by something or someone, this victim consciousness reflects a *feeling* of powerlessness within the tribal culture, whether because of a sexual preference, lack of money, or lack of social status. These Latin Americans believe they lack any means of protecting themselves. HIV-positive Latin American women, even those married to successful men, cannot challenge their husbands' behavior because their culture does not, as yet, value the female voice. Viewed symbolically, the HIV virus emerged into U.S. culture just as the issue of victimization became mainstream. The cultural energy of our own country is being depleted by the need that some have to feel empowered at the expense of others deemed less valuable. Challenges to our biological immunity will follow accordingly.

Maintaining the health of our individual first chakra depends upon addressing our personal tribal issues. If we feel victimized by society, for example, we should deal with this negative perception so that it doesn't cause us to lose energy. We can, for instance, get therapeutic support, become skilled at an occupation, seek a more symbolic view of our situation, or become politically active to change society's attitudes. Nurturing bitterness toward the cultural tribe embroils our energy in a continual inner conflict that blocks access to the healing power of the sacred truth *All Is One*.

Our respective tribes introduce us to life "in the world." They teach us that the world is either safe or dangerous, abundant or poverty-ridden, educated or ignorant, a place to take from or to give to. And they transmit their perceptions about the nature of reality itself—for instance, that this life is only one of many or that this life is all there is. We inherit from our tribes their attitudes toward other religious, ethnic, and racial groups. Our tribes "activate" our thinking processes.

Everyone has heard ethnic generalizations such as "All Germans are very organized" or "All Irish are great storytellers." We have all been told some view of God or the unseen world and how it interacts with us, such as "Don't wish evil upon someone because it will come back to haunt you," or "Never laugh at anyone because God

might punish you." We also absorb numerous sex-linked perceptions, such as "Men are smarter than women," "All little boys love to
play sports, and all little girls love to play with dolls."

The tribal beliefs we inherit are a combination of truth and fic-
tion. Many of them, such as "Murder is forbidden," hold eternal
value. Others lack that quality of eternal truth and are more
parochial, designed to keep tribes separate from one another, in violation of the sacred truth *All Is One*. The process of spiritual development challenges us to retain the tribal influences that are positive
and to discard those that are not.

Our spiritual power grows when we are able to see beyond the
contradictions inherent in tribal teachings and pursue a deeper level
of truth. Each time we make a shift toward symbolic awareness, we
positively influence our energy and biological systems. We also contribute positive energy to the collective body of life—the global
tribe. Think of this process of spiritual maturation as "spiritual
homeopathy."

The Energy Consequences of Belief Patterns

Regardless of the "truth" of familial beliefs, every one of them
directs a measure of our energy into an act of creation. Each belief,
each action has a direct consequence. When we share belief patterns
with groups of people, we participate in energy and physical events
created by those groups. This is the creative, symbolic expression of
the sacred truth *All Is One*. When we share support for a candidate
running for office, and that candidate wins, we feel that our energy
and physical support helped; further, we have some sense that he or
she represents our concerns—which is a way of physically experiencing the power of unity in the truth *All Is One*.

Carl Jung once remarked that the group mind is the "lowest"
form of consciousness because individuals involved in a *negative*

group action rarely, if ever, accept responsibility for their personal role and action. This reality is the shadow side of the truth *All Is One.* In fact, unwritten tribal law holds that the leaders accept responsibility, not the followers. The Nuremberg trials following World War II are a classic example of the limitations of tribal responsibility. Most of the Nazi defendants on trial for masterminding and conducting the genocide of eleven million people (six million Jews and five million others) stated that they were "only following orders." No doubt, at the time, they were proud of their ability to fulfill their tribal responsibilities, but they were completely unable to accept any personal consequences at the trials.

Given the power of unified beliefs—right or wrong—it is difficult to be at variance with one's tribe. We are taught to make choices that meet with tribal approval, to adopt its social graces, manner of dress, and attitudes. Symbolically, this adaptation reflects the union of individual willpower with group willpower. It is a powerful feeling to be in a group of people or a family with whom you feel spiritually, emotionally, and physically comfortable. Such a union empowers us and energetically enhances our personal power and our creative strength—and it continues as long as we make choices consonant with the group's. We unite to create.

At the same time we have within us a relentless congenital desire to explore our own creative abilities, to develop our individual power and authority. This desire is the impetus behind our striving to become *conscious.* The universal human journey is one of becoming conscious of our power and how to use that power. Becoming conscious of the responsibility inherent in the power of choice represents the core of this journey.

From an energy perspective, becoming conscious requires stamina. It is extremely challenging, and often very painful, to evaluate our own personal beliefs and separate ourselves from those that no longer support our growth. Change is the nature of life, and external and internal change is constant. When we change inwardly, we out-grow certain belief patterns and strengthen others. The first belief patterns that we challenge are tribal because our spiritual develop-ment follows the structure of our energy system; we clear out ideas from the bottom up, starting with the earliest and most basic.

Evaluating our beliefs is a spiritual and biological necessity. Our physical bodies, minds, and spirits all require new ideas in order to thrive. Some tribes have very little awareness of the importance of exercise and healthy nutrition, for example, until a family member develops an illness. A new physical regimen and more appropriate diet may be prescribed for the ill person. As a result, other family members will have an entirely different reality introduced into their minds and bodies concerning the need to make more responsible and conscious choices in their personal care, such as learning to appreci-ate the healing power of nutrition and exercise.

Seen symbolically, our life crises tell us that we need to break free of beliefs that no longer serve our personal development. These points at which we must choose to change or to stagnate are our greatest challenges. Every new crossroads means we enter into a new cycle of change—whether it be adopting a new health regimen or a new spiritual practice. And change inevitably means letting go of familiar people and places and moving on to another stage of life.

Many of the people I encounter in my workshops are stuck between two worlds: the old world that they need to release and the new world that they are afraid to enter. We are attracted to becom-ing more "conscious," but at the same time we find it frightening because it means we must take personal responsibility for ourselves—and for our health, career, attitudes, and thoughts. Once we accept personal responsibility for even one area of our lives, we can never again use "tribal reasoning" to excuse our behavior.

In tribal consciousness personal responsibility does not exist in well-defined terms, so it is much easier to avoid the consequences of personal choices in the tribal milieu. Tribal responsibility extends mainly to the *physical* areas of our lives, meaning individuals are accountable for their finances, social concerns, relationships, and occupations. The tribe does not require members to take personal responsibility for the attitudes they inherit. According to tribal reasoning, it is acceptable to excuse one's prejudices by saying, "Everyone in my family thinks this way." It is extremely difficult to give up the comfort zone that accompanies such excuses; just think of how many times you have said, "Everyone does it, so why shouldn't I?" This dodge is the crudest form of the sacred truth *All Is One*, and it is commonly used to evade responsibility for all manner of immoral acts, from tax evasion to adultery to keeping the extra change from a sales clerk. Spiritually conscious adults, however, can no longer utilize tribal reasoning. Tax evasion becomes a deliberate act of theft; adultery becomes the conscious breaking of a marriage vow; and keeping extra change becomes equal to stealing from the store.

Often one needs to examine one's attachments to tribal prejudices before healing can begin. A man called Gerald contacted me for a reading, saying that he was exhausted. As I scanned his energy, I received the impression that he had a malignant tumor in his colon. I asked him if he had been through any medical tests; he hesitated for a moment, then said he had just been diagnosed with cancer of the colon. He said that he needed my help in order to come to believe he really could heal. Part of him was trying to unplug from his tribe's attitude about cancer because everyone in his family who had ever developed cancer had died, neither he nor his family believed cancer could be healed. We talked about a number of ways he could get assistance, such as the many therapies that help people develop a positive attitude through visualization. Most significantly, Gerald had already intuitively recognized that his energy connection to this tribal attitude was as serious a problem as the physical illness itself. In his healing process, Gerald enlisted therapeutic support to help him break free of his tribal belief patterns about cancer. He was willing to try every option open to him.

Challenging Toxic Tribal Power

From our tribe we learn about loyalty, honor, and justice—moral attitudes that are essential to our well-being and sense of personal and group responsibility. Each of them expresses the sacred truth of the first chakra, sacrament, and sefirah: *All Is One*. Each can, however, become restrictive or toxic if interpreted narrowly.

Loyalty

Loyalty is an instinct, an unwritten law that tribal members can rely upon, particularly in times of crisis. It is thus part of the tribal power system, and it often is more influential than even love. You can feel loyalty toward a family member you do not love, and you can feel loyalty toward people who share your ethnic background, even though you do not know them personally. An expectation of loyalty from a group holds enormous power over an individual, especially when one feels conflicted over allegiance to someone or some cause that holds great personal values.

In a reading that I did for a young man who complained of chronic fatigue, I received the impression that his legs were symbolically in his hometown; his first chakra was literally transferring power from his lower body and spirit back to his hometown. The rest of his body was with him, so to speak, where he presently lived, and this fragmentation was the cause of his chronic fatigue. When I told him my impression, he remarked that he had never really wanted to leave his hometown because his family was so dependent upon him, but he had been transferred by his company. I asked him whether he liked his job. He said, "So-so." I suggested he quit and return home, given that he had very little invested in his occupation. Two months later I received a letter from him. A few days after our conversation, he said, he had turned in his resignation and gone home within the week. His chronic fatigue was healed, and though he had not yet found another job, he felt terrific.

Loyalty is a beautiful tribal quality, most especially when it is conscious loyalty, a commitment that serves the individual as well as the group. Extremes of loyalty that harm one's ability to protect oneself, however, qualify as a belief pattern from which one needs to free oneself. The following case history involves a primary tribal violation and exemplifies the symbolic meaning of the sacrament of Baptism.

Tony, thirty-two, is the son of Eastern European immigrants. He was five years old when his family moved to the United States, one of seven children. During those early years of establishing a home in this country, his parents found it extremely difficult to provide the family with the basics, including food. At the age of eight, Tony got a job at a local candy store, helping with small maintenance tasks.

Tony's family was deeply grateful for the extra ten dollars a week. After two months the boy was bringing home almost twenty dollars a week and feeling proud of himself—he could see how much his parents appreciated his contribution to the family funds. But once that dynamic of appreciation was in place, the store owner began to make sexual advances toward Tony. They began as subtle physical contact, but eventually they led to a situation in which this pedophile totally controlled the young boy. Tony was soon so completely dominated that he had to call the store owner every evening to assure him that everything was still "their secret."

As his double life continued, Tony's psychological state became understandably fragile. He knew that his frequent encounters with the "candy man" were immoral, yet his family was now counting on his monthly household contribution of almost a hundred dollars. Tony finally found the courage to describe to his mother—in limited detail—what he had to do in order to earn his monthly wage. His mother responded by forbidding him ever to speak of such things again. The family members were counting on his keeping that job, she said.

Tony remained at the candy store until he was thirteen years old.

The effects of his abuse extended into his student life. He barely made it through his sophomore year in high school, and at fifteen he was a dropout. To earn his way Tony took a job as an apprentice to a construction worker and, simultaneously, began to drink.

Alcohol helped repress Tony's nightmarish experiences of being sexually molested and calmed his nerves. He began to drink every evening after work. By sixteen he was an adept street fighter and a neighborhood troublemaker. The local police brought him home several times for starting fights and for minor vandalism. His family tried to force him to stop drinking but could not. During one incident when Tony's friends brought him home after an evening of drinking, he screamed in rage at his parents and his brothers for not rescuing him from the "candy man." He knew that his mother had told his father about the molestation because even though they did not tell Tony to quit his job, his parents had forbidden his younger brothers to go to that store. And he later realized that his brothers understood what had happened, too, but treated it as a joke, implying at times that he enjoyed it.

At twenty-five, Tony started his own small construction company; he and his crew of four men performed minor repair work on neighborhood homes. He managed to maintain this business fairly successfully until he reached twenty-eight. At that time his drinking became so severe that it triggered attacks of paranoia in which he believed that demons were surrounding him, telling him to kill himself. By twenty-nine Tony had lost his company and his home. As a coping mechanism, he turned completely to alcohol.

I met Tony only a month after he began working again. He had been hired to repair a home near mine, and we met quite accidentally. Even while he was managing his small crew, he was drinking on the job. I made a comment about it. He responded, "You'd drink too if you had my memories." I looked at him, and by the way he held his body, I knew instantly that he had been molested as a child. I asked him if he wanted to talk about his childhood. For some reason he opened up, and that dark chapter of his life poured out of him.

We met a few times after that to talk about his past. I realized in listening to him was that the pain of knowing that his family had not tried to help him was greater than the pain of the sexual abuse. In fact, his family now considered him a drunkard and fully expected him to fail again and again in his life. The pain of family betrayal was destroying him. Curiously, he had already forgiven the candy man. His unfinished business was with his family.

Two months after we met, Tony decided on his own to enter an alcohol treatment program. After he completed it, he contacted me and shared with me the healing impact of the therapy sessions in the program. He knew that he would now have to deal with his negative feelings about his family.

In therapeutic circles reconciliation more often than not means confronting the people with whom you have unfinished business and cleaning out your wounds in front of them. In the best of cases, the people who wounded you will apologize, and some form of renewal or closure will occur. Tony, however, realized that his family would never be able to acknowledge their betrayal of him. His parents in particular would be too ashamed even to listen to his history. They were emotionally incapable of admitting that they knew what he had had to do to earn that money so many years ago. Tony, instead, turned to prayer and continual psychotherapy.

When his sobriety and his commitment to prayer had continued for more than a year, he told me that his anger toward his family was gone. I believed him. Given his parents' fear of survival in a new country with very little money, he said, perhaps they had made the only choice they were capable of making. He worked at renewing his bonds with his family, and as his new business grew, his family spoke proudly of his success. To him, that represented their apology for the events of long ago.

Tony was able to bless his family and see them as the source of the strength that he discovered within himself. His journey from ostracism to healing to love and acceptance embodies the symbolic meaning of the sacrament of Baptism.

Another man, George, arrived in one of my workshops because his wife had pressured him to attend. He was not a typical participant. He introduced himself as a "spectator" and let it be known right from the start that all this "hocus-pocus" was his wife's interest, not his.

I began the workshop with an introduction to the human energy system. George worked on a crossword puzzle. He napped during the part of the lecture about the relationship between attitudes and physical health. At the break I brought George a cup of coffee. "Can I interest you in a drink?" I asked, hoping he would get the hint that I prefer my students to keep their eyes open.

After the break I turned to the first chakra and the nature of tribal influence. George perked up a bit. At first I thought it was the caffeine kicking in, but as I lectured on the influence of early programming on our biological makeup, George remarked, "You mean to tell me that all the things my folks said to me are still in my body?" His tone verged on sarcasm, yet something about the subject obviously had hit a nerve with him.

I told him that perhaps not everything his parents told him was still in his energy, but certainly many things were. "For instance," I said, "what memories do you have about how your parents approached growing older?" I asked because George had just turned sixty.

Silently, all the workshop participants waited for George to reply. As soon as he realized he had their attention, he became almost childlike and very self-conscious. "I don't know. I've never thought about that."

"Well, think about it now," I said, and repeated the question. George's wife was on the edge of her seat, wanting to answer for him. I gave her a look that said, "Don't even consider it," and she leaned back.

"I don't know what to say. My parents always told me to work hard and save my money because I had to be able to take care of myself in my old age."

"And when do you intend to get old?" I asked. George couldn't answer that question, so I rephrased it. "When did your parents get old?"

"When they reached their sixties, of course."

"So that's when you decided to get old, when you reached your sixties," I said.

"Everyone gets old in their sixties," George said. "That's just the way life is. That's why we retire in our sixties, because we're old."

An afternoon's discussion opened up around George's comments. George shared with the group that he always believed that old age began at sixty because that message had been continually reinforced by his parents, neither of whom had lived to see seventy.

We talked about what it means to unplug from a belief pattern that has no truth but nonetheless has "power" over you. Much to the surprise of everyone, including his wife and myself, George grasped the concept immediately, as though someone had given him a new toy to play with. "You mean that if I unplug, as you say, from an idea, that idea doesn't have any say-so in my life anymore?"

The ultimate moment came when George looked at his wife and said, "I don't want to be old anymore, do you?" His wife started to laugh and cry at the same time—as did the entire workshop. I still cannot explain why George's understanding "took off" as fast as it did. I have rarely seen anyone grasp something as fast and as deeply as he did when he recognized that the main reason he was aging was that he thought he had to at sixty. George has been enjoying life since he began honoring his own internal sense of age rather than being ruled by society's concept.

Honor

A tribe is bonded not only by loyalty but by honor. Every tribe's code of honor is a combination of religious and ethnic traditions and rituals. Rituals such as Baptism or other tribal blessings energetically bond new members to the group's spiritual power. A sense of honor radiates strength within us, aligns us with our blood and ethnic relations, and teaches us the significance of keeping our word and acting with integrity.

While honor is not usually considered a component of health, I have come to believe that it may well be among the most essential, equal even to love. A sense of honor contributes a very forceful and positive energy into our spiritual and biological systems, the immune system, and our bones and legs. Without honor, it is very difficult, if not impossible, for an individual to stand up for himself with pride and dignity, because he lacks a frame of reference for his behavior and choices and thus cannot trust himself or others.

A sense of honor is part of what a tribe teaches its members about the fundamental tribal ritual of marriage. As one woman, who was the last member of her family, describes it, "My father told me, as he was dying, to promise him that I would have a child. I told him that I had not found a man that I wanted to marry. His last words to me were 'Marry anyone, just continue the family.'"

The way in which married partners behave teaches ethical standards to the next generation. Adultery is forbidden; yet tribal elders who commit adultery are nonetheless giving the children permission to bend that rule when they too are adults. A father supports his family; yet a father who walks away from this responsibility leaves his children with a very distorted meaning of commitment and responsibility. People are taught to treat others with respect; yet parents who do not show respect themselves produce children who become disrespectful adults. Without the moral stability of a code of honorable behavior, children grow into adults who cannot create stable lives for themselves.

You have to be able to give your word and keep it—whether it is to another person or to yourself. You have to be able to trust yourself to complete something and to honor your commitments. When you don't trust yourself, everyone and everything around you feels temporary and fragile because that is how you feel within yourself. One man said, "I don't want to live the way my parents did, always lying to each other. But I keep thinking that somehow I inherited that trait, and that given the right circumstance I will behave in the same way." The absence of individual honor extends beyond the boundaries of personal tribes into society in general.

I met Sam in a workshop, where he openly shared his life story. He had grown up in poverty, without a father figure. He desperately needed to be a leader, even if it was a gang leader, which became his way of feeling a sense of honor. He earned almost $75,000 per week as a major drug dealer. He had a staff of "employees" who assisted him in deals involving enormous sums of money.

One day while driving in his car, Sam turned on the radio to a talk show. As he was reaching over to change the channel, the guest speaker commented on the existence of angels. She said that each person has a guardian angel and that these angels watch over us and all our activities. As Sam later recalled, "I didn't want to hear any more of that stuff, but all of a sudden, all I could think about was how my grandmother used to tell me stories when I was growing up about how my angel was always looking after me. I'd forgotten all about that until I heard that woman talking on the radio."

Sam was on his way to a drug delivery, only now he was plagued by a sensation that his angel was watching what he was doing. "All I kept thinking that day was, when I die, how am I going to explain what I did for a living?"

For the first time in his life, Sam felt he had a problem that he did not know how to cope with. "I mean, I had a lot of guys who were counting on me for their money. I couldn't just say to them, 'Hey, listen, we gotta change things now because we've got these angels watching us and we don't want to get them angry.' These are tough characters, and I didn't know how to get out of this situation."

One night just a few days after that radio program, Sam hit a lamppost in his car and sustained fairly serious injuries to his legs and lower back. His "employees" assured him they would continue the business, but Sam saw the accident as his opportunity to change the direction of his life. His doctors told him that regaining the use of his legs would be a long, slow process, and that he might still have to endure chronic pain for the rest of his life. Sam started to read books on healing—and on angels.

"I had this feeling that if I made a promise not to return to the streets, I would be able to heal my legs. I told my guys that I just couldn't handle the pressure anymore, and for some reason, they believed me. I think it was because they wanted my share of the take, and that was fine with me. I moved out of the neighborhood as soon as I could and started my life all over again."

Sam eventually became involved with a different type of "gang"—a youth group that met in the evening at a neighborhood YMCA. He became dedicated to helping them avoid the life he had formerly led. "I hardly make any money these days compared with what I used to make, but believe me, that doesn't matter at all. I get by. And when I see these kids and they tell me about their dreams, I tell them anything is possible, because I know it's true. I even talk to them about how important it is to take pride in what they do, and sometimes I talk to them about their angels. These kids make me feel like I have a purpose for my life. I never had that feeling before, and I gotta tell you, it's a better high than any drug I ever sold. For the first time in my life, I know what it feels like to be clean down to your soul and to be proud of who you are." He has become a different type of "gang leader," inspiring honor among the children he works with.

Sam walks with a limp today, but he is walking. He jokingly commented, "Who would have thought that I would stand up better with a limp?" He still experiences bad pain days, as he calls them, but his attitude about life is endless joy. He inspires everyone he comes in contact with, and he radiates a quality of self-esteem that comes from genuinely loving his life. I have no doubt that his healing was enhanced by discovering a life purpose for himself.

Justice

Our tribes introduce us to the concept of justice: usually the law of "an eye for an eye," or "Do unto others as you would have them do unto you," or the law of karma: "What goes around, comes around." Tribal justice maintains social order and can be summarized this way: It is just to seek revenge for harmful actions that are without cause; it is just to do all that is necessary to protect oneself and one's family; it is just to assist other family members in actions of protection or vengeance. It is unjust to put any family member at risk for personal gain; it is unjust not to follow through on a tribal command; it is unjust to assist anyone whom the tribe recognizes as a threat. The injunction against bringing shame upon the family exerts an extremely controlling force over each member.

When a tribal member accomplishes something of value to others, the other members automatically share an "energy reward." It's not unusual for a tribal member to "live off the power" of another tribal member who has earned a public reputation. "What's in a name?" we sometimes ask, scornfully. But a great deal is in a name—the energy of pride or shame that is transmitted from a person's first chakra. Violating tribal justice, on the other hand, can cause a loss of power to an individual's energy system—so much so that one may feel permanently "ungrounded" and have difficulty forming connections to other people.

The tribe usually believes that there is a "humanly logical" reason for why things happen as they do. Such beliefs cause terrible grief. Some people futilely spend years trying to discover "the reason" they had to endure certain painful events; when they cannot find a satisfactory reason, they end up living in a fog—unable to move forward yet unable to release the past. Although tribal law is necessary in order to maintain social order, it does not reflect the reasoning of heaven. By thinking symbolically about the sacrament of Baptism, one can find a spiritual passageway out of the trap of human justice and into the nature of Divine reasoning. If we can view our tribal circumstances as "arranged" to promote spiritual advancement, not physical comfort, we can consider painful events as being essential to our personal development rather than as punishments for our actions.

When tribal justice obstructs our spiritual advancement, we need to free ourselves from its authority over our individual power of choice. This challenge is one of the most difficult associated with the first chakra because it often requires a physical separation from our family or from a group of people to which we have become bonded.

Patrick was an amazingly charming man who attended one of my workshops. He flirted with every woman who came within ten feet of him. Everyone who met him thought he was jovial, warm, and loving. An emergency room paramedic, he was also a gifted storyteller; when he shared bits and pieces of his life he mesmerized the other participants. Few seemed to notice that Patrick was also suffering from chronic pain in his legs and lower back. He could not sit through a whole lecture but had to stand up and stretch his body for a few moments every now and then. He walked with a mild limp.

Everyone assumed Patrick was as lighthearted privately as he appeared to be in public, even though he was from Northern Ireland, known for its endless religious and economic conflicts, and had probably seen more than his share of gunshot wounds and car bomb victims in his emergency room.

One morning Patrick and I met for breakfast, and he asked me to do a reading on him, though he was uncomfortable making the request. I asked him for his age, and when I was in that drifty state that allows impressions to begin, he nervously said, "So how much do you think you can see?" Instantly, I received the impression that he was currently in the military and that his intense leg pain was due to being severely beaten to the point of almost permanent injury to his legs.

"Why am I receiving the impression that you lead a double life—half in the military and half in the hospital? Are you involved in some type of military organization?"

Patrick's entire body and manner immediately stiffened. As he changed from a warm, loving human being into an ice-cold stranger, I realized that I had just crossed a dangerous boundary.

Patrick answered, "You have to be prepared to protect yourself in my part of the world," obviously referring to the long-running conflicts in Northern Ireland. Yet I knew immediately that his energy involved not self-defense but aggression. I said, "I believe the pressure of your connection to a militarylike organization is the cause of your inability to heal your chronic pain. In my opinion, you need to reduce your association with this group, if not leave it entirely."

He responded, "Some things are possible, some are not. A person can't leave the power of history, no matter how much we might want to. And a person can't easily change the ways things are done. Vengeance leads to more vengeance; one week it's my legs, next week it's theirs. It's a fool's road, but once you're on it, you can't get off."

We sat still for a few moments, neither of us speaking, and then he said, "I need to be leaving now. We've said enough." I thought he meant that he needed to be leaving the breakfast table, but actually he left the workshop, and I never saw him again.

I do not know if Patrick was ever forced to take a person's life, but I do know that the burden of his double life was the reason his legs were unable to heal. He was simply incapable of breaking away from his "military tribe," regardless of the cost to his personal health and conflict between his sense of personal justice and the atmosphere of righteous vengeance that surrounded him.

The ultimate first chakra lesson is that the only real justice is divinely ordered. I understood the depth of this lesson while doing a reading on a woman who was filled with cancer. As I was receiving impressions from her, I saw an image of the crucifixion. This image was connected not to her religion, but rather to her feeling of suffering from a "Judas" experience—the challenge of healing from a profound betrayal.

As I pondered the meaning of this image, I realized that the Judas experience is an archetype. It conveyed the meaning that human reasoning and justice always fail us at some point and that we do not have the power to reorder events in our lives and remake all things according to how we would want them. The lesson of a Judas experience is that putting faith in human justice is an error and that we must shift our faith from human to Divine authority. It is to trust that our life is governed "with Divine justice," even though we cannot see it. We must strive not to become bitter or cling to victimhood when we are betrayed or cannot attain what we want, as did the woman who developed cancer as a result of her betrayal experience. We need to trust that we have not been victimized at all and that this painful experience is challenging us to evaluate where we have placed our faith. Erik's story is a classic illustration of exactly this challenge.

I met Erik several years ago at a workshop in Belgium. He sat silent during the entire workshop, and when it was over, he announced that he was my ride to Amsterdam. I was exhausted and wanted to sleep, but once we were on our way, he said, "Let me tell you all about myself." At that point I found the prospect about as appealing as a stick through my eye. Nevertheless, I said, "Okay, you've got my attention," and to this day I am grateful for his insistence.

Ten years before, Erik's entire life had crashed. Two business partners with whom he was trying to get a couple of business ventures off the ground announced that they had decided they no longer wanted to work with him. Because they were two against one, he could not do much about their decision. They made him a settlement offer: he could take the equivalent of $35,000 in cash, or he could have all of the stock in a company they mutually owned, which was actually worthless.

Stunned, Erik left the office and went home. As he entered the house, he said to his wife, "I need to tell you something," to which she replied, "I need to tell you something too. I want a divorce. I've met someone else."

Erik said to me, "All three of my partners divorced me in one day. I was so overwhelmed that even though I was an atheist, I concluded that only heaven could mess up someone's life this much. That night I decided to pray. I said to God, 'If You are behind this, talk to me. I will follow whatever direction You give me.'

"That night I had a dream. In the dream I was driving a car across the Alps during a horrible storm. The roads were treacherously icy, and I had to cling to the steering wheel in order to keep the car from slipping off the road. At one point I almost lost control of the car and seemed to be heading off the side of the mountain, but I didn't. I finally made it across the top of the mountain, and once I was over the top, the storm was gone, the sun was shining, the roads were dry and safe. I continued along the road to a small cottage, where a candle was burning for me in the window and a warm meal was waiting at the table.

"I decided from that dream to take my partners' offer of all the stock in that worthless company—because the company was a cat-food company, and the car I was driving in the dream was a Jaguar. My partners were delighted with my choice, thinking that they had just saved themselves $35,000. I knew, though I wasn't sure why, that in accepting this offer, I had to release them and my wife without anger. I had to bid them all farewell, even though, ironically, it was they who thought they were getting rid of me. Shortly afterward, several opportunities to help this little company came into my life, and as the dream foretold, the early months of getting it off the ground were seriously challenging. But I knew, because of that dream, that I would make it, so I hung on.

"Today I have one of the most successful companies in Belgium and spend a great deal of my time in entrepreneurial ventures. And I am remarried to the most wonderful woman, someone who is a life's partner in every meaning of the word. I never anticipated anything that I am doing now—only God could have known this plan. Each morning I begin my day in prayer, thanking God for separating me from my earlier life, because I would never have had the courage to leave those three people on my own. Now, when I meet people whose lives are upside down, I tell them, 'God is behind you. There is nothing to worry about. I know that for a fact.'"

All of these case studies are examples of situations in which we can learn the sacred truth *All Is One*. The spiritual power contained within the sefirah of Shekhinah and the sacrament of Baptism combines with the energy of the Tribal chakra to give us "first chakra intuition," to help us to live honorably with each other and to evolve beyond misperceptions that contradict the truth *All Is One*. The next stage of our development is to explore second chakra themes and the sacred truth *Honor One Another*.

Questions for Self-Examination

1. What belief patterns did you inherit from your family?
2. Which of those belief patterns that still have authority in your thinking can you acknowledge are no longer valid?
3. What superstitions do you have? Which have more authority over you than your own reasoning ability?
4. Do you have a personal code of honor? What is it?
5. Have you ever compromised your sense of honor? If so, have you taken steps to heal it?

6. Do you have any unfinished business with your family members? If so, list the reasons that prevent you from healing your family relationships.

7. List all the blessings that you feel came from your family.

8. If you are now raising a family of your own, list the qualities that you would like your children to learn from you.

9. What tribal traditions and rituals do you continue for yourself and your family?

10. Describe the tribal characteristics within yourself that you would like to strengthen and develop.

CHAPTER 2

The Second Chakra: The Power of Relationships

The second chakra is the Partnership chakra. Its energy begins to pulsate and become distinct around the age of seven. At that age children start interacting with other children and adults, more independently of their parents and outside the home environment. Through these initial interactions they begin to individuate, form relationships, and explore their power of choice. With the second chakra energy shifts from obeying tribal authority to discovering other relationships that satisfy personal, physical needs. Still a lower chakra energy that pushes us toward relating to external forces, the second chakra is a powerful force.

Location: Lower abdomen to navel area.

Energy connection to the physical body: Sexual organs, large intestine, lower vertebrae, pelvis, hip area, appendix, and bladder.

Energy connection to the emotional/mental body: This chakra resonates to our need for relationships with other people and our need to control to some extent the dynamics of our physical environment. All the attachments by which we maintain control over our external lives, such as authority, other people, or money, are linked through this chakra to our energy field and physical body. The illnesses that originate in this energy center are activated by the fear of losing control. Prostate or ovarian cancer, chronic pain in the lower back and hips, and arthritis are a few of the more common health problems.

Problems at menopause, such as hot flashes and depression, are second chakra energy dysfunctions. Fibroids result from second chakra creative energy that was not birthed and from life energy that is directed into dead end jobs or relationships.

Symbolic/perceptual connection: The energy in this chakra enables us to generate a sense of personal identity and protective psychological boundaries. As we continually assess our personal strength in regard to the external world and its physically seductive forces—such as sex, money, addictive substances, or other people—the second chakra energy of a healthy physical ego keeps us able to interact with that world without having to negotiate or "sell" ourselves; it is the energy of self-sufficiency, a survival instinct for being in the world.

Sefirot/Sacrament connection: The second chakra is aligned to the sefirah of Yesod, which represents the phallus, the male energy of procreation. This Partnership chakra also holds the energy of "covenant." This procreative energy is both biological and spiritual: we desire to create children and also to bring our creative ideas into physical form, which is as crucial to our physical health as to our spiritual. The sacrament of Communion resonates to the energy of this chakra and symbolizes bonds we form with people. Communions of many types are symbolized by the act of "sharing bread together."

Primary fears: Fears of loss of control, or being controlled by another, through the dominating power of events or conditions such as addiction, rape, betrayal, impotence, financial loss, abandonment by our primary partner or professional colleagues. Also, fear of the loss of the power of the physical body.

Primary strengths: The ability and stamina to survive financially and physically on one's own and to defend and protect oneself; the "fight or flight" instinct; the ability to take risks; the resilience to recover from loss whether of family members, partners, property, occupation, or finances; the power to rebel and reestablish a life; and personal and professional decision-making ability and talent.

Sacred truth: The sacred truth inherent in the second chakra is *Honor One Another.* This truth applies to our interactions with each other and with all forms of life. From a spiritual perspective every relationship we develop, from the most casual to the most intimate, serves the purpose of helping us to become more conscious. Some relationships are necessarily painful because learning about ourselves and facing our own limitations are not things we tend to do with enthusiasm. We often need to be spiritually "set up" for such encounters.

The archetypal energies of the sefirah of Yesod and the sacrament of Communion and the physical energy of the second chakra all symbolize that relationships are essentially spiritual messengers. They bring into our lives—and we into theirs—revelations about our own strengths and weaknesses. From relationships within the home to those at work to community or political activity, no union is without spiritual value; each helps us grow as individuals. We can more easily see the symbolic value of our relationships when we release our compulsion to judge what and who has value and instead focus on honoring the person and the task with which we are involved.

The second chakra's energy has an inherent duality. The unified energy of the first chakra, represented by the tribal mind, becomes divided into polarities in the second chakra. This division of forces has been given many names: yin/yang, anima/animus, male/female, sun/moon. Understanding the significance of these opposites is the key to working with second chakra issues. The energies of the sefirah of Yesod and the sacrament of Communion combine with these dual energies of the second chakra to ensure that we "attract" to ourselves relationships that help us come to know ourselves. Well-known expressions such as "Like attracts like" and "When the student is ready, the teacher will appear" acknowledge that an energy working "behind the scenes" seems to organize when and where we meet people—and always at the right time. The spiritual challenge of the second chakra is to learn to interact consciously with others:

to form unions with people who support our development and to release relationships that handicap our growth.

Physical science recognizes second chakra energy as the law of cause and effect (for every action, there is an equal and opposite reaction) and the law of magnetism (oppositely charged objects attract). Applied to relationships, these laws mean that we generate patterns of energy that attract people who are opposite us in some way, who have something to teach. Nothing is random; prior to every relationship we have ever formed, we opened the door with energy that we were generating. This fact is what makes learning about second chakra dualism so delicious; the more conscious we become, the more consciously we can utilize the energy of the second chakra.

The Power of Choice

The energy of the second chakra helps us evolve beyond the collective energy of the tribe. Choice is born out of opposites, and the duality of the second chakra is forever challenging us to make choices in a world of opposing sides, of positive and negative energy patterns. Every choice we make contributes a subtle current of our energy to our universe, which is responsive to the influence of human consciousness.

Managing the power of choice, with all its creative and spiritual implications, is *the essence of the human experience*. All spiritual teachings are directed toward inspiring us to recognize that the power to make choices is the dynamic that converts our spirits into matter, our words into flesh. Choice is the process of creation itself.

The fact that our choices weave our spirits into events is the reason the major spiritual traditions are formed around one essential lesson: Make your choices wisely, because each choice you make is a creative act of spiritual power for which you are held responsible. Further, any choice made from faith has the full power of heaven behind it—which is why "faith the size of a mustard seed can move a mountain." And any choice made from fear is a violation of the energy of faith.

Choice has a mysterious aspect, however, for we will never completely know the full outcome of any choice we make. A primal lesson of the second chakra is the paradoxical nature of choice: what seems right can turn out wrong; what appears good can end up bad. Just when everything is going smoothly, chaos breaks things up.

Paradoxically, while the energy of the second chakra inclines us to try to control our lives, the lesson of the second chakra is that we cannot be in control. We are physical beings and energy beings, but since the physical world cannot be controlled, the task before us is to master our inner responses to the external world, our thoughts and emotions.

Nevertheless, we all struggle in a seemingly never-ending cycle of disappointment in which we attempt to control our lives. We search endlessly for the one grand choice that will put everything in our lives into permanent order, halting the motion of change long enough to establish final control over everyone and everything. Is that choice the right career? The right marriage partner? The right geographic location? In seeking this one right choice constantly, we give form to our fear of the changing rhythm that is life itself. In looking for this single external person or thing that will forever bring us peace, stability, love, and health, we dismiss the more authentic power that lies "behind our eyes and not in front of them." The truth contained within the paradoxical nature of dualism is this: It is not *what* we choose that matters; our power to influence an outcome lies in our *reasons* for making a certain choice.

The challenge of the second chakra is to learn what motivates us to make the choices we do. In learning about our motivations, we learn about the content of our spirits. Are you filled with fear, or are you filled with faith? Every choice we make contains the energy of either faith or fear, and the outcome of every decision reflects to some extent that faith or fear. This dynamic of choice guarantees that we cannot run away from ourselves or our decisions.

Choice and Relationships

Second chakra energy is extremely volatile because it seeks to create. It is also linked to the issues of physical survival: sex, power, and money, the currencies of relationships. As we set out to carve a place for ourselves in the physical world, our internal conflict between faith and fear is often buried underneath the survival issues that dominate our thoughts: Can I earn a living? Can I find a partner? Can I take care of myself?

The shadow side of second chakra issues consists of our most prevalent fears: rape, betrayal, financial loss and poverty, abandonment, isolation, impotence, and the inability to care for ourselves. Each of these fears has the power to control us and to direct our actions for an entire lifetime. In the language of the Scriptures, these fears qualify as "false gods."

In order to learn about our motivations—to discover our personal "false gods"—we need relationships. To form a relationship, we use some of our energy or personal power. Once the relationship is formed, we may ask, often unconsciously: Is this relationship drawing power from me, or am I drawing power from it? Where do I end, and where does the other person begin? What is my power, and what is the other's power? Am I compromising myself, in exchange for safety, or money, or status? While these questions are essentially healthy, in most relationships we begin thinking in terms of psychologically divisive and conflict-inducing opposites: me or you, mine or yours, good or bad, winner or loser, right or wrong, rich or poor.

Symbolically, these conflicts represent most people's relationship to God: my power or Yours—are You really with me on this earth, or must I try to control everything myself? And even if a Divine power is maneuvering behind the scenes, how do I know what choices to make? This primary conflict of faith is present in every one of our relationships.

Paradoxically, our challenge in managing these conflicting energies is to maintain them in the consciousness of the inherent oneness of the universe. We begin this journey by exploring conflict within relationships: Relationships generate conflict, conflict generates choice, choice generates movement, and movement generates more conflict. We break free of this cycle by making choices that transcend dualism and the perceived divisions between ourselves and others, and between ourselves and God. So long as we focus on trying to control another person and forget that that person is a mirror reflecting back to us our own qualities, we keep conflict alive within ourselves. Seeing ourselves and others in symbolic unions, however, helps us accommodate differences. This is the symbolic meaning of the Sacrament of Communion.

The Challenge of Managing Creative Energy

Second chakra energies need to create life, to "move the earth," to make an impression or contribution to the continuum of life. Creative energy, unlike inspiration—a seventh chakra quality—is essentially physical, of the earth or grounded. It is the sensation of being physically alive. Second chakra energy gives us our basic survival instincts and intuitions, as well as our desire to create music, art, poetry, and architecture, and the curiosity to investigate nature in science and medicine. Our creative energy draws us into an internal dialogue with the polarities of the self, our conflicting inclinations, and it compels us to form external relationships to resolve these polarities.

Creative energy breaks us out of habitual patterns of behavior, thoughts, and relationships. Habit is a hell to which people cling in an attempt to stop the flow of change. But creative energy defies the repetition of habit. These two forces, repetition and creativity, are at odds with each other within the human psyche and impel us to invest and reshape the chaos of our world with personal meaning.

Second chakra energy is one of the primary resources we have for coping with the day-to-day events of our lives, providing creative solutions to mental, physical, and spiritual problems or issues. Blocking this energy can give rise to impotence, infertility, vaginal infections, endometriosis, and depression. It also interferes with our spiritual maturation, as if stating, "I don't wish to see anymore, I don't wish to understand any deeper, I don't wish to interact with the learning processes of life." If allowed to flow, creative energy will continually act to reshape our lives and reveal more meaning for why things happen as they do than we could determine on our own.

A woman named Kate contacted me for a reading after her husband, a man in his early thirties, died in a car accident. She was left to support two children, with seemingly minimal options for coping with life, with neither formal education nor skills. Kate told me she simply had no energy left "to go on living."

It was obvious to me, and to Kate herself, that she was suffering from depression. During the reading I noted that she had a benign ovarian cyst, about which she did not yet know. We spoke about the importance of releasing the past and finding a reason to move forward, but that challenge seemed overwhelming to Kate. I told her to see her physician for a checkup regarding the cyst and also to do some small task that would represent her intention to rebuild her life. She was to visualize that task as bringing new energy into her life. That she would have a growth in her ovarian area was not surprising, because not only had she lost her mate, she had lost a way of life and was now confronting her ability even to survive physically and financially. Survival is a major issue of the second chakra.

The task Kate chose as symbolic of her new beginning was to plant flowers, which represented new life. With each flower she planted, she said, "I am planting a new beginning for myself and my children." Each day she worked more consciously to bring her energy into the present. She refused to allow herself to dwell on the past life she had had with her husband. She also went for a physical, and her physician confirmed that she had a benign ovarian cyst. She was in no immediate danger, he said, but this cyst had to be checked periodically. Kate then added another task to her gardening; as she weeded the garden, she would say, "I am pulling the cyst out of my body."

After six weeks Kate began to get ideas about how to create an income for herself. She had always been good at domestic activities, such as cooking and sewing, but she had never considered earning a living from these skills. Then one day a friend called to say that she had just sprained her wrist and was unable to sew all the costumes that she had committed to make for a local theater production. Would Kate take over the task?

Kate accepted, went to the theater, received instructions about the costumes, and returned home with fabric and measurements. As she looked over the designs, she began to fiddle with them, noting where she could make improvements. She phoned the person in charge of costumes and suggested some changes, all of which met with approval. Her costumes were a success. Shortly afterward Kate's phone began ringing with requests for her to assist in other theater projects and personal design work.

Kate has since opened her own design shop and has a thriving business. Her ovarian cyst has dissolved. She has recommended to numerous people that when they feel themselves at a dead end and need to start over, they should plant flowers in a garden with the thought, "I am now planting a creative idea for myself."

Kate's story illustrates how creative energy can propel us along paths that we may never have anticipated and enhance the power of our positive choices. A creative idea has its own energy field and can generate the synchronistic involvement of people and circumstances required to carry the idea through to the next stage of life. Symbolically, Kate's story also represents the presence of the spiritual energies of the Sefirah Yesod—the need to create—and the Sacrament of Communion—the magnetic force we radiate that draws help to us when we need help the most.

Because creative energy is so volatile, however, and so powerful, one of our greatest challenges is to use it consciously. We most frequently utilize our creativity in the privacy of our thoughts, but creative energies are also present in our interactions with other people. We may, for example, creatively change the details of stories we tell others to suit our own purposes; or we may manipulate someone to get something we want. These are acts that use energy in negative ways. Gossip and manipulation drain power from the second chakra.

Negative acts and negative thoughts originate in fear. To the extent that the fear of betrayal by another person, for instance, or of violation within a relationship, or of being taken advantage of financially has authority within us, it determines the extent to which we will behave in negative ways. Faith in anything, be it positive or negative, produces results. Putting faith in fear generates destructive results, beginning with the disintegration of our ability to relate confidently to the external world.

When we are motivated by fear, we can easily be seduced by the false gods of sex, power, and money and all that they represent. Once seduced, we abdicate our control to the seductive authority: the dysfunctional personal relationship, the external source of money or security, the experience remembered long after it should have been put to rest, or the addiction to drugs or alcohol. Hypnotized by the voice of fear, one is unable to think or act with clarity, because one is contaminated with fears that short-circuit creative energy and ideas, which gather their energy from the second chakra. Literally and symbolically, the second chakra is the birth canal. Although newborn ideas have their own energy field and will fight for survival, just as newborn infants do, fear will often abort a new idea. Some people are afraid to give ideas—or relationships— the "breathing room" they need in order to thrive. You might feel threatened, for instance, when an idea you have reaches a point where you need expertise other than your own for support. Or you may assume a position of ownership over an idea—meaning that because you "birthed" the idea, it's yours, and therefore you control everything and everyone attached to it. Both responses frequently result in "energy suffocation," the smothering effect of a controlling, fearful parent or partner.

A man named John attended one of my workshops because he wanted to discover intuitively a new direction for his career. He had always been expected, he said, to start his own video production company. As he approached his fortieth birthday, he felt that the time was "now or never." He found two partners, and together they launched what they all hoped would become a successful corporation. Together the three of them developed a business plan and set out to find investors. During the planning or "dream time" of the project, all went well among the three partners. They thrived on their energy and ambitions and felt that they were marked for success—a belief that became even stronger when they secured five different investors.

Yet the infusion of capital unexpectedly set them against one another. Instead of propelling them into the next creative stage of development, the money changed John's attitude. He began to imply subtly that all the ideas were largely produced by his creativity and that therefore he should really be in charge of the next phase of decisions. John's competition with his partners derailed their creative impetus, and six months later, a good portion of their initial investment capital spent, they had still failed to produce one video project. The three of them were finally forced to terminate their partnership and declare bankruptcy. John blamed his partners for the failure, convinced that they were jealous of his talent.

Inherent in the second chakra's potential to create is also the potential for conflict. The sacred truth and theme of the second chakra, *Honor One Another*, contain enormous spiritual power and the solution to the management of this spiritual challenge. When we act in alignment with this truth, we bring out the best in ourselves and in others. Symbolically, the energies of the sefirah of Yesod and the sacrament of Communion are meant to be used to honor another human being, whether by intuiting the right thing to say to someone or by acknowledging the equal importance of the other person in a union. Creation is a form of communion, uniting the life-generating energies of people toward a common goal. Creativity is frequently referred to as sowing seeds, which is yet another metaphor representing the phallus energy of the sefirah of Yesod.

John was unable to acknowledge the fact that his business partners also had talent, creative ideas, and ambition. Instead of respecting and working with them, he felt threatened by them. When I did a private reading on him, hoping to help him understand the source of his fear, I received the impression that his biggest fear was impotence and that he associated sexual impotence, and financial and creative impotence, with shared authority. At the same time he was attracted to the idea of creating with other people. While this kind of conflict could be resolved in therapy, John resisted this suggestion. He said that, in his opinion, every business should have only one leader and that his problem would be resolved if he were to find a group of talented people who understood that. Therapy, said John, would not change how he felt about the dynamics of running a business; therefore, therapy would have no value. Until John became motivated to challenge his own beliefs, he would continue to lead ventures that would fail. Indeed, he left the workshop determined to find another team of people to lead.

Energy and physical abortions that result from fear have emotional and often physical consequences. Women who have abortions because their husbands reject them or the child or because they are terrified that they will be unable to provide a home for the child may have disorders of the reproductive system—fibroids, for instance. In one incident, Norm Shealy called me in to consult on a patient who had severe vaginal bleeding with no known physical cause. As I evaluated her energy, I noted that she'd had two abortions, neither of which she had wanted. I asked Norm, "Did she tell you about her two abortions?" Norm asked the patient about her feelings about her abortions, which she had not mentioned during his medical evaluation. She broke down emotionally, and out poured the grief and guilt that had burdened her for years. These traumas were the energy cause of the bleeding.

The women whom I've met who have had an abortion by choice have not reported feeling traumatized by the experience. Rather, their feeling that the time was not right for them to become a mother or to have another child and the fact that they knew they had the right to make the decision played a significant role in their ability to live comfortably with their choice. One woman told me that prior to having an abortion, she conducted a ceremony, sending a message to the spirit of the child she was carrying. She communicated to the child that she could not provide a stable environment. She felt convinced that the message was received because, following the abortion, she had a dream in which she met a spirit who said to her, "All is well."

Energy abortions, the aborting of an idea or project, occur with far greater frequency than physical abortions, and men and women both experience them. Just as fetal abortions can cause enormous emotional and physical scars, so too can energy abortions leave their imprint. In both men and women energy abortions contribute to physical problems, among them infertility. Many career women who are extremely involved in the birthing of their careers have difficulty becoming pregnant. Some men in the same position also experience prostate problems and difficulty with sexual potency.

One man recalled how he had invested a great deal of his time, energy, and money in planning a new business. Since he didn't have enough money to start it on his own, he sought financial backing from several acquaintances. On the strength of their assured support, he set about making plans. After several months of hammering out the details, he approached his partners for the money they had promised. They all backed out. His creation never came into being, and he was deeply hurt. He said he couldn't "give birth" to the idea. For years he carried the "death" of his plan in his body like an abortion. Eventually he developed a malignant tumor in his colon from which, years later, he died. His need to give birth to life, which is equal in the male and female psyches, caused him to suffer this energy abortion.

Another man told me his wife once had an abortion without telling him because she felt the decision was hers alone. When he found out, he carried the energy of that abortion—the anger and guilt—in his system. As a result, he became impotent: his body refused to produce life again.

The Challenge of
Managing Sexual Energy

Sexuality and all of our attitudes toward it are patterned in the second chakra. Sexuality is raw power, the power to form strong bonds and an intimate union with another person with whom we can produce and sustain life. Having a mate and forming a family, with or without children, represent stability for us as adults. Finding a life's partner also includes forming a union with a person of the same sex. Breaking through the cultural restraints that have held people to confined and limited forms of sexual expression has allowed individuals to seek companionship according to their needs, and this has permitted the homosexual community to begin its journey toward achieving dignity within a dominantly heterosexual world.

The second chakra contains the desire, as well as the ability, to create life. Pregnancy and birth unite the "dualistic" forces between two people more tangibly than any other expression of unity.

Besides creating life, sex is an avenue of self-expression, a means of making a statement about our comfort in relating physically to the world around us. Sexuality connects us to our own bodies and physical needs as well as to our potential for exploring our erotic and sensual aspects. Sexual eroticism is a form of physical and emotional liberation as well as of spiritual liberation. Why spiritual? Erotic pleasure is, by nature, "in the moment," an encounter in which we drop most of our physical boundaries in order to enjoy the full measure of human contact. Explored without shame, erotic energy can elevate the human body and spirit into sensations of ecstasy, at times producing altered states of consciousness.

Women are physical examples of the ongoing life pattern of energy becoming matter through pregnancy, labor, and delivery. Women's life cycle expresses a natural progression of sexual energy. For most women, for instance, kundalini, or sexual-spiritual energy, begins to rise naturally around the age of forty. As it rises, it activates the chakras through which it passes. Any unfinished business residing in the lower chakras will make itself known during the premenopausal and menopausal years. For women who have had limited sexual pleasure, for instance, the blocked kundalini energy or unused sexual juice may manifest as hot flashes. Unused creative energy or creative conflicts may also be expressed as hot flashes.

In a woman younger than forty, problems with menstruation, cramps, and PMS are classic indications that she is in some kind of conflict with being a woman, with her role in the tribe, and with tribal expectations of her. Most problems with bleeding and irregular periods frequently come from having too much emotional stress combined with the belief that one has no power over one's life choices, that one's choices are controlled by others. Bleeding abnormalities are often exacerbated when a woman internalizes confusing signals from her family or society about her own sexual pleasure and sexual needs. For instance, a woman may desire sexual pleasure but feel guilty about it or be unable to ask directly for it. She may not even be conscious of this inner conflict..

Tubal problems and problems with fertility are centered on a woman's "inner child," while the tubes themselves are representative of unhealed childhood wounds or unused energy. The flow of eggs can be blocked because a woman's own inner being is not "old" or nurtured enough, or mature or healed enough, to feel fertile. This energy pattern can underlie tubal problems. One part of a woman may remain in prepuberty due to her own unconscious indecision about her readiness to produce life if, on some level, she's not "out of the egg" herself.

Kundalini energies are contrary energies of the psyche and body. They wind around the spine, from its base in the first chakra to the crown of the head, following and spiraling around all seven chakras. Kundalini yoga teaches a way of managing this energy and of bringing about a kundalini experience, an ecstatic state of spiritual ecstasy reached through disciplining one's sexual energy. Rather than allowing the normal release of sexual energy through a physical orgasm, Kundalini spiritual practice directs the sexual energy to rise up the spine and culminate in a spiritual union with the Divine. Numerous mystics have been said to experience altered states of consciousness during deep moments of meditation that included orgasmic release.

Sexual eroticism normally produces orgasm, and the release of this voltage of energy is essential to physical, mental, and psychological health. Orgasm is one way—certainly one of the more pleasurable ways—of releasing the "energy debris" we collect through ordinary human contact. Exercise and creativity are other well-known avenues of release. When a person has no release, however, this energy backs up in the system and, without conscious management, can produce reactions that run the gamut from depression to violence. Spontaneous kundalini experiences do occur, however.

Once upon a time I would have scoffed at the idea of a sexual union leading to a spiritual bond. But the profound truths contained in kundalini and tantric teachings are evident in the following story.

I met Linda several years ago when we were both house guests of a mutual friend. Because I was having some premenstrual cramping, I asked Linda if she had any aspirin, commenting casually, "You know how it is." She responded, "No, I don't. I've never had a period in my entire life." Seeing my look of disbelief, she said, "I'm not kidding. You can do a reading if you want." So I did.

I immediately received the impression that Linda had had a hysterectomy, but the impression was extremely peculiar because I kept seeing the image of a child having the operation. At the same time, I received the impression of intense sexual energy flowing in a very healthy stream through her second chakra—an image that is rarely found in the energy of women who no longer have their sexual organs. I shared my impressions with Linda and confessed that I was very confused by them.

Linda, smiling, confirmed that she had had a hysterectomy. The rest of the imagery would make sense, she assured me, when she filled me in on her story.

Linda and her husband, Steve, had been high school sweethearts in the early sixties. In those days it was still rare for teens to relate to each other sexually. Linda admitted that she had dreaded the moment when her relationship with Steve would become sexual because at sixteen she had been diagnosed with underdeveloped sexual organs (which explained why I later received the image of a child). A normal menstrual cycle was impossible for her, much less a pregnancy. Linda was embarrassed by her condition and kept it a secret from Steve because if he learned that she was unable to bear children, she feared, he might not marry her because she was not a "normal" woman. He might not even find her sexually appealing anymore. She had no idea whether she could even have sexual relations with a man, but she very much wanted to marry Steve.

In high school Linda had developed a fondness for playing the dulcimer, a stringed American folk instrument. As a graduation present Steve made her a dulcimer and gave it to her the night they graduated. That night Linda and Steve made love. She did not tell him her secret, terrified that he would somehow discover something wrong with her, some abnormality in the sex act, which was her first.

While they made love, Linda began breathing heavily, not so much from passion as from fear. Simultaneously she repeated a prayer in her mind, asking God to let them be together for the rest of their lives. In the midst of this combination of spiritual fervor and sexual love, Linda felt an energy rush move through her body and into Steve's. It made her feel as if she and Steve had become one system of energy. In that moment she felt convinced that they would marry, even though she was unable to bear children.

Within a week of that powerful graduation night, however, Steve announced that he wanted to go out on his own for a while. The suddenness of his announcement, coupled with their new physical intimacy, convinced Linda that he was leaving because something was wrong with her sexually. He had decided that he did not want to be with her, she imagined, and leaving town was his way of telling her. They parted.

Four years later, they both got married to other people. Curiously, they both married in the same month. While Linda intended to give this marriage her best shot, she had never stopped loving Steve. In fact, by the time she married, she no longer cared whether her inability to bear children or have a normal sex life was an issue to any man, not even a husband. A year and a half into her marriage, Linda had a hysterectomy because of indications that a growth was developing there.

In both their marriages, Linda and Steve moved to cities away from their hometown. Both marriages lasted five years, and as unbelievable as this may seem, Linda and Steve divorced within a week of each other. Both also returned to live in their hometown the same month. They had been out of touch with each other during all these years and had had no contact with former mutual friends.

After moving back to her hometown, Linda became financially

strapped, so much so that she had to pawn all her valuables, including her precious dulcimer, her last tie to Steve. Two hours after Linda left the pawnshop, Steve walked in to pawn some of his jewelry. He spotted the dulcimer. How long had the dulcimer been in the shop? he asked. When told that the seller had practically just left the shop, he set out to find her, dulcimer in hand. That evening Linda and Steve were reunited, and they have never been apart since. When he spotted his handmade dulcimer, he told her, memories of her instantly saturated his body, and he felt flooded with love. He knew that she was in desperate financial trouble because she would never have pawned her dulcimer otherwise.

That same evening Linda told Steve about her health condition, including her belief that he had left her because she was unable to be a fully sexual being. Steve confessed that the reason he left her was that on their graduation night, as they were making love for the first time, he felt an energy rush going through his body, the likes of which he had never before experienced. He felt as if his entire being were united with her forever, and in that moment, the feeling was euphoric. But as he thought about it a few days later, the sensation frightened him, and all he could think about was running away. Linda was dumbfounded.

Also that evening, Steve and Linda decided to marry, and within the week. As they made love on the night of their reunion, that same rush of energy returned and they both were conscious of it. They thought the rush was merely from their delight at being together again, but as their sexual life continued on a regular basis, the energy increased. Steve had read about kundalini and introduced Linda to the practice of consciously utilizing the rush of energy for both physical and spiritual pleasure. Steve and Linda's history explained my impression of rushes of healthy energy flowing through her second chakra, despite her hysterectomy.

Sexual union, for all its physical pleasures, also symbolizes a spiritual union of two people. It may well be that sexual energy opens a current of spiritual energy that forms a transcendent bond between two people who are deeply in love. It allowed Linda and Steve to attain the state of consciousness described as the kundalini experience, a total expression of the united power of the sefirah of Yesod, the sacrament of Communion, and the second or Partnership chakra.

The need to strive to *Honor One Another* is easily and frequently eclipsed in sexual encounters, largely because sexual energy is so often controlled by fear or unrestrained desires. Men are made afraid of not being potent or masculine enough, yet most tribes permit their boys to act out of control sexually until they reach a certain "maturity." At that point, their capacity to act sexually responsible is expected to kick in automatically. A common tribal perception is that young men have to "sow their wild oats" before they can settle down, freeing promiscuous males from condemnation or accountability for their behavior. Biological urges, after all, control them.

Women, however, are still not given the same license to explore their sexual natures, despite the three-decades-old women's liberation movement. Women are still required to behave, to control their sexual energy, while men still enjoy license. Many women are made to fear losing control or even being thought of as sexual beings. One of my workshop participants described how her mother always made her feel "dirty" whenever she dressed up to go out with her friends. Her mother's sexual innuendos made her feel that attracting the attention of any man was equivalent to prostitution. This mother's emotional invasiveness was a violation of her daughter's energy.

The view of sexual energy as necessary but always "potentially out of control" contributes enormously to our society's schizophrenic tribal attitude toward sexual expression. It encourages women to look sexy, act sexy, and dress sexy; yet if they are attacked as a result, the social mind is still uncomfortable with blaming the rapist or batterer or murderer. Women who have been raped are still scrutinized for what they were wearing and their private sexual lives.

Women who are battered or raped by their boyfriends or husbands receive support from groups organized specifically for their protection but not actually from society as a whole. The social mind still asks raped and abused women questions such as "If he is really so bad, why didn't you just leave him?"—implying that these assaults are matters to be resolved through therapy, not serious enough for legal action. The minor criminal sentences rapists receive communicate the tribal attitude that sexual violations are still only somewhat illegal, as opposed to genuine social atrocities.

The dualism of second chakra energies carries through the societal view of sexual energy as out of control, on the one hand, and the high value our tribe places on self-control, on the other. We view sexuality as a continual threat to our ability to manage ourselves or control others. Relationships of any kind bring out in us our need to protect ourselves, but sexual bonds bring out extreme fears, especially of betrayal, a fear so strong that it can threaten an intimate relationship.

Cultural views of sexuality are different in different societies. The puritanical history of American culture, combined with the value we place on sexual control, contributes substantially to the widespread shame people feel about their bodies and sexual natures. During many of my workshops, participants who share personal stories of their unfulfilled sexual lives are as numerous as those who come to workshops to improve their health. Many report having lived with a mate for years, even decades, yet never having had one conversation about their personal sexual needs. The reasons given are all variations of the identical feeling, ranging from embarrassment to a lack of awareness about what it means to have personal sexual needs.

This sexual shame, so prevalent in our tribal mind, contributes to American society's need to generate rules setting proper and improper sexual behavior—yet another paradox of the second chakra. Since the natural energy of the second chakra moves away from the self and toward the "other," its characteristic fear produces a need to control sexual behavior. Thus, the tribe validates married and monogamous couples and attempts to shame others. Some states consider certain types of sexual behavior to be criminal rather than merely improper, regardless of the fact that sexuality is voluntary between consenting adults. Most particularly, this legal condemnation is directed at homosexuals.

Shame about sexuality carries over into shame about sexual diseases, such as syphilis, herpes, and AIDs. Inevitably, people with a sexually transmitted disease feel compelled to offer a profile of their personal sexual history, to prevent the inference that the illness was picked up through indiscriminate sexual encounters.

Criminal sexual violations—rape, incest, and child molesting—are more than physical violations—they are also energy violations. One can rape someone's energy field with verbal abuse or destructive, disempowering attitudes. Bill, a workshop participant, had a relationship with his father that exemplifies emotional violation or attitudinal rape.

Bill's father continually belittled him as he was growing up, saying he would "never amount to anything in this life." Bill spent years trying to prove his father wrong but never succeeded. When his father died, never having retracted his condemnation, Bill was emotionally paralyzed. He suffered from chronic depression, could not keep a job, and was impotent. Although Bill's father had derogated his son's potency in the material world, not his sexuality, financial productivity and sexuality are both second chakra energies and are intimately linked.

Rape and incest of an energy field are motivated by the desire to cripple a person's ability to be independent and thrive outside the control of another person. The sexual organs warehouse the damage inflicted by these negative beliefs and actions. Numerous people who suffer from sexual problems ranging from impotence to infertility to reproductive-organ cancer remember having been constantly criticized about their professional skills, ambitions, and accomplishments as well as their physical appearance. In effect, their parents "raped" their children, stripping them of the personal power they needed for health and success.

Energy violations of this type may be even more common than physical rape and incest. When rape and incest are defined in energy terms, as violations of energy, men and women in equal numbers admit to having been violated. When I ask workshop participants, "How many of you have ever felt that your dignity or your self-esteem was raped within your working or living environment?" almost everyone holds up a hand.

When I ask, "How many of you are, or have been, energy rapists?" the response is, not surprisingly, a bit more restricted. Yet when the physical talents of another person intimidate us and we either hold negative attitudes about that person or engage in verbal combat, we are attempting to rape that person, to deprive him or her of power. Our physical bodies warehouse our own negative intentions in our sexual organs: acts of energy rape harm the rapist as much as they do the victim. Violations of other human beings poison the violator's energy system and therefore contaminate the violator's biological system. Energy violations have a karmic quality of inherent justice that transcends physical justice—although people appear to get away with criminal behavior, especially in incidents of rape or incest, justice is always served at the energy level, whether or not anyone witnesses it. For this reason, spiritual teachings emphasize forgiveness and encourage people to get on with their lives. Spiritually, it is understood that Divine Order is a force that works constantly to restore balance in our lives, a force that is enhanced when we can release our need to determine a just outcome. Whether or not we witness the unfolding of justice is irrelevant, and that is a "spiritual fact" that we often find hard to digest.

Sexuality is a form of exchange and, in certain circumstances, a type of currency. Many people use sex as a means to an end, only to find themselves feeling like rape victims when their efforts to manipulate someone fails. A person who exchanges sex for a desired job or uses it to get close to a person in power risks creating a situation in which someone ends up feeling used. If however, sex is used for what a person would describe as a "fair exchange," then the energy vibration of rape is absent from the body.

The oldest form of sexual currency is, of course, prostitution, the most disempowering act in which a human being can participate. Prostitution of one's energy is a more common violation than is physical prostitution, for countless women and men remain in situations that represent physical security while feeling that they are selling a part of themselves in the process.

The Energy of Money

Within each of our psyches lives an element of the prostitute—a part of ourselves that could possibly be commanded by the right financial figure. Whether our inner prostitute emerges in business dealings or in personal relationships, we will inevitably meet up with it.

Money, like energy, is a neutral substance that takes its direction from the intention of the individual. A more fascinating aspect of money, however, is the fact that it can weave itself into the human psyche as a substitute for the life-force. When people equate money with their life energy—an often unconscious substitution—the consequences are usually negative, for every dollar a person spends is also an unconscious expenditure of energy. A scarcity of money translates into a scarcity of energy in the body itself—again, unconsciously.

The misperception of money as the life-force, coupled with a sudden loss of money, can activate any of several health crises: prostate cancer, impotence, endometriosis, ovarian problems, and lower back and sciatic pain. The fact that so many of the physical problems created by financial stress manifest in the sexual organs is a symbolic expression of the energy of the phallus, represented by the sefirah of Yesod: money has been equated to a sexual force.

To some degree we all unite money and the life-force within our psyches. Our challenge is to achieve, if we can, a relationship with money in which it is separate from our life-force yet attracted to our energy easily and naturally. The more impersonal our relationship to money is, the more likely we are to command its energy into our lives as we need it.

There is no denying that money does have clout in the symbolic or energy world. Expressions such as "Put your money where your mouth is" and "Talk is cheap; money speaks" refer to the cultural view that what people do with their money says more about their motives than any spoken intention.

Money is the means through which we make our private beliefs and goals public. Energy precedes action, and the quality of our intentions contributes substantially to the results.

Beliefs about money affect spiritual attitudes and practices as well. The belief that God blesses those who strive to do good by giving them financial rewards is extremely prevalent, as is the belief that helping others out financially through charity serves to ensure that we ourselves will be protected from poverty. These and many other beliefs of the same genre reflect the grander notion that God communicates with us through our finances and, conversely, that we communicate with God by our financial actions.

Whether these attitudes are based on mythology or truth is irrelevant. We believe in these social adages far more than we disbelieve in them, and from that fact alone, we should understand that we have linked money and faith. The wisest relationship we can have with money is to see it as a substance that faith can attract into our lives.

Putting faith before money reduces money from its status as leader to that of servant, its more appropriate position. Faith that transcends money frees a person to follow his or her intuitive guidance without giving over unnecessary authority to financial concerns. Obviously, so long as we are a part of the physical world, we must honor its codes of debt and payment and assume a commonsense relationship to money, but money deserves no more of our attention than that.

Even beginning to establish such faith is a mark of spiritual maturation. A spiritually mature person can act according to guidance that would strike the financially motivated person as foolish or risky. In many spiritual myths heaven contacts the person who has faith and then directs that person by providing daily "manna from heaven," so that the person can accomplish an appointed task. Such myths partake very much of the symbolic meaning of the sefirah of Yesod. Part of the manna received includes financial energy. Nowhere in the spiritual literature, as far as I know, is there one reported incident of a person regretting following Divine guidance.

Andrew, twenty-seven, contacted me for a reading because of a dream he kept having that he wanted help interpreting. In his dream Andrew moved to a town in Montana. He had no job, no home, and no friends or contacts there, since he had never been to Montana. He tried to dismiss the dream, as if it were a movie scene that got lodged into his unconscious. But gradually the dream produced the sensation that the only reason he was in his present job was for the financial benefits. He asked me what I thought the dream meant, and I said, "I'd seriously consider moving to Montana."

Andrew said that he'd never even been to Montana and had no desire to go there. Perhaps he should make a trip to Montana just to see how the place felt to him, I replied. He said he'd think about that and would let me know.

About six months later, I heard from Andrew. The dream was continuing, only now the sensation about financial benefits was making Andrew feel like a prostitute. He thought of himself as a man of honor, and when the dream suggested that he was compromising his honor, he found it difficult to get through the day. I again encouraged him to visit Montana, only now I told him to make the trip as soon as he could. He said he would give it some serious thought.

The next morning, Andrew called to tell me that he had quit his job. A feeling had come over him when he walked into his office that morning, he said, and he simply had to act on it. When he announced that he was moving to Montana, his associates figured he had landed some great new position there. He told them that not only did he not have a job or any promise of one, he was, in fact, following a dream.

Within a month of his resignation, Andrew moved to Montana. He ended up renting a room in the home of two people who owned a ranch. They needed some help with ranch chores and hired him. One thing led to another, and as the months passed, Andrew was working more with his hands than with his head—a new experience for him. When the holiday season arrived, Andrew decided to stay with his newfound friends rather than visit back east. The ranchers had a daughter, who came to visit at Christmas. The next summer Andrew married the daughter, and over the next five years he learned how to manage the substantial ranch that he and his wife would eventually inherit.

By following his dream, Andrew declared himself a free man, whether or not he realized it. His actions were a statement before heaven that it was more important to him to face the unknown than to compromise his honor for financial security. In return, he received far more than he ever dreamed possible.

Given the numerous negative sexual messages that are a part of our culture, it is not easy to develop a healthy sex life, as illustrated in the following case study.

Allen, twenty-eight, contacted me for a reading, stating that he was afraid of women and needed help understanding why. As I did his reading, I recognized that he was impotent, and I received very strong impressions that Allen saw himself as a sexual pervert; yet I did not get the sense that he had actually molested anyone. He also did not have the energy of someone who had been molested as a child, so I was confused by this imagery. During our conversation I shared my impressions with him and I asked him why he thought of himself as a sexual pervert. He said that when he was a teenager, he and a group of other boys participated in a "circle jerk," as he called it, a group act of masturbation. A mother of one of the boys walked in unexpectedly and screamed that they were all perverts and that they should be ashamed of themselves. She telephoned each boy's mother, telling them all about the incident, and then telephoned the school principal and told him too, adding that these boys couldn't be trusted around the girls and the small children in the town. Gossip spread throughout the town, and for the remainder of their high school years, all the boys were socially shunned. As soon as Allen graduated from high school, he moved away, but by then, he believed that he was a deviate.

Allen admitted that he was impotent and then said that he had still not had a date. I remarked that "circle jerks" are actually very common, so common that they can almost be considered a rite of passage for teenage boys. "I don't believe that," Allen replied. We agreed that he would seek counseling to work through this problem, and to learn for himself that this experience was not an indication of sexual perversion.

About a year later I received a letter from Allen, sharing the progress he had made in therapy. He wrote that he was beginning to feel "socially normal," which for him was a new sensation. He had begun a relationship with a woman with whom he felt comfortable enough that he could tell her about his traumatic experience. She responded compassionately and wasn't repelled by it. Allen was optimistic that he would soon heal completely.

The energies of the second chakra subtly bring up memories that need to be released, constantly presenting us with the desire to act to become more whole in body and spirit.

Ethical Energy

The second chakra is the ethical center of the body. While laws are connected to the first chakra, personal ethics and morals reside in the second chakra. The energy of the sefirah of Yesod and the sacrament of Communion spiritually influence us to have a strong personal code of ethics, drawing us into one-on-one relationships and alerting us intuitively to the dangers of betraying our honor code.

The second chakra organs "record" all our interactions in which we "give our word" to other people, make promises and commitments to them, or accept their promises. A strong personal code of ethics radiates a perceptible quality of energy. This part of our biology also records the promises we make to ourselves, such as New Year's resolutions and other decisions to "repattern" certain behaviors in our lives.

The physical order of which the first chakra is in charge makes us feel safe, and its laws make us feel that control exists within our environment. The ethics and morals of the second chakra provide us with a language through which we can communicate what we accept and don't accept in human relationships. Ethics hold enormous bonding power: we seek out the company of those who hold the same sense of right and wrong as we do; when people deviate from their ethical or moral character, we often disqualify them as intimate companions. We also want our god to be an orderly god, and we are forever trying to crack through the Divine code of right and wrong and reward and punishment, attempting to reason why "bad things happen to good people." We take comfort in believing that if human justice fails us, Divine justice will see that all receive their "just desserts."

Because the second chakra harbors all our individual survival fears, we have constructed an external legal system that supports some semblance of fair play, which is crucial to our well-being. Exercising legal power, or even using legal vocabulary, provides a release valve, of sorts, for pressures that build up in the second chakra. The legal system, at least in theory, is a means of determining guilt and punishing violations; frequently, an "innocent" verdict is seen as a matter of honor, and the financial settlement that the victim gains represents the return of some personal dignity. This dynamic is the social version of the sacred truth *Honor One Another.*

The need for fair play and law and order is felt in our biology, where we observe physical laws of health, such as exercise, proper nutrition, the conscious regulation of stress, and a measure of consistency and order. These laws signal our physiology that we are physically safe and trust our environment. Instability, by contrast, keeps our adrenaline flowing full strength and our "fight-or-flight" mechanism on continual alert. The physical body cannot endure prolonged stress without producing negative biological response. Ulcers and migraines are two of the more common indicators that the chaos in a person's life has become unbearable.

Paul, forty-two, is an attorney who contacted me for a reading because, he said, the stress related to his job was getting to him. While doing his reading, I received impressions that toxic energy was trying to penetrate into his second chakra, as if someone or something was trying to control him. Then I realized that Paul suffered from chronic pain, from migraines to backaches to neck and shoulder pain.

When I shared my impressions with him, Paul verified them, saying that he had been in varying degrees of pain for the past ten years. He had tried therapy, but it hadn't helped. He popped pain pills like candy, which explained my impression that something was trying to control him: he was terrified of becoming addicted to his pain medication. The source of his pain, I pointed out to him, was his compulsion to want everything to go according to his plans. As a part of this control obsession, he had to win, no matter what he was doing, be it a matter of law, sports, card games, or even getting somewhere first. He was driven by the need to control, and now that he was taking a pain medication, he was tormented by the possibility of becoming controlled by something. For Paul, such a development would mean losing his sense of honor. Paul believed that if he was dominated by something or someone, he was but inches away from compromising his integrity; this was his personal code of honor.

I suggested that since Paul was an attorney, he should draw up a contract with himself through which he would, step by step, reorder his life. He could make his controlling but honorable nature work with him by gradually changing his need to control outcomes. With each success, I told him, the energy generated by his success would be more likely to ease his pain. He loved the idea, no doubt because he could control the content of the contract. He said he would draw up the agreement immediately and fax me a copy, which he did—the next day.

Three months later Paul sent me a note commenting that he had made progress with his healing ever since he put himself "under contract" to heal. As a way of beating his need to win, he forbade himself to place bets on anything. He allowed his winning compulsion to continue only in legal matters, where it was appropriate. He had never realized, he said, that everyone who knew him interpreted his need to win as an "obnoxiously competitive nature." His pain was healing, his migraines were becoming more infrequent, and his back pain was improving to the point that he could once again exercise.

Paul's story conveys the symbolic meaning of taking communion with oneself; that is, agreeing with yourself to make yourself whole and balanced. So long as a dysfunctional part of your nature negatively influences the rest of your system, your energy will be depleted, divided against itself. Paul was able to make a successful contract with himself and heal.

Because humans are, by nature, a species that seeks law and order, we fall easily under the sway of people who project authority and seek to control. Our instinct to trust the people with whom we live and work is an extension of the energy of *Honor One Another*; it is unnatural to feel that you have to look over your shoulder while trying to create something together with others. Yet many people misuse power to control rather than support others.

Within personal relationships it is normal to create a set of rules that both parties agree to follow: no extramarital affairs, no gam-

bling, no major purchases without mutual agreement, and so on. Setting rules in order to control another person's emotional, mental,
psychological, or spiritual growth, however, is energetically destructive. In general, if a couple cannot expand their original rules and
boundaries to accommodate personal growth, the relationship disin-
tegrates. Parents sometimes violate their children spiritually and
emotionally through imposing harsh rules as a way to establish
parental authority.

Personal vengeance is yet another misuse of second chakra energy.
The second chakra is our center of self-defense and of weaponry,
which is designed to be worn around the second chakra. Although
newspapers today are filled with reports of people delivering justice
with bullets, most often acts of "taking the law into one's own
hands" are based on personal, psychological, and emotional laws of
honor, like the desire to "get even" with someone who has injured
us in some way. The energy of vengeance is one of the most toxic
emotional poisons to our biological system, causing dysfunctions
ranging from impotence to cancers of the genital area.

The Personal Power
of the Second Chakra

While creativity, sexuality, morality, and money are all forms of second chakra energy or power, the desire for personal power also needs
to be discussed. Power is a manifestation of the life-force. We require
power in order to live, to thrive, to function. Illness, for example, is the
natural companion of powerless people. Everything about our lives is,
in fact, involved in our relationship to this energy called power.

At the level of the first chakra, we feel a sensation of power when
we are with a group of people to whom we are bonded in some way,
like an electrical current. The enthusiasm of sports fans or of participants in political rallies—uniting people behind the same team or
cause—exemplifies this type of power. The quality of power in the

second chakra, however, expresses this energy in physical forms, like materialism, authority, control, ownership, sexual magnetism, sensuality, eroticism, and addiction. Every physically seductive form that power can take is energetically connected to the second chakra. And unlike the group nature of first chakra power, the second chakra has a one-on-one nature. Each of us as an individual needs to explore our relationship to physical power. We need to learn how and when we are controlled by external power and, if so, the type of power to which we are most vulnerable.

Power is the life-force, and we are born knowing this fact. From the time we are young, we test ourselves and our capacity to learn what and who has power, to attract power, and to use power. Through these childhood exercises we discover whether we have what it takes to draw power to ourselves. If we do, we begin to dream of what we would like to accomplish as adults. If we decide that we are unable to attract the life-force, however, we begin living in a type of "power debt." We imagine ourselves surviving only through the energies of other people, but not on our own.

For people who are confident of their ability to attract power, ordinary dreams can turn into power fantasies. In the worst of cases they may fill their minds with delusions of grandeur. Then the reasoning mind becomes eclipsed by a desire for power that stretches the parameters of acceptable behavior to include any and all means that fulfill this end. The appetite for power can become an addiction that challenges the will of God. The craving for power for power's sake alone is the subject of numerous scriptures and myths of humans who are ultimately humbled by Divine design.

For all of us the challenge is not to become "power celibate" but to achieve sufficient internal strength to interact comfortably with physical power without negotiating away our spirits. This is what it means to be "in the world but not of it." We are fascinated by people who are immune to the seductions of the physical world; they become our social and spiritual heroes.

Gandhi had a clean rapport with power. His desire to improve the lives of the people of India had transpersonal more than personal motivations. Within his personal life, to be sure, he suffered great torments over power, specifically regarding sex. But his personal sufferings only lend more credibility to his global achievements: he recognized his own imperfections and consciously attempted to separate his weakness from his social work while trying to use it to evolve spiritually.

The movie character Forrest Gump won the hearts of millions, primarily because of his ethical comportment toward power in the physical world. Curiously, Gump was not overtly spiritual, and he did not reject sex, power, or money. Rather, he attained all of these second chakra goals through his innocence and his imperviousness to contamination by the business of living. He never negotiated his spirit, regardless of his fear or loneliness.

During workshops, when I ask participants to describe their relationship to power, the atmosphere in the room usually changes dramatically. The tension only makes me want to pursue this question more. Most people shift position in their chairs in order to cover up their second chakras. They cross their legs, for example, or they lean over their second chakras, placing their elbows on their thighs and holding up their heads with their hands. They look at me in a way that says, "My, what an intriguing question, but don't come any closer."

When they offer responses, the first chorus invariably includes descriptions of power as the ability to maintain control over one's environment, or as a vehicle for getting things done. The second chorus describes power as the internal strength to control oneself. The most striking feature of all the combined responses is that the majority define power as having an *object*, whether that object is something in the external world or the self. Although internal power is certainly recognized as the ideal, in practice it is less popular than external power, first because external power is so much more practical, and second because internal power in some way requires giving up our relationship to the physical world.

At this point in our evolution, both as a culture and as individuals, we can recognize that external or physical power is necessary for health. Health is a direct consequence of the spiritual and therapeutic principles we absorb into our everyday life. Both contemporary spirituality and psychotherapy emphasize that personal power is fundamental to material success and spiritual balance. It is involved directly in the creation of our personal worlds as well as our health.

David Chetlahe Paladin (his real name) shared his personal story with me in 1985; he passed away in 1986. It is a testimony to the human potential to achieve a quality of internal power that defies the limitations of physical matter. When I met him, he radiated a quality of empowerment that was rare, and I had to know how he had achieved what so many people were seeking to achieve. David was one of my finest teachers, a person who mastered the sacred truth *Honor One Another* and who fully transmitted to others the energy of the sefirah of Yesod and the sacrament of Communion.

David was a Navajo Indian who grew up on a reservation during the 1920s and 1930s. By the time he was eleven, he was an alcoholic. He left the reservation in his mid-teens, wandered around for a few months, then got a job on a merchant marine ship. He was only fifteen but passed himself off as sixteen.

On board ship, he became friends with a young German and another young Native American. Together they traveled to ports of call throughout the Pacific Ocean. As a hobby, David took up sketching. One subject that he sketched was the bunkers that the Japanese were building on the various islands in the South Seas. The year was 1941.

David's bunker drawings eventually fell into the hands of the American military. When he was drafted into military service, he assumed that he would continue his work as an artist. Instead, he became part of a secret operation against the Nazis. The Army had enlisted Navajo and other Native Americans for a spy network. The operatives were sent behind enemy lines and transmitted information back to the main base of military operations in Europe. Because all radio transmissions could be intercepted, Native American languages were used to guarantee that a message picked up could not be interpreted.

While David was behind enemy lines, he was caught by a group of Nazi soldiers. The Nazis tortured him by, among other things, nailing his feet to the floor and then forcing him to stand for days in that condition. After surviving that horror, David was sent to an extermination camp because he was "of a lesser race." While he was being shoved into a train car, he felt a rifle push him in the ribs, ordering him to move faster. He turned to face the Nazi soldier. It was the German fellow David had befriended on board the merchant marine ship.

David's German friend made arrangements for David to be transferred to a prisoner of war camp, where he spent the remaining years of the war. When the camps were liberated, American soldiers found David unconscious and dying. Transported to the United States, David spent two and a half years in a coma in a military hospital in Battle Creek, Michigan. When he finally came out of the coma, his body was so weakened from his prison camp experiences that he could not walk. He was fitted for heavy leg braces and, using crutches, he could drag himself short distances.

David made up his mind to return to his reservation, say a last good-bye to his people, then enter a veterans' hospital and stay there for the rest of his life. When he arrived at the reservation, his family and friends were horrified at what had become of him. They gathered together and held council to figure out how to help him. After the council meeting the elders approached David, yanked the braces off his legs, tied a rope around his waist, and threw him into deep water. "David, call your spirit back," they commanded. "Your spirit is no longer in your body. If you can't call your spirit back, we will let you go. No one can live without his spirit. Your spirit is your power."

"Calling his spirit back," David told me, was the most difficult task he ever had to undertake. "It was more difficult than enduring having my feet nailed to the floor. I saw the faces of those Nazi soldiers. I lived through all those months in the prison camp. I knew that I had to release my anger and hatred. I could barely keep myself from drowning, but I prayed to let the anger out of my body. That's all I prayed, and my prayers were answered."

David recovered the full use of his legs and went on to become a shaman, a Christian minister, and a healer. He also returned to his drawing and earned a reputation as a highly talented artist.

David Chetlahe Paladin radiated a quality of power that felt like grace itself. Having survived a confrontation with the darkest side of power, he transcended that darkness and spent the rest of his life healing and inspiring people to "call back their power" from experiences that drain the life-force from their bodies.

The core issue in uniting the dualistic energies of our relationships is to learn how to *Honor One Another.* Using the energy of the second chakra, the creative force of the sefirah of Yesod, and the symbolic sight of the sacrament of Communion, we can learn to cherish the sacred unions we form with each other through the days of our lives.

So much of the way we respond to the external challenges is determined by how we respond to ourselves. In addition to all the relationships we have with people, we must also form a healthy and loving relationship with ourselves—a task that belongs to the energy of the third chakra.

Questions for Self-Examination

1. How do you define creativity? Do you consider yourself a creative person? Do you follow through on your creative ideas?

2. How often do you direct your creative energies into negative paths of expression? Do you exaggerate or embellish "facts" to support your point of view?

3. Are you comfortable with your sexuality? If not, are you able to work toward healing your sexual imbalances? Do you use people for sexual pleasure, or have you felt used? Are you strong enough to honor your sexual boundaries?

4. Do you keep your word? What is your personal code of honor? of ethics? Do you negotiate your ethics depending upon your circumstances?

5. Do you have an impression of God as a force that exerts justice in your life?

6. Are you a controlling person? Do you engage in power plays in your relationships? Are you able to see yourself clearly in circumstances related to power and money?

7. Does money have authority over you? Do you make compromises that violate your inner self for the sake of financial security?

8. How often do survival fears dictate your choices?

9. Are you strong enough to master your fears concerning finances and physical survival, or do they control you and your attitudes?

10. What goals do you have for yourself that you have yet to pursue? What stands in the way of your acting upon those goals?

CHAPTER 3

The Third Chakra: Personal Power

Third chakra energy, the energy of the Personal Power chakra, becomes the dominant vibration in our development during puberty. It assists us further in the process of individuation, of forming a "self," ego, and personality separate from our inherited identity. This energy center also contains most issues related to the development of personal power and self-esteem.

The third chakra completes the physical trilogy of the human energy system. Like chakras one and two, it primarily relates to a physical form of power. Where the first chakra resonates to group or tribal power, and where the second chakra resonates to the flow of power between the self and others, the third chakra relates to our personal power in relation to the external world.

Location: The solar plexus.

Energy connection to the physical body: Stomach, pancreas, adrenals, upper intestines, gallbladder, liver, and the middle spine, located behind the solar plexus.

Energy connection to the emotional/mental body: The third chakra, often called the solar plexus, is our personal power center, the magnetic core of the personality and ego. The illnesses that originate here are activated by issues related to self-responsibility, self-esteem, fear of rejection, and an oversensitivity to criticism.

Symbolic/perceptual connection: The third chakra mediates between the primarily external (which is characteristic of the first and second chakras) and the internalization of consciousness. The first chakra has an external center of gravity and is always located within a group mind. The second chakra, too, has an external gravitational center but focuses on relationships and their effects on us. In the third chakra, however, the gravitational center is partly internalized, as our focus shifts from how we relate to people around us to how we relate to and understand ourselves.

Sefirot/Sacrament connection: The sefirah of Nezah represents the Divine quality of *endurance,* and the sefirah of Hod symbolizes the *majesty* (or integrity) of the Divine. In the chakra system these two qualities are partnered because within the Kabbalistic tradition both represent the qualities we need in order to "stand up" as individuals. Thus, Nezah and Hod are symbolically illustrated as the legs of the body. They are also considered the source of prophecy and the center of symbolic sight. The symbolic meaning of Nezah and Hod forms a powerful spiritual bond with the sacrament of Confirmation. This sacrament represents the emergence of the "conscious self," or that part of the human personality that is eternal and naturally aligned to the sacred.

Primary fears: Fears of rejection, criticism, looking foolish, and failing to meet one's responsibilities; all fears related to physical appearance, such as fear of obesity, baldness, or aging; fears that others will discover our secrets.

Primary strengths: Self-esteem, self-respect, and self-discipline; ambition, the ability to generate action, and the ability to handle a crisis; the courage to take risks; generosity, ethics, and strength of character.

Sacred truth: The sacred truth of the third chakra is *Honor Oneself,* a theme supported by the spiritual energies of the sefirot of Nezah (endurance) and Hod (majesty), and by the symbolic meaning of the sacrament of Confirmation, as well as by the power inherent in the third chakra. The energies that come together in this chakra have but one spiritual goal: to help us mature in our self-understanding—the relationship we have with ourselves, and how we stand on our own and take care of ourselves. The spiritual quality conferred by the sacrament of Confirmation is self-respect. This sacrament also symbolizes the passage from childhood to adulthood. We all have faced or will face an experience that reveals to us our own internal strengths and weaknesses as separate from the influence of our elders. The spiritual quality inherent in the third chakra compels us to create an identity apart from our tribal self.

Developing Self-Esteem

All three spiritual currents merge to form the intuitive voice of our solar plexus. As we develop a sense of self, our intuitive voice becomes our natural and constant source of guidance.

How we feel about ourselves, whether we respect ourselves, determines the quality of our life, our capacity to succeed in business, relationships, healing, and intuitive skills. Self-understanding and acceptance, the bond we form with ourselves, is in many ways the most crucial spiritual challenge we face. In truth, if we do not like ourselves, we will be incapable of making healthy decisions. Instead, we will direct all of our personal power for decision-making into the hands of someone else: someone whom we want to impress, or someone before whom we think we must weaken ourselves to gain physical security. People who have a low sense of self-esteem attract relationships and occupational situations that reflect and reinforce this weakness.

One man told me that he had never expected to be loved in his marriage. He married for companionship alone, believing that love was something that happened to other people, but never to people like him. No one is born with healthy self-esteem. We must earn this quality in the process of living, as we face our challenges one at a time.

The third chakra in particular resonates to the boundaries of the physical body. Are we physically strong or weak? Able or handi-capped? Beautiful or scarred? Too tall or too short? From a spiritual perspective, any and all physical assets and limitations are illusory, mere "life props." Yet a person's acceptance of or resistance to them is critical to entering spiritual adulthood. From a spiritual perspec-tive, in fact, the entire physical world is nothing more than our class-room, but the challenge to each of us in this classroom is: Given your particular body, environment, and beliefs, will you make choices that enhance your spirit or those that drain your power into the physical illusion around you? Again and again, the challenges of the third chakra will cause you to evaluate your sense of power and self in rela-tion to the external world.

Consider, for instance, the third chakra challenges of a person in a wheelchair. The fact that the physical world is an illusion does not mean that the wheelchair does not exist or that her physical problem is not real. Rather, it means that nothing in the physical world can contain or limit the power of the human spirit. The woman may never regain the use of her legs, but she still has the power to decide whether being in a wheelchair will handicap her *spirit*. If she chooses to make the best of life in a wheelchair, she does far more than make a healthy psychological decision; she makes a spiritual decision that engages the full energies of the sefirot of Nezah and Hod.

I met a woman named Ruth while I was conducting a weeklong workshop in Mexico. Ruth was staying at the same hotel—she was not part of my workshop. She was wheelchair-bound due to crippling arthritis, a case about as extreme as I have ever seen.

One morning I got up uncharacteristically early and went out to the patio with a cup of coffee to make notes for my lecture that day. I noticed Ruth sitting by herself, listening to classical music with an old tape recorder. I had met her the day before, but this morning I couldn't stop staring at her, although I didn't think she noticed because she had her back to me. I was wondering how she coped with her terribly crippled body, which had also become obese because of her inability to move. Suddenly she turned her head, smiled, and said, "You're wondering how I manage to live in this body, aren't you?"

I was so stunned that I couldn't cover my tracks. "You caught me, Ruth," I said. "That's exactly what I was thinking."

"Well, come on over here, and I'll tell you."

As I pulled my chair up to hers, this seventy-five-year-old woman said to me, "You like New Age music?"

I nodded, and she said, "Good. I'll put this tape on while I tell you about myself."

With Kitaro playing in the background, this remarkable Jewish woman told me her story. "I was widowed when I was thirty-eight years old, left with two daughters to support and few ways to do it. I became the most manipulative person you could ever imagine. I never stole anything, but I came close to it.

"When my older daughter was twenty-two, she joined a Buddhist community. I raised my girls in a traditional Jewish household in New York City, and she enters a Buddhist community! Every time she came over to visit me, I asked her, 'How could you do this to me? After all I've given up for you, how could you?' We must have had that conversation a hundred times. Then one day she looked at me and asked me, 'Mom, are my clothes dirty? Am I unclean in some way? Am I doing anything at all that offends you?'

"I said, 'You must be on drugs. That's it—they've got you on drugs.' She responded, 'Yes, I've tried drugs.' So you know what I said to her then? I said, 'Get me some,' and she did. She brought me some LSD. I was fifty-five years old, and I dropped acid."

I nearly fell out of my chair. I could hardly picture her taking LSD.

She continued, "Do you believe in angels?"

"Yes, of course," I said.

"Good, because that's what happened to me next. I took the LSD, and I had an out-of-body experience. I found myself floating above my body, lighter than air itself. And I met this lovely being who said she was my angel. She complained to me, 'Ruthie, Ruthie, do you know how difficult it is to be your angel?'

"I said I'd never thought about it, and my angel said, 'Let me show you what you look like to me.' And then she pointed to my double—only my double was completely tied up in thousands of rubber bands. My angel said, 'That's how you look to me. Each one of those rubber bands is a fear that is controlling you. You have so many fears that you can never hear me trying to talk to you, to tell you that I've got everything under control.'

"Then my angel said, 'Here's a pair of scissors. Why don't you cut all those rubber bands and free yourself?' And that's just what I did. I clipped every single one of them, and with each one I cut, I felt this unbelievable surge of energy come into my body. Then my angel said, 'Now, don't you feel better?' I told her that I felt lighter than air and happier than I had ever felt in my life. I couldn't stop laughing. My angel said, 'You're going to have to get back into your body now, but before you do, I have to show you something.'

"She showed me the future, and I saw myself full of arthritis. She couldn't tell me why I would have to endure this condition, just that I would have to. But she said she would be with me every step of the way. Then she put me back into my body. I told my daughter everything that had happened, and both of us laughed almost continually for two months. She and I have been close ever since that experience. When this arthritic condition began ten years ago, I thought, oh, well, this isn't being crippled. I was far more crippled when I could walk: I was always so afraid of being alone, of taking care of myself, that I wanted to keep my daughters near me so I would never have to take care of myself. But after that experience I never felt afraid again. I believe that my physical condition is a way to remind me never to have fear. Now I talk to my angel every day, and I still laugh more each day now than I ever did before."

I wish I could take Ruth with me wherever I go so she could tell her story to my workshop participants. To me, Ruth and her angel are twins. Her story represents the choice to believe that the non-physical world of Divine energy has more authority than the physical world of form and matter. This choice caused what might have been a handicap gradually to become a source of inspiration. Her limitations became an asset. This is the influence of the sefirot of Nezah and Hod, our spiritual "legs."

Enhancing Inner Power

We "reorder" our lives when we choose spirit over the illusions of physical circumstances. With each choice we make, we either become more involved in the illusory physical world, or we invest energy into the power of spirit. Each of the seven chakras represents a different version, or manifestation, of this one essential lesson. Each time we choose to enhance our internal power, we limit the authority of the physical world over our lives, bodies, health, minds, and spirits. From an energy point of view, every choice that enhances our spirits strengthens our energy field; and the stronger our energy field, the fewer our connections to negative people and experiences.

I met Penny in a workshop when she had already begun actively reconstructing her life on her own. Penny had been married for eighteen years to a man with whom she had a business partnership. She was the brains of the operation. She was also an alcoholic—a condition that suited her husband just fine because he was an alcoholic too. He wanted her to drink because keeping Penny semiconscious gave him more control in the marriage and business.

On an average day in their relationship, Penny would come home from work and tend to the dogs and the household. Her husband would pour her a glass of wine and say, "Now you go and rest. I'll take care of dinner." By the time dinner was ready, she was already "in her cups."

After about seventeen years Penny realized she had a problem.

She thought about attending an Alcoholics Anonymous meeting but reconsidered. "We lived in a small town," she explained. "If people saw me at that meeting, the word would be out." So she would drive by but never walk in. Then Penny bottomed out. Instead of falling back on her husband, she phoned a friend and said, "Help! I need help." The friend directed Penny to her first AA meeting.

Sobriety changed her life. When she came to her senses, she realized that nothing in her world, least of all her marriage, worked. As frightened as she was of leaving her marriage—which also meant leaving her job—she did so one step at a time. She moved to a different part of the country, continued attending AA meetings, and took courses in personal development, which was when we met. She went for a makeover, changed her hairstyle, and dropped twenty pounds. In short, she came back to life. She decided to divorce her husband, even though it would put her in a more vulnerable financial position, because it was "what my spirit needed to be free." As she took all these steps, Penny and I would discuss each new move and how it would change her life and comfort. Although the divorce would change her financial status, she needed to discover whether she could earn an income on her own. She decided that she believed in herself enough to expect that she could. She worked to become a trainer in neurolinguistic programming (NLP). She eventually met James, a wonderful man who suited her now-high standards of health and personal development. They married and now conduct seminars on personal development throughout Europe.

Penny's story speaks of the unlimited potential in each person to transform his or her life, given determination and a strong sense of personal responsibility. These qualities of power are inherent in the third chakra. Penny's commitment to her own healing is the symbolic meaning of the sacrament of Confirmation. She unplugged from negative people and circumstances, called forth her own spirit, and discovered that she had endless endurance (Nezah) and dignity (Hod), through which she could rebuild her life. Because Penny was able to face her fears, she was also able to release them and become empowered, healthy, and successful.

The stronger our spirits become, the less authority *linear time* can exercise in our lives. To some extent linear time is an illusion of the physical world, tied in to the physical energy of the first three chakras. For physical tasks, we need this physical energy; for example, when we need to take an inspiration from thought to form, we run it through linear steps. But in terms of our belief in our ability to heal, our concept of time should be reexamined.

The illusion that healing takes a "long time" holds considerable authority in our culture. Believing it makes it true. In the Book of Genesis, Yahweh "breathed into his nostrils a breath of life, and thus man was born." By choosing to believe something, we breathe our breath into that belief, giving that belief authority.

Our culture believes that healing painful childhood memories requires years of psychotherapy, but that need not be the case. If one believes it, healing painful memories and releasing the authority they have within one's life can happen rapidly.

The length of healing processes becomes calibrated to the time that the tribal mind attributes to them. For instance, the group mind currently believes that certain cancers take six months to kill us, that people with AIDS can live for six to eight years, that grieving a mate's death requires at least one year, and that grieving a child's death may never end. If we believe these assessments, we give the tribal mind power over our lives instead of exercising our personal power. If your spirit is strong enough to withdraw from the authority of a group belief, it is potentially strong enough to change your life, as Margaret's unusually rich story shows.

I met Margaret at a workshop I gave in New Hampshire. She described her upbringing as "plain, ordinary, and strict." Her parents screened everything she read and determined who would be her friends. Margaret was never allowed to attend any functions that her parents felt were too "radical." At times, she even had to sneak-read a newspaper. She grew up controlled by her parents' fear of the unknown. When she went to school, her parents told her that because she was a woman, she essentially had two occupations open to her: teaching and nursing.

Margaret decided to become a nurse. Shortly after graduating from nursing school, she married a man who was, in her words, "plain, ordinary, and strict. I duplicated my parents."

Margaret and her husband moved to a small town, where she practiced home-care nursing. The town, a typically sweet community, had its local characters, particularly a woman named Ollie. Ollie had somehow earned the reputation of being "dangerous." No one would talk to her, and no one invited her to any social events. The children tormented her every Halloween, as they had for ten years.

The day came when Ollie phoned the home-care nursing office, requesting assistance. The staff nurses all refused to respond—except Margaret. She felt a bit apprehensive as she approached Ollie's home, but once she was inside, she met, in Margaret's words, a "lonely, harmless fifty-year-old woman starved for affection."

As Margaret cared for Ollie, they developed a friendship. When Margaret felt comfortable enough, she asked Ollie how she had come to have her reputation. Ollie paused for a moment, then shared with her that a "power" had "come on her suddenlike" when she was a child. This power could heal people. Ollie's father began to sell her healing services to those in need. Ollie's father made a good deal of money this way—until the power "just seemed to stop one day." Her father thought she was just being stubborn, so he tried to beat her to make the power come back, but it didn't.

When she was old enough, Ollie left home and moved to a town where no one knew her. She worked as a cleaning woman and married when she was thirty-two. She and her husband had two children. When their youngest child was five, he became seriously ill with leukemia. The doctor told Ollie and her husband to prepare for his death because it was inevitable. Only then did Ollie tell her husband about the power she had had as a child, and she asked him to join her in prayer, asking God to restore that ability to her once more, to heal their son. Ollie knelt by her son's bed, prayed, then put her hands on him. Within two days he was showing signs of improvement, and within a week he was on his way back to health. He healed completely within two months.

The doctor asked Ollie and her husband what they had done, what treatment they had given their son. Ollie asked her husband not to tell their physician, but he revealed exactly what had happened regardless. The physician's response was that Ollie was "dangerous," and he advised Ollie's husband to be "careful around that woman. After all, she could be a witch or something."

Five months later Ollie came home to find that her husband had taken their two children and left her. The divorce was granted him on the grounds of her insanity. Ollie was devastated and told Margaret that she had tried in vain several times to find her children. She had not seen them since.

The bond between Margaret and Ollie grew stronger with each visit. Ollie's "power" inspired Margaret to read literature on healers, the power of healing, and spirituality. Ollie had opened a new world to her. The more she learned, the more she thought of her parents, their fear of new ideas, and their efforts to ensure that she would learn only "ordinary things, in keeping with their ordinary lifestyle."

Margaret attempted to share with her husband all that she was learning, hoping that he would find the information as inspiring as she did. But her husband felt threatened by Ollie and these new ideas, and the day finally came when he forbade her to see Ollie again.

By this time, Margaret needed to see Ollie not only because she cared so deeply for her but because Ollie was teaching her about a power of healing that was the energy of love from a Divine source. This time she did not want to be controlled by someone else's fears.

Margaret entered into the darkest crisis of her life, not only because of Ollie but because she was "between two worlds of thought." She knew that, with or without ever seeing Ollie again, she could never go back to her earlier beliefs about healing and spirituality. She wanted to keep learning and eventually told her husband that she would continue her home-care nursing duties with Ollie, regardless of how he felt.

Margaret's husband began to say things like "That woman's got you under a spell," and "I wonder what else is going on between you two." The atmosphere in Margaret's home finally became unbearable and she moved into an apartment. She hoped a temporary separation would help heal their marriage.

Margaret's colleagues as well as her friends sided with her husband. Margaret was sacrificing her marriage for a dying crazy woman, they told her. No one understood her reasons for doing what she was doing. She "prayed for a miracle without restrictions," meaning she did not care how God resolved her crisis—she just wanted it to end.

About four months later, Margaret got a message from her husband saying that they had to meet. She thought that he was going to ask for a divorce, but instead, he told her that he had just been diagnosed with colon cancer. He was scared, he said—and then came the miracle. Would Ollie be able to help him? he asked. Margaret trembled with emotion. They went immediately to Ollie's house.

Ollie told Margaret's husband that her power came from God and that he should focus his attention on that. She did a laying-on-of-hands over him, lasting no more than ten minutes. The man recovered from his colon cancer within three months. He became passionate about caring for Ollie, so much so that he insisted that she move into their home, where she lived until her death.

"Now my husband can't do enough for me, or for others. We have healing services in our home where we pray with others and offer instructions on healing. I would never have believed this could happen, and I can't tell you how many times my husband has said to me, 'I thank God every day in my prayers that you had the courage to stand up to me and to hold on to your beliefs. I am alive today because of you.'"

Without a doubt, our childhood memories can be the source of great pain. Yet like Margaret we may be given opportunities to use that pain to inspire other choices as adults.

Self-Esteem and Intuition

When I began to teach workshops on intuitive guidance, I gave the participants internal exercises and meditation practices. But most people who meditated reported a lack of success in developing their intuition. I realized during one workshop that getting in touch with intuition was not really the challenge. For the most part, the participants were already in touch with their intuition, but they completely misunderstood the nature of their intuition.

Every single participant in this workshop had confused intuition with prophetic ability. They thought intuition was the ability to foretell the future. But intuition is neither the ability to engage prophesy nor a means of avoiding financial loss or painful relationships. It is actually the ability to use energy data to make decisions *in the immediate moment*. Energy data are the emotional, psychological, and spiritual components of a given situation. They are the "here and now" ingredients of life, not nonphysical information from some "future" place.

For the most part information that is accessible to intuition makes its presence known by making us feel uncomfortable, depressed, and anxious—or at the other extreme, drifty and detached, as if we were suddenly cut off from all of our own feelings. In dreams of an intuitive nature, we receive symbols of change or chaos. Such dreams often occur more intensely during emotional crises. Energy or intuitive sensations signal that we have reached a crossroads in our lives and that we have an opportunity to influence the next stage of our lives, at least to some degree, through the choice we make now.

The intuition and the independence of the third chakra together give us the capacity to take risks, to follow through on gut hunches. Evan, twenty-eight, contacted me because he was suffering from a severely ulcerated colon. As I evaluated him, I kept receiving the impression of a horse being led to the starting gate but never running the race. Evan's third chakra was like an open hole, pouring out energy. He seemed to have no energy left to stand on his own. In fact, he seemed to have fled from the opportunities life had given him because he was afraid of failure. He would not take even one chance to seek confirmation of an intuition.

In his own words, Evan's life had been a series of false starts. He had considered all sorts of business ventures, but had decided against each of them. He was forever studying the stock market, looking for a formula that revealed the rise-and-fall pattern of stock prices. Obsessed with this ideal, he had carefully accumulated statistics. Actually, he had become pretty good at identifying stocks that were about to increase in value. When I asked him why he didn't just go ahead and invest in some of those stocks, he said, "The formula is not yet perfect. It has to be perfect." Yet, he was filled with bitterness toward himself because he knew he would have earned a great deal of money had he followed through on some of his hunches. In fact, he would have become fairly wealthy. When I commented that, having done so well on paper, he was equally likely to succeed in an actual investment, Evan responded that the stock market is volatile, and he could never be certain that his hunches would prove accurate.

With the ulcerated colon, Evan's body was being ripped apart by his inability to act on his gut hunches. He could not bring himself to invest even a little money in a stock. His fear of taking a risk was literally destroying his body, yet he was completely obsessed by a business that is nothing but risk. Telling Evan to use a relaxation technique would have been about as helpful as telling a teenager to be home on time. Evan needed to release his computerlike mind and shift to his gut instincts. He insisted his gut instincts don't provide "proof" of outcomes, but only suggest possibilities.

My workshop participants, too, were in touch with their intuition—but they assumed that intuition meant clear direction rather than intuitive guidance. They hoped that one good intuitive "hit" would give them the power to reorder their lives in complete harmony and happiness. But intuitive guidance does not mean following a voice to the Promised Land. It means having the *self-esteem* to recognize that the discomfort or confusion that a person feels is actually directing him to take charge of his life and make choices that will break him out of stagnation or misery.

If a person suffers from low self-esteem, she cannot act on her intuitive impulses because her fear of failure is too intense. Intuition, like all meditative disciplines, can be enormously effective *if, and only if*, one has the courage and personal power to follow through on the guidance it provides. Guidance requires action, but it does not guarantee safety. While we measure our own success in terms of our personal comfort and security, the universe measures our success by how much we have learned. So long as we use comfort and security as our criteria of success, we will fear our own intuitive guidance because by its very nature it directs us into new cycles of learning that are sometimes uncomfortable.

In one of my workshops, a woman named Sandy commented proudly that she had spent six years living in an ashram in India developing her meditation practice. Every morning and evening she entered into an hourlong meditation and was able to receive very clear spiritual guidance. In a private moment she asked me if I had received any impressions about where she should live and how she should earn her living. Why wasn't she receiving this type of information in her own meditations? I asked, adding that occupational counseling was not my specialty, so to speak. She replied that her guidance was only for spiritual matters. But her occupation was part of her life, I objected, and therefore was part of her spirituality. She said that she just couldn't get that type of information. Then I asked her, "What's the worst possible intuition you could receive in your meditation about where you should live and what you should do?" She instantly responded, "That's easy—go back to teaching in the inner city of Detroit. I've actually had nightmares about that." I said, "I'd consider doing that, if I were you. Sounds like guidance to me."

A year later I received a letter from Sandy telling me that after my workshop she had been plagued by urges to go back to teaching. She fought them so strongly, she ended up developing migraines and a sleep disorder. Meanwhile, she was earning a living as a clerk in a bookstore, which did not pay her enough. So when she received an offer to do some substitute teaching in her former school district, she accepted. Within two months, she introduced an extracurricular class on meditation for high school students that met twice a week after school. The class was so successful that it was put into the regular curriculum the next year, and Sandy delightedly signed a teaching contract. Her migraines and sleep disorder ended shortly afterward.

Belief in oneself is required for healing. Before I realized the significance of self-esteem for developing intuitive skills, I would have stated that faith is the most important factor in healing. I now equate faith with self-esteem and personal power, because low self-esteem reflects one's lack of faith in oneself as well as in the powers of the unseen world. Unquestionably, faith is vital for managing the challenges of our everyday existence.

For instance, a woman in her late twenties named Janice contacted me because she wanted to learn about managing her health. Janice had a number of serious health challenges, but she did not ask me why she had to cope with them; she was only interested in beginning to heal.

When Janice was in her teens, she had gone through surgery for a blockage in her colon. When I met her, she was married, the mother of one child, and in the hospital for her seventh abdominal surgery. Most of her intestinal tract had been removed, and she would have a colostomy for the rest of her life. She could no longer eat solid food and had to be fed liquids via a catheter surgically implanted into her upper chest. This, too, would remain for the rest of her life. She had to hook up to her liquid nutrition just before going to sleep; during the night it would drip into her body. Because this liquid nutrition, called hyperalimentation, had just been developed, it was not covered by her insurance. Travel, even weekend trips, was now a major ordeal, because she had to take so much medical equipment with her. On top of all her physical problems and as a result of them, Janice and her husband were accumulating an insurmountable debt.

On my way to the hospital to meet Janice, I expected that she would be overwhelmed by her circumstances and would dread the future. But much to my surprise, she radiated a positive attitude and energy. She wanted to learn about energy techniques like meditation and visualization so she could use them to improve her health. During our conversation she remarked, "When I was having a catheter put in, I have to admit to feeling sorry for myself, not to mention guilty. I felt that I had only become a financial burden to my husband and was hardly a suitable wife. Then I walked down a few of the halls in the hospital and I saw some of the conditions other people faced. I decided that my situation wasn't so bad, and I told myself that I can handle this."

After her last surgery, Janice went back to school to complete her degree in nursing. Just as she was getting her life back together, her husband asked her for a divorce. She telephoned me, and we arranged to meet. During our conversation she remarked, "I'm not all that surprised that Howard wants a divorce. He's given me as much support as he could during these last twelve years, but it hasn't been much of a marriage for him. I can't afford to be bitter; I have a son who needs me, and I deeply believe that negativity will only further my physical problems. But I'm frightened—what do I do now? Is there a visualization that makes courage suddenly appear in your gut?"

We decided that getting through the divorce was her first priority and that she should have as much support around her as possible during the months ahead. While she was in the final stages of her divorce, Janice found a job at a local hospital. She and her ten-year-old son moved into a new apartment, and she worked very hard at meeting new friends. She made her spiritual life a priority, and each morning she and her son would visualize their lives as happy and complete—an action that tapped into the spiritual energies associated with the third chakra: endurance, stamina, and self-respect. She was determined to "stand on her own" through her ordeal. Ultimately she succeeded. Her health remained stable throughout this transition period, and a year after her divorce, she met a wonderful man and remarried. Her story illustrates well the capacity of the human spirit to transcend physical limitations and personal challenges by choosing a courageous response to them. Janice had her bad days, to be sure, but she realized that self-pity was more harmful to her than her physical condition. Her attitude and her daily spiritual practice kept her body and mind in balance, symbolizing the energy support of the sefirot of Nezah and Hod and the sacrament of Confirmation.

The *symbolic* meaning of the sacrament of Confirmation is that we become "alive" inside by becoming internally empowered. Self-esteem and conscious personal power sometimes develop at a memorable point in life that signifies an initiation into spiritual adulthood. Perhaps, in a sudden flash of insight, you saw how you could accomplish a task that had been previously overwhelming. Perhaps you saw yourself as powerful and realized that you could accomplish goals of all sorts, from physical fitness to financial success.

Developing the confidence to pursue goals is one way that personal power becomes an agent of personal change. At the same time an equally impressive level of change can occur within a person's spiritual or symbolic life. Becoming internally empowered shifts a person's center of gravity from external to internal—a mark of spiritual passage.

Most cultures practice a rite of passage for young people, a rite that represents the coming of age of spirit: bar mitzvahs in the Jewish culture, for example, and confirmation in the Christian. In many Native American traditions, at least historically, young men were sent away from the tribe for a time to live alone in the wilderness in order to be initiated as warriors. These ceremonies mark the symbolic ending of a young person's dependence upon the protective energy of tribal power and his acceptance of responsibility for his physical and spiritual life. The rite also marks tribal recognition of that acceptance. Once "initiated," a young person is subject to the more mature expectations of friends and family.

An empowered sense of self can also develop in stages, over the course of our lives, in a series of mini-initiations. Every time we advance in self-esteem, even in a small measure, we have to change something about our external dynamics. For the most part we abhor change, but an initiation represents the necessity to change. We may end a relationship because we have become sufficiently empowered that we need a stronger partner. Or we may quit a job because we need to break out of our safe and familiar patterns and test-fly our own creativity. Too much change that happens too rapidly can be overwhelming, so we try to manage our own empowerment by taking on only one challenge at a time. As we do, one by one, the changes we undergo form a pattern in our journey toward personal power.

The Four Stages of Personal Power

Self-esteem became a popular word beginning in the 1960s, a decade of revolution that redefined our view of the empowered individual. Only then did self-esteem become accepted as essential to women's and men's health which was redefined to include psychological and spiritual health as well as physical health.

Each of the next three decades seemed to refine further this new definition of self-esteem. Symbolically, the social trends between the 1960s and the 1990s reflect the developmental stages of self-empowerment that we each undergo as individuals. After the 1960s decade of revolution came the 1970s—the decade of involution. The raw energy released during the 1960s, which broke down external barriers, led to the 1970s task of breaking through internal barriers. This was the decade that made *psychotherapy* a household word.

The 1970s merged two new psychological forces. First, the exceedingly powerful word *self* was released from its puritanical prison, in which the only allowable suffix had been *ish*. That one word alone, *selfish*, had for centuries been strong enough to prevent the vast majority of people from pursuing any form of personal development. The 1970s made *self* an acceptable and commonly used prefix—as in *self*-motivated, *self*-healing, *self*-awareness. That simple shift was equal to giving each of us our own key to the "secret garden," where, with a little help, we would all discover that we can indeed walk on our own.

Not surprisingly, this fascination with the self was taken to an extreme. To test how far the power of our new "selves" could take us, the theme of the 1980s became the *indulgence* of the self: narcissism. Its narcissistic atmosphere made us feel as if we were suddenly free to satisfy all of our physical desires. And indulge we did, to every extreme. How fast could we become rich? How fast could we transfer information? How fast could we convert our world into a techno-planet? How fast could we become thin? How fast could we become healed? Even the goal of becoming conscious, formerly a sacred task that required a lifetime's dedicated work, became something people believed they could achieve in a week, if they paid enough money.

Even self-indulgence reaches a saturation point, and by the time we entered the 1990s, the pendulum had once again swung from the external world to the internal world, directing all these energy patterns toward personal evolution—forming a self that is powerful enough to be "in the world but not of the world," a self that can enjoy the magnificence of the physical world without allowing the world's many illusions to deplete its soul.

Revolution, involution, narcissism, and evolution are the four stages through which we progress to attain self-esteem and spiritual maturity. A spiritual adult inconspicuously involves his or her inner spiritual qualities in everyday decisions. One's "spiritual" thoughts and activities are inseparable from other aspects of life: all becomes one.

A person may spend years in each phase or only months, but regardless of how long each phase lasts, she will inevitably grapple with its particular challenges to her character, ethics, morality, and self-respect.

We have to work to discover ourselves, to understand why we keep secrets, or have addictions, or blame others for our own errors. We must work to understand why we find it difficult to receive or give a compliment, or whether we carry shame within us. We need to become comfortable with taking pride in our character and accomplishments. We need to learn the parameters of our character, how much of ourselves we will compromise, and where we draw the line—or even if we draw the line. Creating an identity for ourselves is based upon self-discovery and not upon biological and ethnic inheritance. This first stage of self-discovery is revolution.

Stage One: Revolution

Developing self-esteem requires an act of revolution, or several mini-revolutions, in which we begin to separate from group thought and establish our own sense of authority. We may suddenly realize we hold an opinion different from our family or our peers, but in either case we will have difficulty freeing ourselves from the group's energy, whose strength depends upon numbers and opposition to most expressions of individuality.

The act of finding our own voice, even in mini-revolutions, is spiritually significant. Spiritual maturity is measured not by the sophistication of a person's opinions, but by their genuineness and the courage necessary to express and maintain them. By courage, I do not mean the intractable stubbornness of two people locking horns; that dynamic is a second chakra power play. Spiritual maturity, in contrast, is the capacity to stand one's ground as a reflection of a genuine inner belief.

Jerry contacted me for a reading because he was suffering from ulcers. I received a very strong impression that he was involved with a woman who was violating his moral code. I sensed that he felt both protective of this woman as well as disappointed in her, and that he was equally disappointed in himself because he was unable to confront her about his feelings. When I shared my impressions with Jerry, he told me that Jane, his partner, was a drug addict. He had met her when she was "clean," and after a month she had moved in with him. Everything seemed to go well for about two more months, and then Jane's behavior started to change. He asked her if she was using again, but she said no, adding that she was moody because she wanted to leave her job but had no idea where to go. Initially he believed her, but then he noticed money missing from his wallet. When he asked her about it, Jane told him that she needed money for household supplies and apologized for not mentioning it to him. Jerry's stories of Jane's lies filled thirty minutes of our conversation.

I asked Jerry to connect the dots. He had never had ulcers before living with Jane. His problem was not Jane, I said, but the fact that he desperately wanted to tell her that he didn't believe her excuses. He paused for a moment, then said that he didn't want to think he had developed ulcers because of Jane. He had made a commitment to her, it was wrong to abandon a person in need, and he was terrified that if he confronted Jane, she would leave him. I asked him, "Which would you rather lose, your health or Jane?" adding that he was already confronting Jane—only his ulcer was doing the talking. Two days later Jerry called to say that he had asked Jane to move out. Much to his surprise, he said, he felt relieved by his decision: "I didn't think I had it in me, but I just couldn't live like that anymore. I'd rather be alone than live a lie."

For Jerry, challenging Jane was a personal revolution. In that one experience, he learned that he needed to honor his personal values and that he did have the courage to make the choice he needed to make.

When we develop this kind of inner strength, even in small measure, we are more capable of introspection and self-examination. In this way we gradually replace the influences of our tribal or group mind with our own inner or intuitive guidance. Once this process has begun, the next natural step is "involution," the exploration of our interior self.

Stage Two: Involution

Every new encounter or pursuit we have asks our inner self, "What else do I believe? What else do I think? I want to know myself better. This is a request for information." In every new situation, information pours into our gut. We get feelings about new people and new circumstances. In this phase, involution, we assess our external world and how well it is serving our needs. Often, this self-examination leads us to want to focus on our relationship with God and our life's purpose, but we first need to develop a level of internal stamina that gives us the strength to handle the consequences of self-examining thought. During my workshops people have admitted to me that when I ask them certain self-reflective questions, they prefer to "zone out" because they don't want to know themselves that well. Or they may say, "I don't know. I've never thought about that," to which I respond, "Well, think about it now!" Why is this response so common? Because self-knowledge promotes choice and action, and many people feel unready for either.

During one of my workshops, I met Emma, a woman in her late

fifties who had just completed chemotherapy for colon cancer. She had six children, all of whom were now young adults. She told me that her cancer had been her inspiration. During her recovery period she had realized that while her children did indeed love her dearly, they loved the "servant" part of her most. Much to her own grief, four of her children had remarked during her recovery that they now had to find someone else to do this or that for them; and when did she think she would be ready to go again? Emma realized she needed to reevaluate her role in her own life and what she needed to heal herself. Her revolution led her to an involutionary period, during which she read a great deal of material on self-healing and self-awareness. She came to realize that she had lived for her children, and now she wanted to live for herself. It took her a few months to gather the courage to change the rules in her household, but change them she did. She announced to her children that she could no longer be counted upon for endless baby-sitting jobs; that she would no longer always fix the major meals; and that she would no longer drop what she was doing to run their errands. In short, she claimed the right to say no. Her children were so upset by her announcement that they actually called a family meeting (tribal gathering) to discuss how to handle her. Emma stuck to her position and told her children that they would have to adjust to the fact that she was an individual with needs as well as their mother, and that she was retiring her mother role permanently.

Emma's story shows how the involution stage is followed by a narcissistic birthing of a new image of oneself.

Stage Three: Narcissism

Although it has a bad rap, narcissism is sometimes an extremely necessary energy for us as we work to develop a strong sense of self. Giving ourselves a new image—a new hairstyle, new clothes, perhaps even a new body shape from personal training—indicates that changes are also occurring within us. While we are in this vulnerable stage, we may get major critical reactions from our tribal or group associates, but narcissistic energy gives us the backbone to re-create ourselves and our boundaries in the face of opposition. The changes in this stage prepare us for the more significant internal changes to follow.

Gary described this stage beautifully when he commented in a workshop that he had suddenly begun to dress up formally for concerts and plays, whereas he had previously always worn blue jeans and sweatshirts. Even though he would break out into a cold sweat at the thought of breaking away from his friends' habits, he saw this change as a major step in his personal development because he wanted to know what it was like to be "stared at with envy." It wasn't that he wanted to be envied; he wanted to break free from the group control his friends had exerted in determining his continually projected humble image. Gary said that he was homosexual, and when I asked if he was open with his family about it, he replied, "Not yet. I'm working on achieving that level of self-esteem one step at a time. As soon as I can get strong enough to wear what I want, then I'll work on becoming strong enough to be who I want."

Being who we want captures the significance of the fourth stage: evolution.

Stage Four: Evolution

This last stage in developing self-esteem is an internal one. People who can maintain their principles, their dignity, and their faith without compromising any energy from their spirit are internally evolved: people such as Gandhi, Mother Teresa, and Nelson Mandela. The world is filled with people of much lesser reputations who have accomplished this level of self-esteem, of course, but these three peoples' spirits took charge of their physical environments—and the environments changed to accommodate the power of their spirits.

All three of these people were, incidentally, thought to be narcissistic during some stage of their development. Mother Teresa, for example, was almost forced to leave two religious communities in her early days because her vision of service to the poor was much more intense than her sisters could abide. During that time she was thought to be self-absorbed and narcissistic. She had to go through a period of deep spiritual reflection, and when the time was right, she acted on her intuitive guidance. Like Gandhi and Mandela, she entered into a stage of evolution in which personality became persona—an archetypal force from which millions of people could draw inspiration. As your own spirit takes command, the world will also yield to its force.

Challenges of the Journey

There is nothing simple about developing self-understanding, independence, and self-respect, even though the journey consists of only four stages. The third chakra is filled with the energy of our personal ambitions, our sense of responsibility, and our respect for our strengths and weaknesses, as well as our fears and secrets that we are not yet ready to face. Because we are often riven with personal conflicts, we meet the spiritual challenge to "becoming empty in order to be made full," to die to old habits and self-images in order to be reborn, with great trepidation. Yet the path to developing independence and maturity is far more than a psychological act of health. Becoming adept at the internal process of self-inquiry and symbolic insight is a vital spiritual task that leads to the growth of faith in oneself.

I love Chuck's story because it captures the spiritual essence of *Honor Oneself*. Chuck came from a very traditional Eastern European family. The influence of his family was strong in every way—social attitudes and religious values. The children were expected to grow up to be like their parents. Chuck was the outsider in his family: he disliked sports and beer parties and was attracted to liberal ideas and friends. By the time he was in high school, he was already leading a double life, keeping his interests and friends separate from his home life. By the end of high school, he knew that he was gay, which intensified his need for his double life since he knew his family would not be able to cope with his homosexuality. Chuck left home to travel abroad and teach in other cultures; he mastered numerous languages.

By the time he finally resettled in his hometown, he had received a number of academic honors, yet he was continually depressed. When I met him, he clearly needed to stop his external travels and venture into himself. We spoke of his life in symbolic terms, recognizing that his real motivation for living abroad was that he had been uncomfortable as the outsider in his family. He desperately wanted to be accepted by them, yet he knew that he had yet to accept himself. He still could not live openly as a gay man, which concerned him because, as he said, "I don't consider that I have accepted being gay if the only people who know are my gay friends. My biggest fear is that if I explore my feelings, I'll find the bottom line is that I genuinely can't accept myself. Then what do I do?"

Chuck was devoted to studies in mysticism and maintained a spiritual practice that included prayer, meditation, and worship in church. I suggested that he make a pilgrimage to the spiritual places about which he loved to read, and direct his spiritual intention toward accepting himself. He quoted a friend who had told him, "Pilgrimage is extroverted mysticism, just as mysticism is introverted pilgrimage."

The next summer Chuck left for Europe to visit Fatima, Lourdes, and several other places that represented the sacred for him. At each place he performed a spiritual ceremony, releasing a painful part of his past and asking for the ability to accept himself fully. By the time he returned home, Chuck was changed. He was free and "alive" in the way we are all meant to be. He had shed his shadow and seemed to radiate light. One of the first things he did on his return was to have his family over and tell them he was gay. He was prepared for any reaction from them, but much to his delight they accepted his news. Chuck's spiritual journey had gained him independence from his past and from his fears of tomorrow, and a deep faith in himself.

We are all on a pilgrimage of sorts, though it is certainly not necessary to travel physically to sacred places and conduct ceremonies to release our past. It *is* necessary, however, to travel spiritually and to shed the fears that block us from recognizing the beauty in our lives, and to come to a place of healing and self-acceptance. We can take this type of journey daily in the privacy of our own prayers and meditation.

The late poet Dorothy Parker once remarked, "I hate writing. I love having written." The same could be said about developing personal power: it feels like heaven once we've arrived, but the journey getting there is long and arduous. Life relentlessly brings us to realize the importance of the words of Polonius, "To thine own self be true." For without personal power, life is a frightening, painful experience.

Working with intuition does not allow us to bypass the challenge of facing our fears. There is no shortcut to becoming a whole person, and certainly intuitive abilities are not the answer—they are simply the natural consequence of having self-esteem.

We are biologically aligned to learning this lesson: our bodies thrive when our spirits thrive. The third chakra embodies the sacred truth *Honor Oneself*—a truth that is supported by the symbolic meaning of the sefirot of Nezah and Hod and by the sacrament of Confirmation. As we gain the strength and stamina that come from living with self-esteem, our intuitive abilities emerge naturally.

Questions for Self-Examination

1. Do you like yourself? If not, what don't you like about yourself, and why? Are you actively working to change the things about yourself that you don't like?

2. Are you honest? Do you sometimes misrepresent the truth? If so, why?

3. Are you critical of others? Do you need to blame others as a way of protecting yourself?

4. Are you able to admit it when you are wrong? Are you open to feedback from other people about yourself?

5. Do you need the approval of others? If so, why?

6. Do you consider yourself strong or weak? Are you afraid of taking care of yourself?

7. Have you ever allowed yourself to be in a relationship with a person you didn't really love, but it seemed better than being alone?

8. Do you respect yourself? Can you decide to make changes in your lifestyle and then stick to your commitment?

9. Are you afraid of responsibility? Or do you feel responsible for everything and everyone?

10. Are you continually wishing your life were different? If so, are you doing anything to change it, or have you resigned yourself to your situation?

The Fourth Chakra: Emotional Power

The fourth chakra is the central powerhouse of the human energy system. The middle chakra, it mediates between the body and spirit and determines their health and strength. Fourth chakra energy is emotional in nature and helps propel our emotional development. This chakra embodies the spiritual lesson that teaches us how to act out of love and compassion and recognize that the most powerful energy we have is love.

Location: Center of the chest.

Energy connection to the physical body: Heart and circulatory system, ribs, breasts, thymus gland, lungs, shoulders, arms, hands, diaphragm.

Energy connection to the emotional/mental body: This chakra resonates to our emotional perceptions, which determine the quality of our lives far more than our mental perceptions. As children, we react to our circumstances with a range of emotions: love, compassion, confidence, hope, despair, hate, envy, and fear. As adults, we are challenged to generate within ourselves an emotional climate and steadiness from which to act consciously and with compassion.

Symbolic/perceptual connection: More than any other chakra, the fourth represents our capacity to "let go and let God." With its energy we accept our personal emotional challenges as extensions of a Divine plan, which has as its intent our conscious evolution. By releasing our emotional pain, by letting go of our need to know why things have happened as they have, we reach a state of tranquillity. In order to achieve that inner peace, however, we have to embrace the healing energy of forgiveness and release our lesser need for human, self-determined justice.

Sefirot/Sacrament connection: The fourth chakra corresponds to the sefirah of Tif'eret, symbolic of the beauty and compassion within God. This energy represents the heart of the Divine—an endless pouring forth of the nurturing life-force. The sacrament of Marriage is congruent to the energy of the fourth chakra. As an *archetype*, marriage represents first and foremost a bond with oneself, the internal union of self and soul.

The challenge inherent in the fourth chakra is similar to that of the third but is more spiritually sophisticated. While the third chakra's focus is on our feelings about ourselves in relation to our physical world, the fourth chakra focuses on our feelings about our internal world—our emotional response to our own thoughts, ideas, attitudes, and inspirations, as well as the attention we give to our emotional needs. This level of commitment is *the* essential factor in forming healthy relationships with others.

Primary fears: Fears of loneliness, commitment, and "following one's heart"; fear of inability to protect oneself emotionally; fear of emotional weakness and betrayal. Loss of fourth chakra energy can give rise to jealousy, bitterness, anger, hatred, and an inability to forgive others as well as oneself.

Primary strengths: Love, forgiveness, compassion, dedication, inspiration, hope, trust, and the ability to heal oneself and others.

Sacred truth: The fourth chakra is the power center of the human energy system because *Love Is Divine Power*. While intelligence or "mental energy" is generally considered superior to emotional energy, actually emotional energy is the true motivator of the human body and spirit. Love in its purest form—unconditional love—is the substance of the Divine, with its endless capacity to forgive us and respond to our prayers. Our own hearts are designed to express beauty, compassion, forgiveness, and love. It is against our spiritual nature to act otherwise.

We are not born fluent in love but spend our life learning about it. Its energy is pure power. We are as attracted to love as we are intimidated by it. We are motivated by love, controlled by it, inspired by it, healed by it, and destroyed by it. Love is the fuel of our physical and spiritual bodies. Each of life's challenges is a lesson in some aspect of love. How we respond to these challenges is recorded within our cell tissues: we live within the biological consequences of our biographical choices.

Learning the
Power of Love

Because love has such power, we come to know this energy in stages. Each stage presents a lesson in love's intensity and forms: forgiveness, compassion, generosity, kindness, caring for oneself and others. The stages follow the design of our chakras: we begin learning love within our tribe, absorbing the many expressions of its energy from our family members. Tribal love can be unconditional, but it generally communicates the expectation of loyalty and tribal support; in the tribal setting, love is an energy that is shared among one's own kind.

As the second chakra awakens and we learn the bonds of friendship, love grows to include "outsiders." We express love through sharing with and caring for others to whom we are not connected through blood. And as our third chakra awakens, we discover love of external things, of our personal, physical, and material needs, which may include athletics, academics, fashion, dating and mating, occupation and home, and body.

All three of these chakras involve love in the external world. At one time in our civilization, these three practices of love were all that life required. Very few people needed more than tribal and partnership love. With the advent of psychotherapy and the spirituality movement, however, love became recognized as a force that influences and perhaps determines biological activity. Love helps us heal others and ourselves.

Life crises that have issues of love at their core—divorce, death of a loved one, emotional abuse, abandonment, adultery—are often the cause of an illness and not just an event that coincidentally precedes it. Physical healing often requires, and may demand, the healing of emotional issues.

Jack, a carpenter, forty-seven, invested a substantial portion of his life's savings in a business venture created by his cousin Greg. Describing himself as a "business rookie," Jack told me Greg always seemed to know exactly what he was doing with investments and promised that this major investment would yield enough for Jack's early retirement. Jack's wife, Lynn, was hesitant about putting all their savings into a venture with no guarantee of financial return, but Jack trusted his cousin and felt that all would turn out exactly as anticipated.

Four months later the business venture failed, and Greg vanished. Two months after that, Jack suffered an accident on the job and injured his lower back. He developed high blood pressure and grew withdrawn and depressed. He showed up in one of my workshops because Lynn had forced him to attend with her, in her desperation to rouse him out of his incapacitated state.

Some disorders are so obvious that any outside person can connect the dots and figure out the cause. Jack's financial stress, coupled with his feeling that his cousin had taken advantage of him, no doubt became a raging fire in Jack's psyche, resulting in weakness in his lower back and sciatic nerve. His anger contributed to his high blood pressure, as he had been brooding over his gross blunder in believing his cousin's promises of abundance. Jack was "heartsick" as a result of Greg's betrayal and his feelings of having let down his wife.

When my lecture turned to the subject of forgiveness, Jack became so irritable that he asked to leave the room. I did not want him to leave because I knew that he needed to hear the information I was presenting, but as I looked at his face, it was clear to me that staying would only add to his discomfort. Lynn addressed Jack as if only the two of them were in the room, took his hand, and told him that although he was punishing himself for what he now considered an act of stupidity, as far as she was concerned, he had acted out of love. "I will never believe that an act of love is rewarded with pain," she continued, "I believe that if you change your perspective and hold to the truth that you supported someone you love because it felt right, then—somehow—all this will work out just fine for us. I don't want the anger you feel toward your cousin to ruin the rest of our lives, so I say we just keep going."

Jack began weeping, muttering words of apology and gratitude to his wife. The other workshop participants were also deeply affected and took a break to give Jack and Lynn some privacy. As I was leaving the room, Lynn asked me to join them, then told me, "I think we can leave now. Jack and I will be just fine."

I contacted Jack and Lynn a few months later to check up on them. Lynn said that Jack had returned to work and that his back was still giving him problems but did not hurt as much. His blood pressure was normal, and he was no longer depressed. Both of them were feeling remarkably liberated from their financial misfortune because they were both genuinely able to forgive what had happened and move on. "We haven't heard a word from Greg," she added, "but we suspect that these days he's thinking about this mess much more than we are."

This couple is an example of the spiritual power of heart energy. The compassion that flowed from Lynn's heart into Jack's body gave him the support he needed to forgive his cousin and himself and get on with his life.

Loving Oneself as the Path
to the Divine

The expression "If you can't love yourself, you can't love anyone else" is commonplace. Yet for many people loving oneself remains a vague notion, which we often act out in material ways—through shopping sprees and outrageous vacations. But rewarding oneself with trips and toys is third chakra love—using physical pleasure to express self-appreciation. While this type of reward is enjoyable, it can obstruct our contact with the deeper emotional stirrings of the heart that emerge when we need to evaluate a relationship, or a job, or some other troubled circumstance that affects our health. Loving oneself as a fourth chakra challenge means having the courage to listen to the heart's emotional messages and spiritual directives. The archetype to which the heart most frequently guides us for healing is that of the "wounded child."

The "wounded child" within each of us contains the damaged or stunted emotional patterns of our youth, patterns of painful memories, of negative attitudes, and of dysfunctional self-images. Unknowingly, we may continue to operate within these patterns as adults, albeit in a new form. Fear of abandonment, for example, becomes jealousy. Sexual abuse becomes dysfunctional sexuality, often causing a repetition of the same violations with our own children. A child's negative self-image can later become the source of dysfunctions such as anorexia, obesity, alcoholism, and other addictions as well as obsessive fear of failure. These patterns can damage our emotional relationships, our personal and professional lives, and our health. Loving oneself begins with confronting this archetypal force within the psyche and unseating the wounded child's authority over us. If unhealed, wounds keep us living in the past.

Derek is a businessman, thirty-seven, who attended one of my workshops because he wanted to resolve some painful childhood memories. Derek had been severely abused as a child. Repeatedly beaten and denied food when he was hungry, he was also forced to wear shoes that were too small for him as a form of punishment.

Derek left home after he graduated from high school, put himself through college, and then went into sales. By the time I met him, he was happily married and had two small children. As he put it, the time had come for him to deal with his childhood memories, which, until now, he had managed to keep at a distance—along with his parents. Derek's father had recently passed away, and his mother was eager to regain some kind of contact with him. Derek agreed to see his mother, and in their first meeting he demanded to know why she and his father had treated him so horribly during his childhood.

At first, Derek's mother denied any abuse but eventually put the blame entirely on his father for the few incidents that she did manage to recall, saying that if she had realized Derek was so unhappy, she would have done something. Then she became emotional and asked Derek how he could treat her so harshly, given that she had only recently become a widow. This is a fairly typical response of an abusive parent who is confronted by an adult child.

Derek listened intently to my lecture on individual and tribal memories. He did not believe his parents to be evil people, he told me, just frightened folks, and maybe they didn't realize the consequences of what they were doing. By the end of the workshop, Derek said that he had been given a great deal to think about and was grateful for it.

About four or five months after the workshop, Derek sent me a note. He decided that life was too short to harbor harsh memories, and he chose to believe that his mother's return into his life was his opportunity to show her, through his own marriage and parenthood, a more loving way of life. He was seeing his mother regularly and believed that someday soon "all would be well."

Derek's story speaks of the healing guidance that comes from the sefirah of Tif'eret, which told him he needed to reconsider his emotional memories. As it always does for all of us, this guidance came at a time when Derek was mature enough to act on it. Following our intuitive guidance is the highest form of preventive health care. The spiritual energies of Derek's heart alerted him that his negative memories could begin to harm his physical health. Everyone's intuitive system works in this way; it is rare that it does not alert us to negative currents that can and will harm us or show how we can choose to release these negative energies before they become a physical illness.

Healing is possible through acts of forgiveness. In the life and teachings of Jesus, forgiveness is a spiritual act of perfection, but it is also a physically healing act. Forgiveness is no longer merely an option but a necessity for healing. Jesus always first healed his patients' emotional sufferings; the physical healing then followed naturally. While Jesus' healings have been interpreted by many theologians and Sunday school teachers as a Divine reward for the recipient's confession of misbehavior, forgiveness is an essential spiritual act that must occur in order to open oneself fully to the healing power of love. Self-love means caring for ourselves enough to forgive people in our past so that the wounds can no longer damage us—for our wounds do not hurt the people who hurt us, they hurt only us. Releasing our attachment to these wounds enables us to move from the childlike relationship with the Divine of the first three chakras into one in which we participate with the Divine in acting out of the love and compassion of the fourth chakra.

The fourth chakra energies propel us further into spiritual maturity, beyond a parent-child dialogue with the Divine, beyond praying for explanations for events, beyond fearing the unexpected. The wounded child sees the Divine as operating a reward and punishment system, with humanly logical explanations for all painful experiences. The wounded child does not understand that within all experiences, no matter how painful, lie spiritual insights. So long as we think like a wounded child, we will love conditionally and with great fear of loss.

Our culture as a whole is evolving toward healing from its emphasis on wounds and victimization. Having entered into the power of our wounds, however, it is difficult to see how we let go of this negative power and move ahead to become "unwounded" and self-empowered. Ours is a "fourth chakra culture" that has not yet moved out of our wounds and into spiritual adulthood.

Awakening the Conscious Self

We get out of the fourth chakra by going through it and learning its lessons. When we enter the interior of our own hearts, we leave behind the familiar thought patterns of the lower three chakras and particularly our tribal heart. We are released from the protection of habitual definitions such as "My priority is the needs of my family," or "I can't change jobs because my wife needs to feel secure"—and we are greeted at our heart's doorway with only one question: "What about me?"

That question is an invocation, drawing to ourselves years of repressed but well-recorded emotional data that, in an instant, can determine a new path for ourselves. We may attempt to run back into the protection of the tribal mind, but its capacity to comfort us is now gone.

We begin the formidable task of getting to know ourselves by discovering our emotional nature—not in relation to anyone or anything, but in relation to ourselves alone. With or without anyone else playing a primary role, a person needs to know: What do I like? What do I love? What makes me happy? What do I need for balance? What are my strengths? Can I rely upon myself? What are my weaknesses? Why do I do the things I do? What makes me need the attention and approval of others? Am I strong enough to be close to another person and still honor my own emotional needs?

These questions are different from those of the tribal mind, which teaches us to ask: What do I like *in relation to others*? How strong can I be while still remaining attractive *to* others? What do I need *from* others in order to be happy? What will I have to change about myself in order to get *someone to love* me?

We don't easily pursue these questions of self-exploration because we know the answers will require us to change our lives. Prior to the 1960s this kind of self-examination was the domain of only the more peripheral members of society—the mystics, artists, philosophers, and other creative geniuses. Meeting the "self" activates the transformation of human consciousness, and the consequences for many artists and mystics have included dramatic episodes of depression, despair, hallucinations, visions, suicide attempts, and uncontrollable emotional turmoil—as well as heightened states of ecstasy combined with physical and transcendental eroticism. It was commonly believed that the price of spiritual awakening was too high and too risky for most people and was meant only for a "gifted" few.

But the revolutionary energy of the 1960s led millions of people to chant, "What about me?" Thereafter the human consciousness movement drove our culture through the archetypal doorway of the fourth chakra. It unearthed the secrets of our hearts and articulated details of our wounded childhoods that still shape much of our adult personalities.

Not surprisingly, our fourth chakra culture has seen a nationwide increase in divorce. The opening of the fourth chakra has transformed the archetype of marriage into the archetype of partnership. As a result, most contemporary marriages require a strong sense of "self" for success, rather than the abdication of "self" that was required in traditional marriages. The symbolic meaning of the sacrament of Marriage is that one must be in union with one's own personality and spirit first. After one has a clear inner understanding of oneself, one can create a successful intimate partnership. The increase in divorce is therefore rooted directly in the opening of the fourth chakra, which draws people into self-discovery for the first time. Many people ascribe the breakdown of their marriage to the fact that their spouse had given them no support for their emotional, psychological, and intellectual needs, and as a result they had to seek out a true partnership.

The opening of the fourth chakra has also changed our consciousness about health, healing, and the causes of illness. Whereas disease was once thought of as caused by essentially lower chakra sources—genetics and germs—we now view the origin of disease as stemming from toxic emotional stress levels. Healing begins with the repair of emotional injuries. Our entire medical model is being reshaped around the power of the heart.

The following story reflects this shift. I met Perry, a physician, in one of my workshops. Perry had an enormous practice, which generated the typical level of professional and personal stress. When the medical community became flooded with information on alternative theories and practices, Perry read bits and pieces but continued prescribing conventional treatments for his patients because he did not know enough about alternative treatments to recommend them.

About five years ago Perry decided to attend a seminar on alternative therapies. He was remarkably impressed not only by the scientific validity of the material presented, but by the case studies his colleagues discussed. Immediately upon returning to work, he viewed all his patients differently, and began to ask them about their personal problems during the course of regular exams. Perry read books on holistic health and attended more lectures and seminars on the topic he found most interesting, the emotional component of disease. Little by little, Perry lost faith in conventional treatments. He wanted to discuss his feelings with his colleagues, but they did not share his interest. He reached a point where he no longer felt comfortable writing out prescriptions, but did not yet feel confident enough to recommend simply that a patient seek other treatments. Eventually, he dreaded going to his office so much that he actually considered leaving the practice of medicine.

Then one day, while preparing to meet with a new patient, Perry, at fifty-two, suffered a heart attack at his desk. During his recovery he asked to meet with both a psychotherapist and a spiritual adviser. He received counseling for several months and then took a leave of absence from his practice, during which time he studied alternative care. Eventually, he created a treatment center where the emotional, psychological, and spiritual needs of patients could be attended to along with physical needs.

"I suffered a very severe heart attack," said Perry. "I will always believe that I regained my health because I entered therapy and therefore entered into myself. I never realized that I was heartsick because of my medical practice until my heart literally became sick. What could be more obvious? For my own sake, I need to treat my patients with the care and awareness I now realize they need. I also need to care for myself differently, so I no longer keep the hours I once did in my practice. Now I make care of myself a priority. My entire life is healthier because I became ill and decided to believe that my heart attack was far more significant than merely developing an electrical problem in my coronary system."

Moving Beyond the Language of Wounds

As a fourth chakra culture, we have language of intimacy that is now based upon wounds. Before the 1960s acceptable conversation consisted mainly of the exchange of information about first, second, and third chakra issues: names, places of origin, work, and hobbies. Rarely would someone reveal the details of his or her sexual desires or the depths of his or her psychological or emotional torment. Our culture was not yet comfortable with this level of discussion, and we lacked the vocabulary for it.

Since becoming a fourth chakra culture, however, we have become therapeutically fluent, in the process creating a new language of intimacy that I call "woundology." We now use the revelation and exchange of our wounds as the substance of conversation, indeed, as the glue that binds a relationship. We have become so good at this, in fact, that we have converted our wounds into a type of "relationship currency" that we use in order to control situations and people. The countless support groups for helping people work through their histories of abuse, incest, addiction, and battering, to name a few, serve only to enhance woundology as our contemporary language of intimacy. Within the setting of these well-meaning support groups, members receive—often for the first time—much needed validation for the injury they have endured. The outpouring of compassion from attentive group members feels like a long, cold drink of water on a hot, dry day.

I became aware of the prevalence of woundology a few years ago in an incident with a woman whom I was meeting for lunch. While waiting for her, I was having coffee with two men. When Mary arrived, I introduced her to Ian and Tom, and simultaneously another man approached us to ask Mary if she was free on June 8 because their community was expecting a special guest and they needed someone to escort this guest around campus. Note that the question put to Mary was: "Are you free June eighth?"—a question requiring a yes or no reply.

Instead, Mary responded: "June eighth? Did you say June eighth? Absolutely not. Any other day, but not June eighth. June eighth is my incest survivors workshop, and we never let each other down. We are committed to supporting each other, and no matter what, we are there for each other. Absolutely not that day. You'll have to find some other person. I simply will not break my commitment to this group. We all have a history of broken commitments, and we are dedicated to not treating each other with the same disregard."

Wayne, the man who had asked the question, simply said, "Okay, fine, thanks," and left. But I was spellbound, as were Ian and Tom. Mary and I then left for our luncheon date, and when the two of us were alone, I asked, "Mary, I want to know why you gave Wayne such a dramatic answer to his question about whether you were free June eighth. I mean, within twelve seconds of meeting Ian and Tom, it was obviously extremely important to you to let them know that you had experienced incest as a child and that you are still angry about it. You wanted to make sure these men knew that. From my point of view, it was obvious that you wanted your emotional history to control the conversation at the table. You wanted these two men to tread carefully around you, and you wanted acknowledgment as a wounded person. You relayed all of this information, when Wayne had only asked you if you were free on June eighth—all you had to do was say no. Why did you have to let everyone know your personal history as an incest survivor?"

Mary looked at me as if I had betrayed her and replied, "Because I *am* an incest survivor."

"I know that, Mary. My question to you is, why did you have to let them know that?"

Mary said that I obviously knew nothing about emotional support, particularly for incest survivors. I explained to Mary that I realized that she had endured a very painful childhood, but that healing meant getting over her pain, not "marketing" it. As a friend, I needed to tell her that she had become seriously invested in the authority of her wounds as opposed to actually healing them. She told me that we needed to reconsider our friendship, and when we left the restaurant that day, we left our friendship as well.

But I was captured by what I had just witnessed. She never did answer my question. She was thoroughly entrenched in her wounds, so much so that she had converted her wounds into a type of social currency. She felt she was owed certain privileges because of her painful childhood: the privilege of being able to call in sick at work whenever she needed to "process" a memory; financial support from her father because of what he did to her; and endless emotional support from all her "friends." True friends, according to Mary, were people who understood her crisis and took over her responsibilities for her whenever they became too much for her.

Curiously, the very next day I was scheduled to give a brief lecture in this community. I arrived early and sat down next to a woman who had come to hear my talk. I said, "Hi, what's your name?" She never even turned to face me as she replied, "I am fifty-six years old and an incest survivor. Of course, I'm over that now because I am part of an incest survivors group, and we are each other's support system. My life is filled because of these people." I was shocked, not only because this interaction was a repeat of the experience with Mary but because I had only asked for her name.

Wounds as a language of intimacy have found an arena of expression within relationships as well as in healing support groups. In fact, it is no exaggeration to state that our contemporary romantic bonding rituals practically *require* a wound for "liftoff." A typical bonding ritual looks something like this: two people meet for the first time. They exchange names, hometowns, and possibly some reference to ethnic or religious origins (first chakra data). Next, the conversation moves to second chakra topics: occupations, relationship histories, including marriages, divorces, and children, and perhaps finances. Third chakra sharing comes next, usually in terms of personal preferences in eating habits, exercise schedules, off-hour activities, and possibly personal growth programs. Should they want to establish an intimate connection, they move on to the fourth chakra. One person reveals a wound that he or she is still "processing." Should the other person want to respond in a "bonding" manner, that person will match the wound with something of the same magnitude. If a match is produced, they have become "wound mates." Their union will include the following unspoken terms of agreement:

1. We will be there to support each other through any difficult memories associated with this wound.

2. That support will include reorganizing any part of our social life, or even work life, around the needs of our wounded partner.

3. If required, we will carry our wounded partner's responsibilities as a way of showing how sincere we are in our support.

4. We will always encourage our partner to process his or her wounds with us and to take as much time as necessary for recovery.

5. We will accept, with minimal friction, all weaknesses and shortcomings rooted in wounds, since acceptance is crucial to healing.

In short, a bond based upon wound intimacy is an implicit guarantee that weakened partners will always need each other and that we will forever have open passage to each other's interior. In terms of communication, such bonds represent an entirely new dimension of love, one that is oriented toward therapeutic support and the nurturing of mutual commitments to healing. In terms of power, partners have never had such easy access to each other's vulnerabilities or so much open acceptance for using wounds to order and control our close relationships. Woundology has completely redefined the parameters of intimacy.

Wounded intimacy has found enormous support within the holistic healing community, particularly in the literature on the links between emotional pain and illness and between healing emotional traumas and the recovery of health. Support groups have been created around every possible type of emotional trauma, from incest to child abuse to domestic violence to grief to having a family member in prison. Television talk shows thrive on making public the details of people's wounds. (Not only do we live within our wounds these days, we are entertained by the wounds of others.) The legal system has learned how to convert wounds into economic power: advertisements on television encourage people to consider lawsuits as a way of coping with their injuries.

Before the 1960s the definition of maturity and strength meant keeping one's pain and vulnerability to oneself. Our contemporary definitions, however, include the capacity to expose one's interior weaknesses to another person. While the original intention of these support groups was to help people experience a nurturing, compassionate response to a personal crisis, no one expected them to continue until the person was healed from the crisis, let alone function as the agent of that healing. They were intended merely to be a boat across a river of transition.

But very few members have wanted to get off their lifeboat when they reach the opposite shore. Instead, they have made a transitional phase of their lives into their full-time lifestyle. Once they learned to speak woundology, it became extremely difficult for them to give up the privileges that accompany being wounded in our fourth chakra culture.

Without a schedule for healing, we risk becoming addicted to what we think of as support and compassion; we find ourselves believing we need more and more time to "process" our wounds. Because the supportive response feels so long overdue, support group members frequently hold on to it with a passion that suggests, "I'm never leaving here, because this is the only place where I have ever found support. There is no support for me in my ordinary world. I will therefore live 'in process' and among people who understand what I have been through."

The problem with such support systems is the difficulty of telling someone that he or she has had enough support and needs to get on with the business of living. In many ways, this problem reflects our skewed understanding of compassion. Compassion, a fourth chakra emotion and one of the spiritual energies contained in the sefirah of Tif'eret, is the strength to honor another's suffering while bringing power back into one's life. Because our culture for so long did not allow time for healing the heart nor even recognize the need for it, we have overcompensated for this earlier failing by now failing to place any time boundaries around that healing. We have yet to create a model of healthy intimacy that is empowered yet still vulnerable. At present, we define *healed* as the opposite of *needy*. Therefore, to be healed means to be fully self-contained, always positive, always happy, always sure of oneself, and never needing anyone. No wonder few ever consider themselves "healed."

The Path to the Empowered Heart

Healing is simple, but it is not easy. The steps are few, yet they demand great effort.

Step 1: Commit yourself to healing all the way to the source of the pain. This means turning inward and coming to know your wounds.

Step 2: Once "inside," identify your wounds. Have they become a form of "wound-power" within your present life? If you have converted your wounds into power, confront why you might fear healing. As you identify your wounds, have someone "witness" them and their influence upon your development. You need at least one person, a therapist or a friend perhaps, who is capable of working with you in this way.

Step 3: Once you have verbalized your wounds, observe how you use them to influence or even control the people around you as well as yourself. Do you ever say you are not feeling well because of them in order to cancel an appointment, for instance, when in fact you are feeling fine? Do you ever control another person by saying that his or her actions remind you of your parents? Do you ever give yourself permission to quit something, or not try at all, by dwelling on your past and therefore encouraging depression? Are you afraid that in healing yourself you will lose your intimate connections to certain people in your life? Are you afraid choosing to heal yourself will require you to leave behind some or much of your familiar life? These are questions you need to address honestly, because they are the most significant cluster of reasons that people fear becoming healthy.

As you observe yourself throughout the day, note carefully your choice of vocabulary, your use of therapeutic language, your fluency in woundology. Then formulate new patterns of interaction with others that do not rely upon wound power. Change your vocabulary, including how you talk to yourself. Should changing these patterns prove difficult, recognize that it is often far more difficult to release the power you derive from your wound than it is to release the memory of the painful experience. A person who cannot let go of wound power is a wound addict, and like all addictions, wound addiction is not easy to break. Don't be afraid to seek therapeutic help in getting through this step, or any of the others.

Step 4: Identify the good that can and has come from your wounds. Start living within the consciousness of appreciation and gratitude, and if you have to—"fake it until you make it." Initiate a spiritual practice, and stick to it. Do not be casual about your spiritual discipline.

Step 5: Once you have established a consciousness of appreciation, you can take on the challenge of forgiveness. As appealing as forgiveness is in theory, it is an extremely unattractive personal action for most people, mainly because the true nature of forgiveness remains misunderstood. Forgiveness is not the same as telling the person who harmed you, "It's okay," which is more or less the way most people view it. Rather, forgiveness is a complex act of consciousness, one that liberates the psyche and soul from the need for personal vengeance and the perception of oneself as a victim. More than releasing from blame the people who caused our wounds, forgiveness means releasing the control that the perception of victimhood has over our psyches. The liberation that forgiveness generates comes in the transition to a higher state of consciousness—not just in theory, but energetically and biologically. In fact, the consequence of a genuine act of forgiveness borders on the miraculous. It may, in my view, contain the energy that generates miracles themselves.

Evaluate what you need to do in order to forgive others—and yourself, if necessary. Should you need to contact anyone for a closure discussion, make sure that you are not carrying the message of blame as a private agenda. If you are, you are not genuinely ready to let go and move on. Should you need to share your closure thoughts in a letter to the person, do so, but again, make sure your intention is to retrieve your spirit from yesterday, not to send yet another message of anger.

Finally, create an official ceremony for yourself in which you call your spirit back from your past and release the negative influence of all your wounds. Whether you prefer a ritual or a private prayer service, enact your message of forgiveness in an "official" way in order to establish a new beginning.

Step 6: Think love. Live in appreciation and gratitude. Invite change into your life, if only through your attitude. And remind yourself continually of the message of all spiritual masters worth their salt: keep your spirit in the present time. In the language of Jesus, "Leave the dead and get on with your life." And as Buddha taught, "There is only now."

The curious thing about healing is that depending upon who you talk to, you can come to believe either that nothing is easier or that nothing is more complicated.

The fourth chakra is the center of the human energy system. Everything in and about our lives runs off the fuel of our hearts. We will all have experiences meant to "break our hearts"—not in half but wide open. Regardless of how your heart is broken, your choice is always the same: What will you do with your pain? Will you use it as an excuse to give fear more authority over you, or can you release the authority of the physical world over you through an act of forgiveness? The question contained within the fourth chakra will be presented to you again and again in your life, until the answer you give becomes your own liberation.

The subtle energies of the sefirah of Tif'eret and the sacrament of Marriage continually direct us to discover and love ourselves. This love is the essential key to finding the happiness that we are convinced lies outside of ourselves but that spiritual texts remind us is only found within. Too many people are frightened of knowing themselves, convinced that self-knowledge would mean living alone, without their current friends and partners. While the short-term effect of self-knowledge may well cause changes, its long-term developments—fueled by consciousness, not fear—will be more fulfilling. It makes no sense to seek to become intuitively conscious, then work to keep that consciousness from upsetting our lives. The only path toward spiritual consciousness is through the heart. That truth is not negotiable, no matter what spiritual tradition one chooses as a means to know the Divine. *Love Is Divine Power*.

Questions for Self-Examination

1. What emotional memories do you still need to heal?
2. What relationships in your life require healing?
3. Do you ever use your emotional wounds to control people or situations? If so, describe them.
4. Have you ever allowed yourself to be controlled by the wounds of another person? What are your feelings about letting that happen again? What steps are you prepared to take to prevent yourself from being controlled that way again?
5. What fears do you have about becoming emotionally healthy?
6. Do you associate emotional health with no longer needing an intimate relationship?
7. What is your understanding of forgiveness?

8. Who are the people you have yet to forgive, and what prevents you from letting go of the pain you associate with them?

9. What have you done that needs forgiving? Which people are working to forgive you?

10. What is your understanding of a healthy, intimate relationship? Are you willing to release the use of your wounds in order to open yourself to such a relationship?

CHAPTER 5

The Fifth Chakra: The Power of Will

The fifth chakra embodies the challenges of surrendering our own willpower and spirits to the will of God. From a spiritual perspective, our highest goal is the full release of our personal will into the "hands of the Divine." Jesus and Buddha, as well as other great teachers, represent the mastery of this state of consciousness, complete union with Divine will.

Location: The throat.

Energy connection to the physical body: Throat, thyroid, trachea, esophagus, parathyroid, hypothalamus, neck vertebrae, mouth, jaw, and teeth.

Energy connection to the emotional/mental body: The fifth chakra resonates to the numerous emotional and mental struggles involved in learning the nature of the power of choice. *All* illness has a connection to the fifth chakra, because choice is involved in every detail of our lives and therefore in every illness.

Symbolic/perceptual connection: The symbolic challenge of the Willpower chakra is to progress through the maturation of will: from the tribal perception that everyone and everything around you has authority over you; through the perception that you alone have authority over you; to the final perception, that true authority comes from aligning yourself to God's will.

Primary fears: Fears related to our willpower exist within each chakra, appropriate to that chakra. We fear having no authority or power of choice within our own lives, first within our tribes, then within our personal and professional relationships. And then we fear having no authority with ourselves, being out of control when it comes to our response to substances, to money, to power, to another person's emotional control over our well-being. And finally, we fear the will of God. The notion of releasing our power of choice to a Divine force remains the greatest struggle for the individual seeking to become conscious.

Primary strengths: Faith, self-knowledge, and personal authority; the capacity to make decisions knowing that no matter what decision we make, we can keep our word to ourselves or to another person.

Sefirot/Sacrament connection: The fifth chakra corresponds to the sefirah of Hesed, representing the love or mercy of God, and of Gevurah, representing the judgment of God. These two sefirot are the right and left arms of God, portraying the balanced nature of Divine will. The implication of these sefirot is that the Divine is merciful, and that only God has the right to judge the choices we make. The sefirah of Hesed reminds us to use loving words to communicate with others, and the sefirah of Gevurah reminds us to speak with honor and integrity. The sacrament of Confession is aligned to the fifth chakra, symbolic of the fact that we are all accountable for the way we use our willpower. Through the sacrament of Confession, we are given an opportunity to retrieve our spirits from the "negative missions" we may have sent them on as a consequence of our negative thoughts or actions.

Sacred truth: The fifth chakra is the center of choice and consequence, of spiritual karma. Every choice we make, every thought and feeling we have, is an act of power that has biological, environmental, social, personal, and global consequences. We are everywhere our thoughts are and thus our personal responsibility includes our energy contributions.

What choices would we make if we could actually see their

energy consequences? We can approach this kind of foresight only by abiding by the sacred truth *Surrender Personal Will to Divine Will*. The spiritual lessons of the fifth chakra show us that actions motivated by a personal will that has trusted in Divine authority create the best effects.

One's thoughts and attitudes also benefit from accepting higher guidance. One woman who told me about a near-death experience views every choice she makes as having an energy impact on the whole of life. For while she was in that state between physical and nonphysical life, she reviewed all the choices she had made in her life and witnessed the consequences of those actions upon herself, other people, and the whole of life. She was shown that guidance was always trying to penetrate into her conscious mind. Whether she was choosing a dress or occupation, no choice was so insignificant that it was ignored by the Divine. In purchasing a dress she was shown the immediate energy consequence of that "sale," down a long chain of people who had been involved in its creation and distribution. She now asks for guidance prior to any and every decision she must make.

Understanding the energy consequences of our thoughts and beliefs, as well as our actions, may force us to become honest to a new degree. Lying, either to others or to ourselves, should be out of the question. Genuine, complete healing requires honesty with oneself. An inability to be honest obstructs healing as seriously as the inability to forgive. Honesty and forgiveness retrieve our energy—our spirits—from the energy dimension of "the past." Our fifth chakra and its spiritual lessons show us that personal power lies in our thoughts and attitudes.

The Consequences of Fear

The most costly energy consequences come from acting out of fear. Even when choices made from fear lead us to what we desire, they generally also produce unwanted side effects. These surprises teach us that choosing from fear transgresses our trust in Divine guidance. We all do live, at least periodically, within the illusion that we are in charge of our lives. We seek money and social status in order to have greater power of choice and so that we do not have to follow the choices others make for us. The idea that consciousness requires surrendering personal will to Divine will stands in direct conflict with all that we have come to consider the measure of an empowered person.

Thus, we may repeat the cycle of fear-surprise-fear-surprise, until we reach a point of prayer in which we say: You choose, and I'll follow. Once we release this prayer, guidance may enter our lives, along with endless acts of synchronicity and coincidence—Divine "interference" at its best.

Emily, thirty-five, is a grade-school teacher who lost her left leg to cancer thirteen years before, shortly after she graduated from college. During her rehabilitation she returned home to live with her parents. What they anticipated would be a year's stay turned into a decade because Emily did not regain her independence but instead grew ever more depressed and frightened at the prospect of taking care of herself. She so minimized her physical activity that she would walk no farther than around her block. With each passing year Emily retreated more into her parents' home, eventually ceasing even pleasurable outings.

Emily's parents suggested therapy, but nothing had any impact upon her. As her mother said to me, "All Emily would do, day after day, was dwell upon her belief that the loss of her leg ruined her chances of getting married and having a family of her own, or any type of life on her own. She felt 'branded' by her experience with cancer and would sometimes comment that she wished the cancer would return and 'complete the job,' as she put it."

As a result of her daughter's illness, Emily's mother became interested in alternative treatments. By the time we met, she and her husband were seeking the courage to ask Emily to move out on her own. Emily had to learn to take care of her own physical needs and to heal her psychological state. She needed to rely upon her own willpower again.

Emily's parents rented and furnished an apartment for her, and she moved in—angry and frightened. She told her parents she felt abandoned by them. Within a month she met a neighbor, Laura, a single mother with a ten-year-old son called T.J. This boy always arrived home from school before his mother came home from work. Emily would hear him maneuvering around their apartment, watching TV, eating snacks, waiting for almost three hours alone each day until Laura came home.

One afternoon Emily was coming home from the store just as Laura was coming home from work. They began to discuss T.J., and Laura remarked that she was concerned about his schoolwork and the amount of time he was alone after school. Emily suddenly volunteered not only to keep T.J. company every afternoon but to tutor him in his schoolwork, since she was a qualified teacher. Laura gratefully agreed, and the next afternoon, Emily began to tutor T.J.

Within a few weeks word spread around the apartment complex that a "wonderful teacher" was available to both tutor and care for children after school. Emily was deluged with requests from working parents. She asked the manager of the apartment complex whether a room could be available for three hours every afternoon. A room was available, financial arrangements were made, and Emily—within three months of leaving her parents' home—was, as she put it, "alive again."

As Emily told me her story, she referred several times to the spontaneity with which she volunteered to tutor T.J. Her offer "flew out of her mouth" before she had a chance even to think about it, she said. If she had thought about it, she said, she would never have offered to help. Precisely because this gesture was so out of character, she considered, just for a moment, that she was being "told" by the heavens to tutor T.J. Ultimately Emily decided to believe that she had been intended to tutor T.J., as well as the eleven other children who came under her care before she returned to teaching the following autumn.

For whatever reason Emily had the grace to recognize guidance. As soon as she began caring for others, her own fear of not being cared for abated. She was living proof, she realized, that God attends to the needs of everyone and this renewed her faith.

Faith

The essence of the fifth chakra is faith. Having faith in someone commits a part of our energy to that person; having faith in an idea commits a part of our energy to that idea; having faith in a fear commits a part of our energy to that fear. As a result of our energy commitments, we—our minds, hearts, and lives—become woven into their consequences. Our faith and our power of choice are, in fact, the power of creation itself. We are the vessels through which energy becomes matter in this life.

Therefore, the spiritual test inherent in all our lives is the challenge to discover what motivates us to make the choices we do, and whether we have faith in our fears or the Divine. We all need to address these questions as a matter of spiritual thought or as a result of physical illness. We all reach a moment when we ask, Who is in charge of my life? Why aren't things working out the way I want? No matter how successful we are, at some point we will become conscious that we feel incomplete. Some unplanned event or relationship or illness will show us that our personal power is insufficient to get us through a crisis. We are meant to become aware that our personal power is limited. We are meant to wonder if some other "force" is acting in our lives, and to ask, Why is this happening? What do you want of me? What am I meant to do? What is my purpose?

Gaining an awareness of our own limitations opens us to considering choices we would not otherwise have made. During the moments when our lives seem most out of control, we may become receptive to a guidance that we would not have welcomed before. Then our lives may move in directions we had never anticipated. Most of us end up saying, "I never thought I would be doing this or living here, but I am, and all is well."

It may help you to arrive at the point of surrendering if you can use symbolic sight to view your life as *only* a spiritual journey. We have all known people who have recovered from dire circumstances—and credited the fact that they let the Divine take over. And every one of these people shared the experience of saying to the Divine, "Not my will but Yours." If that one prayer is all that is required, why are we so afraid of it?

We remain terrified that by acknowledging Divine will—by surrendering our will to a greater will—we will become separated from all that brings us physical comfort. So we struggle with our will against Divine guidance: we invite it in, yet strive to block it completely. Again and again I observe people in my workshops who are in this dilemma; they seek intuitive guidance, yet fear what that voice will say to them.

Remember that your physical life and your spiritual path are one and the same. Taking pleasure in your physical life is as much a spiritual goal as achieving a healthy physical body. Both are the consequences of following Divine guidance in making choices of how to live and of acting out of faith and trust. Surrender to Divine authority means liberation from physical illusions, not from the delights and comfort of physical life.

The spiritual energies of the fifth chakra guide us toward that point of surrender. The sefirah of Hesed transfers into our fifth chakra the Divine energy of greatness through love, which directs us to be as loving as possible in all circumstances. Sometimes the greatest act of love is to withhold judgment of another or of oneself. Again and again we are reminded that being judgmental is a spiritual error. Developing the discipline of will allows us to refrain from releasing

negative thoughts toward others or ourselves. By being nonjudgmental, we attain wisdom and defeat our fears. The sefirah of Gevurah teaches us to release the need to know why things happen as they
do, and to trust that whatever the reason is, it is a part of a grander
spiritual design.

Marnie, forty-four, is a healer, a genuinely anointed healer, who
began her work following a seven-year-long "dark night of the soul"
in which she had to heal herself. When Marnie was thirty, she was a
social worker in Scotland, lived an active life, had a number of
friends, and enjoyed her work immensely. Then she was diagnosed
with an "undiagnosable" condition.

With each passing month, Marnie developed increasing pain,
sometimes in her back, sometimes as intense migraines, sometimes in
her legs. Eventually the pain forced her to take a leave of absence
from her job. She spent almost two years going from one specialist to
another, none of whom could help her understand her chronic pain
and occasional loss of balance, or prescribe any effective treatment.

Marnie spiraled into depression. Her friends suggested that she
seek the help of alternative health therapists, in whom she had never
believed. One day, a friend showed up at Marnie's home with a col-
lection of alternative health care books, among which were the writings of Sai Baba, a spiritual master living in India. Marnie read the
material but dismissed it as the type of nonsense that "only cult-
minded creatures would believe."

Six more months of pain forced Marnie to retract those words as
she journeyed to India to try to get a private audience with Sai Baba.
She spent three weeks at his ashram but never saw him privately. She
returned to Scotland even more despondent than before. Yet shortly
after returning home, Marnie had a series of dreams in which she was
continually asked only one question: Can you accept what I have
given you?

At first, Marnie thought the dreams were merely the consequence of her trip to India and her numerous conversations about the nature of God's will for people. Then a friend suggested that she treat the dreams as though she were genuinely being asked a spiritual question. As Marnie put it, "I had nothing to lose, so why not?"

The next time she had the dream, she answered the question: "Yes, I will accept what you have given me." The moment she said *yes*, she felt herself being bathed in light, and for the first time in years she was pain-free. Upon waking up, she hoped her illness would be gone, but it wasn't—in fact, it gradually got worse over the next four years. She dwelled upon that dream again and again, holding to the belief that it wasn't really a dream, yet she continued to experience anger and despair, feeling at times that God was asking her to suffer for no good reason.

One night, while she was weeping, Marnie said she reached "surrender." She thought she had been in that state of consciousness since her dream, but that night she realized, "I was in resignation, not surrender. I was living in this type of attitude that said, 'All right, I'll do this. Now reward me for it by making me feel better.' And then, that night, I realized that I might never feel better, and if that's the case, what would I then say to God? I surrendered completely. I said, 'Whatever you choose for me, so be it. Just give me strength.'"

Marnie's pain instantly eased, and her hands filled with heat—not ordinary body heat, but "spiritual heat." She knew immediately that the heat running through her hands had the power to help heal others, although ironically, she herself might not be able to "drink from that well." She actually laughed at her condition, because it was "exactly like the stories of the mystics of old I had read about—only who would have thought that I would qualify for their tasks?"

Marnie is now a greatly loved and highly respected healer, and while her physical body has healed substantially from the undiagnosed pain, she still has her difficult moments. But in Marnie's words, "I would go through it all again, given who I am today and

what I know, for the privilege of helping others the way I can now."
Her story stands out for me because of her deep understanding of the
difference between surrender and resignation, and because she lived
through the myth that once we say yes to God, everything will be
perfect immediately. Saying yes to our condition is the first part—an
act that may or may not change our condition—and saying yes to
God's timing is the second.

The act of confession reclaims our spirits from the consequences
of our choices. As we learn more about our energy natures, we realize how much our spirits remain attached to negative events and
thoughts, past and present. Confession is much more than the public
acknowledgment of a wrongdoing. In energy terms it is the acknowledgment that we have become conscious of—and therefore empowered over—a fear that had previously commanded our spirits.
Symbolically, confession liberates our spirits from past fears and negative thought patterns. Remaining attached to negative events and
beliefs is toxic to our minds, spirits, cell tissue, and lives.

Karma is the energy and physical consequences of the choices we
make. Negative choices generate situations that recur in order to
teach us how to make positive choices. Once we learn the lesson and
make a positive choice, the situation does not recur because our spirit
is no longer attached to the negative choice that gave rise to the lesson. In Western cultures this kind of karmic lesson is recognized in
social adages such as "What goes around comes around" or "You
don't get away with anything." Acts of confession signify that we recognize our responsibility for that which we have created and that we
realize the error in our choices. In energy terms this ritual liberates
our spirits from painful learning cycles and redirects us into the creative, positive energies of life.

So essential is confession to the health of our minds, our bodies,
and our spirits that we can't stop ourselves from confessing. The
need to purge our spirits of guilt-ridden memories is stronger than
our need for silence. As a prison official told me, "Many criminals get

caught because they have to tell at least one person what they did. And while it may come out as bragging at the time, it is nonetheless a form of confession that I think of as street confessions."

Psychotherapists have become modern-day confessors. With them we try to resolve our psychological and emotional struggles, by exploring openly the dark sides and controlling fears of our natures and psyches. The sweet energy of healing pours into our energy system every time we break a fear's authority over our lives and replace it with a more empowered sense of self. In the language of confession, these therapeutic milestones are the same as calling our spirits back from negative missions on which we have sent them.

Knowing, then, that the fifth chakra teaches us how to use our will, and records the directives we give to our spirits, how do we manage the lessons of this chakra?

Between the Head and the Heart

Since the center of the will is located between the energies of the heart and the mind, we need to learn how to balance our responses to their urgings. Usually as children, we are directed toward one of these two ruling energies: boys are usually pushed to use their mental energy, and girls their hearts.

Mental energy powers the external world, while heart energy powers our personal domains. For centuries our culture has thought that emotional energy weakens our ability to make quick and necessary decisions, and that mental energy is virtually useless in the emotional domain, as noted in the old saying that reason can win no war against a heartfelt choice. For centuries, until the 1960s, this separation was acceptable. Then the decade when the head met the heart redefined a balanced individual to mean one who operates with heart and mind in unison.

If mind and heart are not communicating clearly with each other, one will dominate the other. When our minds are in the lead, we suffer emotionally because we turn emotional data into an enemy. We seek to control all situations and relationships and maintain authority over emotions. When our hearts are in the lead, we tend to maintain the illusion that all is well. Whether the mind is in the lead or the heart, will is motivated by fear and the futile goal of control, not by a sense of internal security.

This imbalance of head and heart turns people into addicts. In energy terms, any behavior motivated by the fear of internal growth qualifies as an addiction. Even behavior that is usually healthy—exercise or meditation, for instance—can be an addiction if it is used to avoid pain or personal insight. Any discipline can become a willful block between our conscious and unconscious minds, saying, "I want guidance, but don't give me any bad news." We even try to direct the very guidance we are seeking. We end up living in a seemingly endless cycle of mentally wanting change but emotionally fearing change at every turn.

The only way to break through this pattern is to make choices that engage the united power of the mind and the heart. It is easy to keep oneself in a holding pattern, claiming that one does not know what to do next. But that is rarely true. When we are in a holding pattern, it is because we know exactly what we should do next, but we are terrified to act on it. Breaking through the repetition of cycles in our lives only requires one strong choice that is aimed at tomorrow and not yesterday. Decisions that say, "No more—I will not take this type of treatment any longer," or, "I cannot stay here one more day— I must leave," contain the quality of power that unites the energy of both of the mind and the heart, and our lives begin to change almost instantly as a result of the authority present within that intense degree of choice. Admittedly it is frightening to leave the familiar contents of one's life, even though one's life is often desperately sad. But change is frightening, and waiting for that feeling of safety to come along before one makes a move only results in more internal torment because the only way to acquire that feeling of security is to enter the whirlwind of change and come out the other end, feeling alive again.

Eileen Caddy, one of the three founders of the spiritual Findhorn community in northern Scotland, has had an interesting life of changes and challenges as she learned to trust in Divine guidance and surrender to its directives. She received guidance that she credits as the voice of "Christ" to leave her first husband and their five children and form a partnership with a man named Peter Caddy. Although she followed this guidance, her next years were tumultuous, partly because Peter himself was married at the time. Eventually Peter left his wife, married Eileen, and took over the management of a declining hotel in a town called Forres in northern Scotland. They had three children, and as Eileen supplied the guidance, Peter soon turned this low-quality hotel into a four-star enterprise. Through these years Eileen had minimal contact with her five other children, although her own guidance told her that she would eventually reconcile with them, which proved accurate. Eileen's guidance, as they both came to realize, came from a deeply spiritual place.

While the hotel was at the peak of its success, much to everyone's surprise Peter was fired. He and Eileen were shocked by the news, never expecting to be rewarded for their leadership with walking papers. But again, Eileen's guidance instructed them to rent a trailer in a local trailer park called Findhorn. There they were instructed to grow a garden—a seemingly preposterous suggestion, given the climate, location, and minimal sunlight. Nevertheless, they did as instructed and were soon joined by a woman named Dorothy McLean.

Like Eileen, Dorothy was a channel, only her guidance came from "nature energies" that instructed her on how to cooperate with them in co-creative ways. The nature energies promised to exaggerate the growth of the garden for exactly seven years, to show what could be accomplished when the spiritual, human, and natural forces of life worked together.

The garden bloomed exactly as promised. Vegetation reached unheard-of proportions. Rumors of this "magical" garden soon hit the airwaves, and people from all over the world traveled to this remote spot to see it for themselves. No one was disappointed; even skeptical horticulturists had to admit the garden was spectacular. When asked about the source of such magnificent production, Dorothy, Peter, and Eileen told the truth: "We follow the will of the Divine."

Eventually a community formed around this garden. Eileen began her remarkable discipline of meditating from midnight until six in the morning in the public bathroom, which was the only place she could find privacy. Their tiny trailer, hardly large enough for one person, now housed six. Each morning Eileen would emerge and turn over to Peter the instructions she had received during the night. He followed them to the letter, utilizing his managerial personality to see that the new community members followed his orders. Buildings were constructed, routines were created, and soon a burgeoning community was up and running.

After the seven years, just as promised, the vegetation returned to normal size. Eileen then received instruction that no more guidance would be given to Peter and that he must now seek his own path to his own voice. That news strained their relationship and led Peter to turn elsewhere in the community for guidance. Soon people were competing to influence Peter. Chaos resulted, and Eileen became depressed. Finally Peter told Eileen that he was leaving her and the community, and that he never really had been in love with her. Emotionally devastated by Peter's revelation and the divorce, Eileen wondered how this could be the reward for following Divine guidance.

Today, Eileen says her struggles and despair, even her divorce, were due to "resistance to God." Though she had followed the guidance that she received, she said, she actually did not want to, and as a result she had been in conflict most of the time. She needed to learn faith and trust in her connection to the "Christ consciousness," as she refers to her guidance. That was her personal spiritual mission.

Now Eileen says that the God-force is a reality within her that directs her always. She is dedicated to a path of service and feels that her rewards have been numerous. "I have a family in the archetypal sense. I am surrounded by a community that is my family. I have a beautiful home, a loving relationship with all my children, and an intimate relationship with God. I feel deeply blessed."

Eileen's bond with the "Christ" energy reflects a contemporary mystical path. Her life has encompassed both old and new spiritual paths: the old, in which the spiritual leader took on hardships and solitary contemplation as the intermediary between others and God; and the new, in which one lives within the spiritual community. Eileen lives with the trials, blessings, and rewards of Divine guidance. Her life is filled with miracles and frequent synchronicities.

Releasing one's will to Divine guidance may result in difficult experiences along with great insight. One may experience the painful ending of many phases of life, such as a marriage or occupation. But I have yet to meet the person who felt that the end result of uniting with Divine authority was not worth the price. No story captures this experience better than the original lesson of surrender, the story of Job.

Job was a man of great faith and great wealth, and he prided himself on both. Satan asked God to be allowed to test Job, claiming that he could cause Job to lose his faith in God. God agreed. Satan first caused Job to lose his possessions and his children, but Job remained faithful to God, believing that if this were God's will for him, so be it. Next, Job was given an illness, and his wife advised him to "rebuke God" for their increasing miseries. Job remained faithful. Job's wife died.

Job was visited by his friends Eliphaz, Bildad, and Zophar, who offered their sympathy and debated the nature of Divine justice. They believed that God would never punish a "just man" and that therefore Job must have done something to offend the heavens. Job protested his innocence and said that his suffering was part of the universal experience of injustice. As Job grew to think that perhaps God was unjust after all in causing him to suffer, a young man named Elihu joined Job and his friends and castigated them for believing that they could know the "mind of God," and for feeling that God owed them an explanation for His choices.

Eventually God spoke to Job and instructed him on the difference between human will and Divine will. God asked Job, "Where were you when I laid the earth's foundation?" and "Have you ever given orders to the morning or sent the dawn to its post?"

Job realized the folly of challenging the will of God, and he repented. He informed his friends of the truth that he had learned: that no mortal could ever know the mind of God, that the only true act of faith is to accept all that God asks of us, and that God owes no mortal an explanation for His decisions. Job then released his will into the hands of God, saying, "I have spoken once, I will not speak again." God gave Job another family and doubled his earthly possessions.

Again and again, the challenges we face cause us to ask, What is God's will for me? We often think of God's will for us as a task, a job, a means of accumulating power for ourselves. But in truth, Divine will will lead us primarily to learn about the nature of spirit and of God.

The greatest act of will in which we can invest our spirits is to choose to live according to these rules:

1. Make no judgments.
2. Have no expectations.
3. Give up the need to know why things happen as they do.
4. Trust that the unscheduled events of our lives are a form of spiritual direction.
5. Have the courage to make the choices we need to make, accept what we cannot change, and have the wisdom to know the difference.

Questions for Self-Examination

1. What is your definition of being "strong-willed"?
2. Who are the people in your life that have control over your willpower, and why?
3. Do you seek to control others? If so, who are they, and why do you need to control them?
4. Are you able to express yourself honestly and openly when you need to? If not, why not?
5. Are you able to sense when you are receiving guidance to act upon?
6. Do you trust guidance that has no "proof" of the outcome attached to it?
7. What fears do you have associated with Divine guidance?
8. Do you pray for assistance with your personal plans, or are you able to say, "I will do what heaven directs me to do"?
9. What makes you lose control of your own willpower?
10. Do you bargain with yourself in situations in which you know you need to change but you continually postpone taking action? If so, identify those situations and your reasons for not wanting to act.

CHAPTER 6

The Sixth Chakra:
The Power of the Mind

The sixth chakra involves our mental and reasoning abilities, and our psychological skill at evaluating our beliefs and attitudes. The Mind chakra resonates to the energies of our psyches, our conscious and unconscious psychological forces. Within Eastern spiritual literature, the sixth chakra is the "third eye," the spiritual center in which the interaction of mind and psyche can lead to intuitive sight and wisdom. This is the chakra of wisdom.

The challenges of the sixth chakra are opening the mind, developing an impersonal mind, retrieving one's power from artificial and "false truths"; learning to act on internal direction; and discriminating between thoughts motivated by strength and those by fear and illusion.

Location: Center of the forehead.

Energy connection to the physical body: The brain and neurological system, pituitary and pineal glands, as well as the eyes, ears, and nose.

Energy connection to the emotional/mental body: The sixth chakra links us to our mental body, our intelligence and psychological characteristics. Our psychological characteristics are a combination of what we know and what we believe to be true, a unique combination of the facts, fears, personal experiences, and memories that are active continually within our mental energy body.

Symbolic/perceptual connection: The sixth chakra activates the lessons that lead us to wisdom. We achieve wisdom both through life experiences and by acquiring the discriminating perceptual ability of detachment. Symbolic sight is partly learned "detachment"—a state of mind beyond the influences of the "personal mind" or "beginner's mind" that can lead to the power and insight of the "impersonal" or open mind.

Sefirot/Sacrament connection: The sefirah of Binah, representing Divine *understanding,* and the sefirah of Hokhmah, representing Divine *wisdom,* are aligned to the sixth chakra. Binah is the womb of the Divine mother, who receives the seed for conception from Hokhmah, identified as "the beginning." The unity of these two forces creates the lower sefirot. Binah and Hokhmah are symbolic of the universal truth that "thought" comes before "form" and that creation begins in the energy dimension.

Binah and Hokhmah remind us to become conscious of that which we create—to use our mind fully as we command energy to become matter. It is that perspective that bridges them to the Christian sacrament of Ordination.

Symbolically, Ordination represents the task one is called to do in service to others. From an archetypal perspective it is recognition from others that you have unique insight and wisdom that lead you to help others: as a mother, healer, teacher, athlete, or loyal friend. The priesthood, of course, is the role traditionally associated with the actual sacrament of Ordination. Symbolically, however, Ordination is any experience or honor in which your community acknowledges that it benefits from your inner-directed path of service as much as you do. This factor of mutual benefit identifies your "ordained" calling. The beauty of the symbolic meaning of Ordination is that it honors the truth that each person is capable of making deeply significant contributions to the lives of others, not just through their profession, but more important, through the quality of person they become. The sacrament of Ordination symbolically seeks to recognize the contributions of our spirits to others' lives far more than the contributions of our tasks.

Primary fears: An unwillingness to look within and excavate one's fears; fear of truth when one's reason is clouded; fear of sound, realistic judgment; fear of relying on external counsel, of discipline; fear of one's shadow side and its attributes.

Primary strengths: Intellectual abilities and skills; evaluation of conscious and unconscious insights; receiving inspiration; generating great acts of creativity and intuitive reasoning—emotional intelligence.

Sacred truth: The sacred truth of the sixth chakra is *Seek Only the Truth.* It compels us to search continually for the difference between truth and illusion, the two forces present at every moment. Separating truth from illusion is more a task of the mind than of the brain. The brain commands the behavior of our physical body, but the mind commands the behavior of our energy body, which is our relationship to thought and perception. The brain is the physical instrument through which thought is transferred into action, but perception—and all that is associated with perception, such as becoming conscious—is a characteristic of the mind. In becoming conscious one is able to *detach* from subjective perceptions and see the truth or symbolic meaning in a situation. Detachment does not mean ceasing to care. It means stilling one's fear-driven voices. One who has attained an inner posture of detachment has a sense of self so complete that external influences have no authority within his or her consciousness. Such clarity of mind and self is the essence of wisdom, one of the Divine powers of the sixth chakra.

Applying Detachment

How does one apply detachment, in practical terms, to one's life? Pete's story shows one practical way of utilizing this skill. Pete contacted me to do a reading on himself during a serious personal crisis. His wife of seventeen years had announced that she no longer loved him and wanted a divorce. Pete was, understandably, devastated, as were their four children. I suggested that just for a moment he try to see this situation from a detached point of view. I suspected his wife was redefining herself beyond the role of caretaker—a role in which she had been living for most of her life. As a child she had taken care of her younger siblings; she had married at seventeen and been a mother at eighteen. Now, at forty, she was waking up to herself and her own needs and was probably having an affair. I told Pete that his wife was likely terrified by what she was feeling and that if she had had a more therapeutic vocabulary, she might have been able to describe the new emotional energies she was experiencing rather than panicking at them. Her affair was her attempt to run away from what was happening inside her. She probably could not care less about the man she was involved with, even though she might not realize it at the time. She chose to have the affair because she could imagine no other way of leaving her husband and children. The option of seeking therapeutic help was not part of her culture or her thinking process.

I told Pete that, as difficult as it might be to accept, the fact was that his wife would have responded the same way at this point in her life no matter who her husband was, because she was going through a process of self-discovery that had nothing to do with him. She did not know herself that she had entered a "dark night" experience. Pete should work at not taking personally her acts of rejection and anger because, while he was certainly a target for her emotional anger, she was far more angry at her confusion than she was at him.

Pete was able to absorb this information and work with it. Though he and his wife decided to divorce, he returned to a more impersonal way of viewing this crisis every time he found himself sinking into the grief and hurt of the breakup of his family. Not long after our first conversation, he discovered that his wife had been having an affair with a friend of his and that it had indeed broken. He realized that his wife was not in love with the other man but was attempting to find an outlet for her own confusion. I told him that she would, more than likely, continue to try to solve her crisis by trying to find another mate, but it would never work. Each relationship was destined to fail because finding another relationship—and thereby becoming the caretaker again—was not the solution to her pain. Eventually she would be forced to go inside herself and work to heal the real source of her pain.

Becoming detached and conscious means getting certain perceptions from our minds into our bodies. It means merging with perceptions that are truth and living them so that their power becomes one and the same as our own energy.

Take, for instance, the truth "Change is constant." Mentally we can absorb that teaching with little difficulty. Yet when change occurs in our lives—when we notice we are aging, when people we love die, or when relationships shift from being intimate and loving to distant—this truth terrorizes us. We often need years to recover from some changes because we had hoped that it—whatever "it" was— would remain the same. We knew all along that it would change, but we can't help hoping that the energy of change will pass by this one part of our lives.

Even when "Change is constant" feels like an enemy that has swept away a happy part of our lives, our lonely times will come to an end and a new part of life will begin. The promise of "Change is constant" is that new beginnings always follow closures.

Consciousness is the ability to release the old and embrace the new with the awareness that all things end at the appropriate time and that all things begin at the appropriate time. This truth is difficult to learn to live with because human beings seek stability—the absence of change. Therefore becoming conscious means living fully in the present moment, knowing that no situation or person will be exactly the same tomorrow. As change does occur, we work to interpret it as a natural part of life and strive to "flow with it," as the *Tao Te Ching* counsels, and not against it. Trying to make things remain the same is useless as well as impossible. Our task is to contribute the best of our energy to every situation with the understanding that we influence, but do not control, what we will experience tomorrow.

Often, after I have lectured on detachment, my groups respond that detachment feels too cold and impersonal. But that is not an accurate perception of detachment. In one workshop I asked each participant to name a situation that they would find extremely threatening. One man said he would find it very difficult to return to his office and learn that the management had taken his responsibilities away from him. I told him to imagine that he was liberated from his attachments to his business and that he could create any options for himself that he wanted. I told him to visualize his business as no more than a drop of energy in his life rather than an ocean of energy, and that an abundance of creative power was rushing through him. And then I told him to imagine that he walked into his office and learned that they had fired him. Now, I said, how would you respond? He laughed and said, given the image of himself that he was holding in his mind at the moment, being fired wouldn't matter to him at all. He would be just fine, he said, because he would be able to attract to himself his next place of employment.

That is the meaning of detachment: the realization that no one person or group of people can determine your life's path. Thus, when change comes into your life, it is because a larger dynamic is moving you along. It may look like a group of people conspired to have you removed from a job—but that is the illusion. If you choose to believe that illusion, it will hold you captive, maybe even for a lifetime. But if it hadn't been the right moment for you to move on, the "conspiracy" would not have been successful. That is the higher truth of this life change, and the symbolic sight that accompanies detachment allows you to see it.

Obviously, none of us wakes up one morning and announces, "I think I'll become conscious today." We are drawn into a desire to stretch the parameters of our minds through the mysteries we encounter. All of us experience, and will continue to experience, relationships and events that cause us to reexamine our understanding of reality. The very design of our minds compels us to wonder why things are as they are, if only within our own personal confusion.

Danny asked for my help because he had been diagnosed with prostate cancer. His only request of me was "Just help me figure out what I'm doing and thinking that I shouldn't be doing or thinking anymore."

As I evaluated Danny's energy, I realized that he was a professional do-gooder to everyone but himself. I asked him what he would like to be doing right now, and he said, "I'd like to leave my job in sales, move to the country, grow my own food, and work as a carpenter." We then discussed the consequences of such a change: he had made commitments to his company, he was an active part of a number of groups, and his family, most of all, was comfortable in their lifestyle. All these relationships would end. Then Danny said, "For the longest time, I've had this idea that I want to think differently. I don't want sales figures in my head. I want to think about other things, like nature. Of course, nature won't pay the bills, so I've never really done anything about it. But I feel this calling to live my life differently. I have for a long time, only now I feel I need to follow this feeling." I replied that he was already filled with guidance. He should listen to it, and by following his feelings, a new world would open up to him, one in which his health would thrive. Two months later Danny contacted me to tell me that his family was in favor of the move and that they were headed southwest come next summer. He had never felt better, he added, and he knew he would never again have a malignant growth in his body.

Danny was willing and able to dismantle his life as a salesman and embrace a new life. By letting go of his self-perception and his occupation, he also let go of his idea that his power in the physical world was limited. By following his internal voice, he opened himself up to evaluating his internal reality: What is life about? What am I meant to do? What is important to learn? He was able to say, "The outside world does not hold that much power over me. I choose to listen to my inside world."

This is how we become conscious—a mystery arises, we take action, and another mystery follows. When we choose to stop that process, we enter a suspended state in which we drift farther and farther away from the life-force. The progression from personal to detached mind, however, can be very natural and easy. A woman named Karen, in one of my workshops, had been fired from three jobs in less than one year. She could not help but wonder if the source of the problem was something in her, she said. And once she had raised that question, she wanted to find the answer. After she took the time to get to know herself, she realized that she had been causing her own problems. She had had absolutely no interest in any of the three jobs. What she really wanted was a career change. That was a revelation. Karen today is involved in many different activities and continues to discover new likes and dislikes, new ambitions, and new fears with every new experience. For her, this is the natural progression of the conscious life. When she remembers the way she was "before the light went on," she wonders how she ever made it through a day without thinking about the things that give her life meaning. "The unconscious life is just that—unconscious. You aren't even aware that you aren't aware of anything. You just think about the basics of life—food, clothing, money. It never occurs to you to wonder about for what purpose were you created. And then, once you ask that question, you can't stop asking it again and again. It always leads to another truth."

Consciousness and
Its Connection to Healing

During the past four decades an enormous amount of information has become available on the role of the mind in health. Our attitudes play a tremendous role in creating or destroying the health of our bodies. Depression, for example, not only affects our ability to heal but directly diminishes our immune system. Anger, bitterness, rage, and resentment handicap the healing process, or abort it entirely. There is great power in having a will to heal, and without that internal power, a disease usually has its way with the physical body. With all these new realizations, the power of consciousness is being given an official place within the medical model of health and illness.

It's amazing how many people credit an experience with illness as their motivation for turning their attention inward and taking a close look at their attitudes and lifestyle. Inevitably they describe essentially the same process of recovery—the journey from the personal to the impersonal mind.

Initially upon learning of a diagnosis, they are full of fear. But once they get a grip on themselves, most report that they had already had a feeling that something was wrong but had dismissed that feeling because of fear. That is significant because our intuitive guidance alerts us to a loss of power in our bodies. As the fear gradually settles down, however, people report that they turned inward and reviewed the content of their minds and their emotional data. This is how people begin the process of becoming mentally and emotionally congruent, or conscious of the distance between what they think and what they feel. Healing requires unity of mind and heart, and generally it is the mind that needs to be adjusted to our feelings, which too often we have not honored in the daily choices we have made.

Thus, people relate story upon story of taking steps to reorganize their lives, giving their feelings a creative voice in their activities. Sylvia's story portrays this journey into consciousness of both mind and heart. Sylvia was diagnosed with breast cancer and had both breasts removed. Her cancer had spread to some of her lymph nodes as well. It would have been natural to think constantly about having cancer, but Sylvia detached from having cancer and focused instead upon the stresses in her life that had contaminated her energy. She reviewed her fears and the control that they exerted within her psyche and recognized that she was terrified of being alone. Her cancer had developed shortly after her divorce. It would have been natural for her to focus on being alone and on her bitterness about her divorce, but instead Sylvia made a commitment to find something of value each day of her life. She resolved not to dwell on yesterday but to appreciate all the good things that had happened to her and release her painful experiences, including her divorce. She frequently felt sadness over her situation, but instead of living in that sadness, she would cry it out and then move on. Sylvia later became involved in supporting other people recovering from cancer, which gave her life new meaning and purpose. From a symbolic perspective, she had become "ordained"—that is, the power she brought to others was returned to her through the recognition and gratitude of those she helped. She had never experienced this degree of self-worth before. Within six months her system was cancer-free.

One aspect of becoming conscious is to live in the present moment and appreciate each day. Sylvia was able to detach from her past and create a new life that had meaning and purpose: this is the definition of becoming impersonal about a crisis in one's personal life. Although she had developed cancer, she reached for the truth that an empowered spirit is capable of healing a diseased body—the impersonal mind carries authority over personal experience. Again and again I have witnessed that healing is a matter of becoming conscious—not of the illness but of a life-force that the person has never before embraced.

Consciousness and Death

Does this mean that people who do not heal have failed to expand their consciousness? Not at all. But the notion that they have failed has become a very controversial aspect of holistic thought. A mechanism in our minds insists on viewing all situations as either-or, win or lose, good or bad. When someone's body does not heal from an illness, people may inaccurately conclude that the individual simply didn't try hard enough.

Death is not a failure to heal. Death is an inevitable part of life. The fact is that many people do heal themselves of their emotional and psychological torments and thus die "healed."

Jackson's story shows what it means to die consciously. Jackson contacted me for a reading because he had a malignant brain tumor. His pain was constant and intense. He was intent upon doing all that he could do to become whole, he said, regardless of whether he lived or died. We discussed every piece of unfinished business we could identify in his life, from relationships that needed closure to fears that needed confronting. He even thought of thank-you notes he should have sent. Jackson focused on completion, but with this emphasis: he was not completing his life—he was completing his unfinished business with his level of consciousness. He asked himself continually, "What am I expected to learn in this life?" Each time an insight or an answer occurred to him, he acted on it. He noted, for instance, that he had never explained to his former wife why he had wanted a divorce. He had just told her one day that he had had enough of being married and wanted out of the vow, as he put it. He knew she had been devastated and confused, and though she had asked for an explanation, he had deliberately refrained from giving one.

This behavior, he realized, was a pattern, because his former wife was only one of several people whom he had hurt in that manner. She was merely the most dramatic victim. Jackson admitted that he had liked the feeling of power that he got when he saw the confusion he created by leaving people or situations. The ability to create chaos had made him feel important. Now he chose to create clarity. He contacted each person who he felt had been a victim of his actions and sent them, via letter, an explanation of his behavior along with an apology. Again and again Jackson examined his shadow side and took every step he could to bring his shadow into the light. Still, he was going to die. Yet he said to me that all was well because he believed he had completed his life's lessons.

The goal of becoming a conscious person is not to outwit death, nor even to become immune to disease. The goal is to be able to handle any and all changes in our lives—and in our bodies—without fear, looking only to absorb the message of truth contained in the change. Regarding the expansion of consciousness, such as through meditation, as insurance against physical illness is to misinterpret its purpose. Mastery of the physical is not the goal of becoming conscious: mastery of the spirit is the goal. The physical world, and the physical body, serve as the teachers along the way.

In keeping with this perception, healing the fear of death and dying is an aspect of the tranquillity that the human spirit is capable of achieving through the journey of becoming conscious. When people who have managed to extend their consciousness across the bridge between this world and the next speak of their comfort with the continuation of life, some of our own fears are disintegrated immediately. I had this opportunity when I met Scott and Helen Nearing. I include their story because they contributed to my own awareness about the nature of human consciousness and our power to heal perceptions that interfere with our ability to live in truth.

Scott and Helen Nearing

Scott and Helen Nearing are known for their contributions to the environmental movement and for promoting a lifestyle of self-sufficiency. They were considered rebels in their younger days because their "back to the land" way of living was practically unheard of in the 1930s, when they became a team. They built their home by hand and lived off the fruits and vegetables they grew themselves. For more than seven decades, they lived in harmony with the land, and Helen continued that lifestyle today, until she died in 1995. They generated a stream of philosophical articles and lectures aimed at getting people to honor the environment and live self-sufficiently, including *Living the Good Life*, in which they describe the benefits of a lifestyle of constant appreciation for the abundance of nature. Their ideals and awareness of a greater cycle of Divine cause and effect continues to inspire countless people today. Scott died in the early 1980s at the age of one hundred. I had the privilege of getting to know Helen when she attended one of my workshops, and she shared with me her husband's choice to die. He had made the choice consciously when he felt he was no longer capable of living in a manner that supported his spiritual growth.

"One day, Scott came into the house carrying wood for the fire-place. He put the wood down and announced to me that his time to die had come. He said he knew this because he was no longer able to do his tasks and carry out his own responsibilities. He said he became 'aware' deep within himself that it was his time to die. He told me that he would welcome death by no longer eating. For three weeks I stayed by his side while he lay in bed, abstaining from food. I did not attempt to offer him any or to change his mind, because I understood the depth to which Scott had made this choice."

Scott Nearing passed away within three weeks of deciding to die because of his inability to live self-sufficiently—the theme of his century-long life. Helen further commented, "I intend to do the same thing as soon as I become anywhere near unable to care for myself. Dying is nothing to fear. You simply embrace your time to leave, and you cooperate with it by not eating. All you're doing is leaving your body. That's not a big deal."

Scott and Helen attained a level of awareness and personal choice that might be controversial—but then again, their entire lives have been controversial. The way they chose to die challenges deeply held tribal beliefs about tampering with the process of death, as well as the religious belief that our time of death lies solely in God's hands. It may well be true, but if we are capable of recogniz-ing that our time has come, are we not free to cooperate with that cognizance? Perhaps Scott, as a consequence of striving to live almost impersonally—aligned to ideals that held only truth—had earned the blessing of being told "internally" that his time had come. Rather than disintegrating through disease, he cooperated with his intuition and left his life fully conscious until his last moment. Isn't this what becoming conscious is all about? Dying consciously is undoubtedly one of the many blessings of having lived a conscious life.

While I was writing this book, in September 1995, Helen also passed away. She suffered a heart attack while driving. She had told me that she would leave this life upon completion of her next book. She kept her word.

So substantial is our fear of death that within our tribal minds, death is very likely to be dominated by superstition. Scott and Helen should be remembered for enhancing our awareness of self-sufficiency, but also as two people who had complete faith in the continuation of life beyond our physical forms.

Sogyal Rinpoche

Sogyal Rinpoche is a noted teacher and author of *The Tibetan Book of Living and Dying*. He has earned a worldwide reputation for himself as the "laughing Rinpoche," because his personality sparkles with humor.

In 1984, I met with Sogyal at his home in Paris. I had never before been in the company of a Rinpoche, but I certainly had read a great deal about Tibetan teachers and was very eager to find out if what I had read was valid. I had read, for instance, that many Tibetan masters have transcended the ordinary laws of time and space, and that some are capable of levitation and of physically running at speeds up to forty miles an hour. I had also read that whenever a Tibetan master is asked directly about his "power," he will always "deflect" any interest in himself, preferring to talk about some other evolved master.

On the way to Sogyal's residence, I wondered what we would have for dinner. Since I had no idea what Tibetan social customs were, I was wondering all sorts of ridiculous things—like, would I have to meditate for hours before dinner? It turned out that Sogyal ordered Chinese take-out for dinner, and we sat on the floor of his office, eating our dinners directly out of the cartons.

As soon as the social atmosphere became conducive to serious discussion, I asked Sogyal, "Is it true that you can levitate?" He laughed—hysterically, I might add—and then said, "Oh no, not me. But my master, he could." Then I asked, "Is it true that because of your meditative practices, you can run at unusually fast speeds?" Again my question was met with laughter, and again he responded, "Oh no, not me. But my master, he could." His responses matched just what I had read: that a Tibetan master being interviewed deflects any attention from his own power to that of someone else. Then it occurred to me: maybe Sogyal was reading my mind and knew exactly what I had read and where my questions were coming from. Finally, I said, "I don't have any more questions. Is there anything you would like to tell me?"

"I would like to tell you about the way my master came to die," he said. "He called his astrologers together and told them to cast a chart for him, noting the perfect time for him to withdraw his spirit from the energies of the earth. His spirit was extremely powerful, and he wanted to leave without causing any type of energy consequence. You may not be aware of such things, but when any spirit leaves the earth, the entire energy field is influenced. And when a very powerful spirit leaves, the influence upon the earth is even more dramatic.

"So his astrologers came up with a day and a time that was the perfect moment for his physical death. He then told his students that on that day, and at that time, he would leave. And that's just what he did. He meditated with his students on the day, blessed them, and then shut his eyes and released his spirit from his body."

I asked Sogyal if his master chose to die because he was ill. Again the question sent Sogyal into near-uncontrollable laughter, and he said, "Ill? What's illness got to do with this? Just as we are all born at the perfect moment for our energy to enter this earth, there is a perfect moment for us to leave this earth. My master wasn't ill. He was complete. We are not meant to die in pain and in disease. The conscious mind is able to release the spirit from the body without having to endure the pain of physical decay. This choice is available to everyone."

Sogyal described the state of spiritual mastery as the attainment of a level of consciousness that "knows no conflict with the Divine," so that one's own choices are the same as Divine choice. His master, according to Sogyal, lived in a state of consciousness in which the dilemma of choice—believing that one choice is better than another—no longer existed. Every choice was the correct choice, as Sogyal described it, at the state of perfection his master had achieved. Sogyal said that his master was an example of a living—and a dying—enlightened mind.

Developing the Impersonal Mind and Symbolic Sight

The Nearings and Sogyal Rinpoche have tapped into the power of the impersonal mind. Describing consciousness on paper has its limitations, however, because of spirituality's ineffable qualities. As the zen koan says, "If you can say what it is, that's not it."

I remember clearly the professor who introduced me to Buddhist and Hindu thought. As a final exam, she took all five of us students to a remote weekend retreat facility and issued the rules: no speaking allowed, and no clocks or wristwatches. During the night she would awaken a student, ask the student to assume a yogic position, then ask questions: How does a Christian speak about the nature of God? How does a Buddhist speak about the nature of reality? What is the truth of eternal life? What is the purpose of this life? The questions were deep and penetrating. It wasn't the quality of our responses that she was evaluating; rather, it was our attachment to any particular school of thought. If she sensed that we were attached to one form of truth more than another, we had failed to learn the lesson of her class: All truth is the same at the level of truth itself. That it becomes "enculturated" is an illusion. For her, this was the essence of what it means to become conscious: to seek truth that is detached from its social or cultural form. In looking back at her influence upon me, I credit her with laying the groundwork for my own abilities in symbolic sight.

How can we work with our own minds to refine our mental perceptual system and become skilled at penetrating illusion? As with all worthy goals, some form of discipline is required to make any substantial progress. The following case represents the wrong way of going about the task of becoming more conscious.

Oliver was a very successful businessman, but he had reached a point in his life where he wanted to do something that had more meaning. So he tried working in various projects that represented meaningful social activities. None felt right to him. He prayed for guidance as to what to do with his life. Finally he arranged a visit with an internationally famous spiritual master. The visit lasted all of ten minutes, during which this spiritual master told Oliver that his task was to "wait and become ready." So he "waited"—he waited in Paris, in Rome, in the Orient. He waited in first-class hotels and while sipping cappuccinos on the Riviera. Finally, he decided that his instruction to "wait" was useless. He returned to visiting projects and writing checks to support them. But his heart remained empty. In my opinion, the spiritual master gave him the one instruction that he could not fulfill by buying something. Had he been able to "wait" in a spiritual sense, to "go inside" and accept whatever humble steps he was asked to take, he would have begun to get his answer.

In many ways the spiritual challenge of "waiting" and becoming a different quality of person makes more of a contribution to this world than financing a new hospital. This may be difficult to understand. We are unaccustomed to giving value to what we cannot see, and we cannot see the power emitted from a healthy psyche. Thus, those whose work is "waiting and becoming" can often appear useless.

But "waiting and becoming" is the symbolic meaning of being "called to ordination"—that is, allowing the Divine to awaken part of your spirit that contains the essence of what you are capable of contributing to others as well as to yourself. The woman who became known as Peace Pilgrim embodies this spiritual process of allowing the Divine to open a doorway.

Peace Pilgrim, which is the only name this woman used for the last twenty-five years of her life, lived a humble and deeply spiritual life, during which she prayed to be shown a path of service. At fifty-two she listened to her inner guidance, which directed her to walk across the country continually on behalf of peace. These were her "ordination" instructions. And so, owning only "the shirt on her back," she began to walk, and she "walked until given a place to rest and ate only what she was offered." Her life became a statement of the power of trusting God completely to provide for one's needs.

During her twenty-five-year pilgrimage Peace Pilgrim touched the lives of hundreds of thousands of people, who were awed by her remarkable rapport with Divine intervention. I heard her tell two stories that touched me deeply. Once as she was walking down a country road, the temperature dropped rapidly. She was unprepared for this sudden change and became chilled to the bone. She was not near any place in which she could find shelter. Then she heard a voice that said to her, "Go under the next bridge." She did as instructed, and there she found a large box, big enough for her to rest in. Inside the box were a pillow and blanket. In relaying this story, she assumed I would understand that these items had been placed there by God.

Peace Pilgrim commented that through her life she had gone through cycles of learning about conflict. She had had to experience external conflict first, then internal conflict. When she had finally surrendered her life to God, she was blessed with the gift of learning without conflict. Peace Pilgrim became a source of endless wisdom, which is the essence of the sefirah of Hokhmah, and of Divine understanding and reasoning, which is the essence of Binah. She became the epitome of the ordained spirit, fluent in symbolic sight, and living in complete harmony and trust with the Divine. Her instructions to others were, in keeping with the nature of truth, ever so simple: "I don't eat junk food, and I don't think junk thoughts." Translation: Honor the body, honor the mind, honor the spirit.

Developing the impersonal mind is a lifetime task, partly because it is such a substantial challenge and partly because it takes us into the depths of our illusions and fears. We have to reconstruct ourselves from the inside out, a process that always brings about numerous changes in our lives. I have yet to find a person pursuing a path of conscious awakening who has not experienced a time of "waiting," during which his or her interior is reconstructed. And as with all matters of the spirit, once we start along the path, there is no turning back.

The following instructions provide a starting point for developing the impersonal mind and achieving symbolic sight, the ability to see through illusion and grasp the energy power behind the scenes. As I drew up these instructions, I kept in mind the sefirot that resonate with the sixth chakra, Hokhmah and Binah. Following these steps may help you attain symbolic sight and increase your ability to reach the dimension of Divine reasoning.

- Develop a practice of introspection, and work to become conscious of what you believe and why.
- Keep an open mind, and learn to become aware when your mind is "shutting down."

- Recognize defensiveness as an attempt to keep new insights from entering your mental field.
- Interpret all situations and relationships as having a symbolic importance, even if you cannot immediately understand what it is.
- Become open to receiving guidance and insight through your dreams.
- Work toward releasing any thoughts that promote self-pity or anger, or that blame another person for anything that has happened to you.
- Practice detachment. Make decisions based upon the wisest assessment you can in the immediate moment, rather than working to create a specific outcome.
- Refrain from all judgments—not just those rendered against people and situations, but those that concern the size or importance of tasks. Rather, remind yourself continually of the higher truth that you cannot possibly see all the facts or details of any situation, nor visualize the long-term consequences of your actions.
- Learn to recognize when you are being influenced by a fear pattern. Immediately detach from that fear by observing its influence on your mind and emotions; then make choices that weaken the influence of those fears.
- Detach from all values that support the belief that success in life means achieving certain goals. Instead, view a successful life as a process of achieving self-control and the capacity to work through the challenges life brings you. Visualize success as an energy force rather than a physical one.
- Act on your inner guidance, and give up your need for "proof" that your inner guidance is authentic. The more you ask for proof, the less likely you are to receive any.

- Keep all your attention in the present moment—refrain from living in the past or worrying about the future. Learn to trust what you cannot see far more than what you can see.

Becoming Conscious

There is nothing easy about becoming conscious. My own life was much easier before I knew about the deeper meaning of choice, the power of choice that accompanies taking responsibility. Abdicating responsibility to an outside source can seem, at least for the moment, so much easier. Once you know better, however, you can't get away with kidding yourself for long.

My heart goes out to people who are working hard to release their negative attitudes and painful memories. "Just tell me how, and I'll do it," they say to me. We are forever looking for the easy meditation, the easy exercise, that will lift us out of the fog, but consciousness doesn't work that way. Ironically, there is a simple way out, only it's not easy: Just let go. Let go of how you thought your life should be, and embrace the life that is trying to work its way into your consciousness.

So many people struggling to find their way are in that necessary but confusing state of waiting. A part of each of them is eager to allow the Divine will to direct their lives, yet they remain tormented by the fear that they will lose all comfort on the physical plane should they actually surrender to it. So they are held in a waiting position until they are strong enough to release that fear and embrace the deeper truth that "all will be well"—not "well" by our definition, perhaps, but certainly by God's.

Toby contacted me for a reading because he was suffering from severe depression, arthritis, and impotence. In evaluating his energy I received the impression that his health had declined almost immediately after his fiftieth birthday. In fact, he believed that once he turned fifty, the best years of his life would be over. As I shared my impression with him, he responded, "Well, just look around you. You see any business opportunities for men my age? I live in constant fear now that I'm going to lose my job to a younger person, and then what will I do?"

I suggested to Toby that he begin a physical exercise program, focusing on rebuilding his physical body. He needed to do something to experience the return of power to his body, and by extension to his life. Much to my surprise, he was open to that suggestion. He had been putting off joining a gym, he said, but he agreed to do it.

Then I told him to read some Buddhist material about illusions, and to begin to think of age and time as illusions. This suggestion stopped Toby in his tracks. "How can time be an illusion?"

"You can make a decision that you will not age according to an ordinary time line. You can decide to throw away your calendar and give every day your best," I replied.

Toby started to laugh. "I'd love to think that could work," he said.

I said, "Then try it. You can always go back to being an old man. That option is always there. But give this a try first." Then, because of the lightness in Toby's voice, I asked, "Do you realize that just for these few moments, you weren't depressed?"

Toby paused for a second. "You're right. I wasn't aware of my depression at all."

"Are you, right now, experiencing any arthritic pain?" I asked.

"I would have to say no, not at the moment. But then, it comes and goes anyway."

"But right now, as you ponder on the possibility of feeling free and good again, you are neither depressed nor in pain, correct?"

"That's correct," he replied.

"So let's just assume that the more positive mental options you give yourself, and the more positive action you take, the better you will feel, and you will recover your power, including your sexual energy."

Toby said, "Okay. But what if I can't maintain a positive outlook? Then it all comes back, right?"

"Right."

"So you're saying I'm in charge of my moods and my arthritis, and that depression increases the pain. So I'm in charge of all of this."

"Looks that way," I said.

"You should have been a lawyer," Toby replied. "You've given me a lot to think about," he added. "I'll do my best."

Four months later I received a postcard from Toby. He and his wife were on a cruise. The card read, "Having a wonderful time—day and night included."

It's not often that one conversation can so thoroughly turn a person's life around, but Toby was willing to look at his attitudes and recognize that he was choosing to dwell on negativity. When a person so readily embraces the energy of wisdom, I can't help but imagine that the spiritual forces present in our energy fields, like Hokhmah, the sefirah of wisdom, are just waiting for an opportunity to penetrate our consciousness.

Carrie, thirty-four, introduced herself to me over the telephone by saying, "Something's wrong with me."

"Okay, what?" I asked.

"I can't do my job anymore. I can't think anymore. I can't do anything anymore," she said.

As I scanned her energy, I noted instantly that her mind, symbolically speaking, was not "in" her body. It was filled with images that had nothing to do with her present life but that involved a spiritual life alone in some remote area of the country.

"What do you read?" I asked her.

Carrie ran down a list of books all related to spirituality. And then she said, "I keep thinking that I belong in New Mexico. I went there for a retreat a year ago, and I had this wonderful feeling that I'm supposed to move my life to New Mexico. I don't know anyone who lives out there, but I can't let go of that idea," she said.

As we discussed the intensity of her feeling, I explained to Carrie, using the symbolic meaning of the sacrament of Ordination, that sometimes people are called to places, and that it might be a wise choice to follow that feeling.

Carrie began to weep, saying she was terrified of leaving and terrified of staying. "I feel as if my life is over here and I just need to break away, but I have no idea of what lies ahead."

I asked her what motivated her to go on a retreat.

She replied that she had been very inspired by the life story of a woman who said to God, "Just show me truth. I don't want anything else in my life." Apparently that woman began to lead a remarkable life once she released that prayer. "I'm not a missionary," said Carrie. "But I want to live an authentic life. I don't feel I'm accomplishing that here, as an attorney in Detroit. I respect the people I work with, and I'm grateful for the opportunity to help people through my work, but I've felt continually empty, and I can't stand it anymore."

I said, "I'm not one to tell people where to live, but I do believe you need to follow that voice you are hearing."

Carrie did move to New Mexico. She gave up the practice of law, and much to her surprise, once she was settled in her new home, she found herself drawn to become a midwife, an occupation she had never considered during her time in Detroit.

She wrote me several times to keep me updated, and each time she expressed a sensation of life coming into her body. "I feel an energy flow into me every time I come near a pregnant woman. I am beginning to understand this substance called energy. I dismissed it as imagination when I lived in Detroit, but I now think there is some conscious force in this universe that continually supports life, and that this force flows through us," she said in one letter.

From my point of view, Carrie had found her ordained path. I am forever awestruck by people whose lives are so filled with the presence of guidance.

The journey toward becoming conscious is often more attractive in theory than it is in practice. Pursuing consciousness theoretically through books and conversations allows us to fantasize about getting to the promised land without actually having to make any changes in our lives. Even the thought that a promised land exists can temporarily make a person feel great. To some extent, "workshop addicts" are doing just that—getting high on conversation, but returning to their homes and their lives exactly as they left them.

The British author Graham Greene once waited two and a half years for a fifteen-minute appointment with the Catholic mystic Padre Pío, who resided in a monastery in Italy. Padre Pío had earned an extraordinary reputation as a "living saint" for a number of remarkable reasons, not the least of which was that he bore the "stigmata"—the "wounds of Christ," which had been imprinted on his body when he was a young priest. On the day Greene was scheduled to meet with the mystic, Greene first attended a mass at which Padre Pío officiated. Their appointment was scheduled to begin after the mass; instead, Greene left the church, headed for the airport, and flew directly back to London. When asked why he broke the appointment, Greene commented, "I was not ready for the manner in which that man could change my life."

Eventually, however, our minds become overloaded with information, and the day comes when we can no longer straddle two levels of perception simultaneously. Try as we will, we cannot forever "visit" truth and then return to illusion. At some point the process of change itself moves us forward.

A few years ago I met a man named Dan, who was taking a class in consciousness and business practices. He said he felt very inspired by the presentation, which focused on applying to business the principles of holistic health—such as having a positive attitude and combining the strength of the mind and the heart. For several weeks after the seminar, Dan said, he openly shared with his co-workers the knowledge he had received. He believed that his enthusiasm would be contagious and that everyone would be inspired to bring a greater sense of personal awareness to their jobs.

The first official test of his new optimism came while his company was launching a new project. He told his co-workers to "visualize" success and abundance. He even gathered them together on the first day of the new project to meditate together. Afterward Dan's boss told him privately that he would appreciate it if Dan kept his newfound "magic" away from the company. When the project failed to produce a successful outcome, Dan—and his new ideas—became the target of unrelenting criticism, so much so that he resigned from the company. For months afterward, he spiraled into confusion and despair. Then one day a former co-worker asked to meet with him. During their conversation she told Dan that all the while Dan was bubbling with his new ideas, several employees had expressed concern that he had joined a cult.

During that conversation Dan realized that he had made an error in judgment. Just because he was ready to live by a new set of internal rules, he had assumed everyone else would be ready as well. They weren't. He wanted his environment to immediately become a living example of the concepts from the seminar—mainly because he knew that he would find it difficult to continue working there with his new internal rules so different from the company's external rules. He finally accepted that no greater gift could have been given to him than motivation to leave his situation so that he could find a more suitable working environment. Shortly thereafter he began to pursue his new life.

Becoming conscious means changing the rules by which we live and the beliefs we maintain. Our memories and attitudes are literally rules that determine the quality of life as well as the strength of our bonds with others. Always, a shift in awareness includes a period of isolation and loneliness as one gets accustomed to the new level of truth. And then always, new companions are found. No one is left alone for long.

Our expansion into the realm of consciousness always uses the energies of the sefirot of Hokhmah and Binah, combined with the inherent desire to find our ordained path—a path of service that allows us to contribute the highest potential of our minds, bodies, and spirits.

Questions for Self-Examination

1. What beliefs do you have that cause you to interpret the actions of others in a negative way?
2. What negative behavioral patterns continually surface in your relationships with others?
3. What attitudes do you have that disempower you?
4. What beliefs do you continue to accept that you know are not true?
5. Are you judgmental? If so, what situations or relationships tend to bring out that tendency in you?
6. Do you give yourself excuses for behaving in negative ways?
7. Can you recall instances in which you were confronted with a more profound level of truth than you were used to hearing and found the experience intimidating?
8. What beliefs and attitudes would you like to change in yourself? Are you willing to make a commitment to making those changes?
9. Are you comfortable thinking about your life in impersonal terms?
10. Are you frightened of the changes that might occur in your life, should you openly embrace a conscious lifestyle?

CHAPTER 7

The Seventh Chakra: Our Spiritual Connector

The seventh chakra is our connection to our spiritual nature and our capacity to allow our spirituality to become an integral part of our physical lives and guide us. While our energy system as a whole is animated by our spirit, the seventh chakra is directly aligned to seek an intimate relationship with the Divine. It is the chakra of prayer. It is also our "grace bank account," the warehouse for the energy we amass through kind thoughts and actions, and through acts of faith and prayer. It enables us to gain an intensity of internal awareness through meditation and prayer. The seventh chakra represents our connection to the transcendent dimension of life.

Location: Top of the head.

Energy connection to the physical body: The seventh chakra is the entry point for the human life-force, which pours endlessly into the human energy system, from the greater universe, from God or the Tao. This force nourishes the body, the mind, and the spirit. It distributes itself throughout the physical body and the lower six chakras, connecting the entire physical body to the seventh chakra. The energy of the seventh chakra influences that of the major body systems: the central nervous system, the muscular system, and the skin.

Energy connection to the emotional/mental body: The seventh chakra contains the energy that generates devotion, inspirational and prophetic thoughts, transcendent ideas, and mystical connections.

Symbolic/perceptual connection: The seventh chakra contains the purest form of the energy of grace or *prana.* This chakra warehouses the energy generated by prayer and meditation and safeguards our capacity for symbolic sight. It is the energy center for the spiritual insight, vision, and intuition far beyond ordinary human consciousness. It is the mystical realm, a dimension of a conscious rapport with the Divine.

Primary fears: Fears relating to spiritual issues such as the "dark night of the soul"; fears of spiritual abandonment, loss of identity, and loss of connection with life and people around us.

Primary strengths: Faith in the presence of the Divine, and in all that faith represents within one's life—such as inner guidance, insight into healing, and a quality of trust that eclipses ordinary human fears; devotion.

Sefirot/Sacrament connection: The sefirah connected to the seventh chakra is Keter, which means "crown." Eastern spiritual traditions refer to the seventh chakra as the crown chakra. Keter represents "nothingness," the energy from which physical manifestation begins. It is thought to be eternal, with no beginning or end. The Christian sacrament related to the seventh chakra is Extreme Unction (or Last Rites), the sacrament administered to the dying. Symbolically, Extreme Unction represents the process of retrieving one's spirit from the various "corners" of one's life that still hold "unfinished business," or releasing regrets that continue to pull at one's consciousness, such as words that should have been spoken but were not, or words that should not have been spoken. Unfinished business would also include relationships we wish we had ended differently or paths we wished we had taken but did not. At the closure of our lives we consciously draw these memories to a final point, accepting the choices we made at the time and releasing the feeling that things could have or should have been otherwise. This is what it means to "call one's spirit back" in order to leave this world and return to the spiritual dimension complete.

The final statements of Jesus, as he hung on the cross, may well have initiated this sacrament. He said to his mother and to his disciple John, "Woman, behold your son. John, behold your mother." Then turning his attention to God, Jesus said, "Forgive them, they know not what they do," and "It is finished. Unto you I commit my spirit." These statements embody the conscious closure of one's life and the preparation to return to an eternal spiritual identity.

From a different symbolic perspective, Extreme Unction represents a ritual that should be a regular part of human life. At many points during our lives, we face a crossroads where we need to let a previous phase of life "die." The less we hold on to the physical world, the more we position ourselves to access consciously the energy of Keter, or the crown chakra, our transcendent link to the Divine.

Sacred truth: Seventh chakra energy motivates us to seek an intimate connection to the Divine in everything we do. This spiritual desire for connection is significantly different from the wish for connection to a religion. Religion, first of all, is a group experience whose main purpose is to *protect the group*, primarily from physical threats: disease, poverty, death, social crises, and even war. Religion is rooted in first chakra energies. Spirituality, on the other hand, is an *individual* experience directed toward releasing fears of the physical world and pursuing a relationship to the Divine. The sacred truth of this chakra is *Live in the Present Moment.*

Seeking a personal spiritual connection shakes us to our core. Our conscious or unconscious prayer to come to know the Divine directly goes something like this: "I no longer want to be protected within the group, nor do I desire to have a mediator filter my guidance for me. I now want You to move into my life directly and remove from my life any obstacle—be it a person, place, or occupation—that interferes with my ability to form an intimate union with You." As Meister Eckhart wrote in *The Soul Is One with God*, the ultimate aim of the mystic is identity: "God is love, and he who is in love is in God and God in him."

In seeking union with the Divine, we are asking to have all physical, psychological, and emotional "illusions" removed from our lives. Once this process of removal begins, we awaken an internal voice of authority that immediately begins to compete with every external authority in our lives, which can throw us into internal turmoil, or even "spiritual schizophrenia."

One man, a social worker, contacted me because he had sensed the presence of angels around him. He had become overwhelmed with a feeling that he was really doing nothing at all to help the poor and desperate people who filled his working hours. "I came home one night, and I fell down on my knees and said to God, 'Are You with these people at all? Can You hear their prayers? They need help, and I feel so helpless.' The next day, as I sat with this one person, trying to help her cope with the struggles in her life, I saw an angel next to her. This angel was smiling. I was stunned. I continued to talk to her as if nothing unusual were going on, but I couldn't contain this ridiculous sense of ecstasy that begin to fill me up. I kept repeating to her, 'Believe me, I know you're going to be fine,' and then she said, 'You know, I do believe, I honestly do,' and then she walked out smiling. I now see angels everywhere. I wish I could tell everyone that they are surrounded by heaven. Before that experience I was in such despair. I had faith, but I also had despair. I know that sounds like a contradiction, but it isn't. I just wanted to do more, from the bottom of my heart."

Spiritual Awakening

Much has been written about the nature of the personal spiritual journey, but one of the first works remains one of the best known: *The Dark Night of the Soul*, written in the sixteenth century by Saint John of the Cross. In this classic work the author articulated the stages of separation from the tribal or group mind (my terminology) that are necessary in order to form a fully conscious bond with the

Divine. At each stage come experiences of exquisite mystical transcendence as well as feelings of depression, madness, and extraordinary isolation unknown to ordinary human experience.

Within the Catholic tradition the work of Saint John of the Cross to some extent gave permission to individuals to separate themselves from group religious experiences and seek personal spiritual development. Monastic life had become a way of transcending the ordinary religious parameters of understanding God to encounter the Divine directly. In the centuries that followed, as Europeans encountered other cultures, it became clear that intense prayer, self-exploration, and self-discipline led to mystical experiences in all cultures.

Like official religious leaders, monasteries and ashrams "contain" the power of the Divine within well-guarded walls. People who reported having visions, hearing voices, experiencing unusually intense telepathic communication, and healing through prayer and touch simultaneously fasted to near-starvation states, meditated for weeks at a time, and fell into depressions that would have brought ordinary mortals to the brink of suicide. Observers, even those inside the monasteries, kept their distance from some of these mystics, lest the "eye of the Divine" blink in their direction. It was well known that few could endure "direct contact" with heaven.

In the 1960s the Vatican Council II was a turning point in the Western religious world. This gathering of the Roman Catholic hierarchy disbanded many centuries-old traditions and initiated a new spiritual freedom for all, regardless of religious background. The word *catholic* alone connotes "universality" of thought—a particularly potent symbol, considering that the Roman Catholic religion was the original Christian church. Now, through Vatican II, this original power structure was transmitting a message of universal spiritual liberalism.

People around the world began to challenge the limits of their own religious traditions and explore the spiritual teachings of others.

Women sought ordination; Christians flocked to Zen Buddhist monasteries and Hindu ashrams; Buddhists and Hindus sought Christian teachings; religious leaders from Eastern and Western traditions held official meetings. Barriers between the East and the West were being broken, not only by rebellious lay people but also by scholars, such as the late Trappist monk Thomas Merton, who in his classic work, *The Asian Journal of Thomas Merton*, articulated the need to explore the mutual truths of Buddhism and Christianity.

For spiritually oriented individuals this new spiritual freedom marked a turning point in the ability to "know God," with revolutionary implications unparalleled since Martin Luther's rebellion. As the "unordained" learned the skills required to interpret the deeper meaning of the scriptures, the education of laypeople weakened the role of the ordained or official religious leader. Symbolically, the walls of the monasteries—which had long contained the most intense form of "Divine Light"—came tumbling down. Indeed, in the 1950s, the Chinese invaded Tibet, forcing the Dalai Lama to flee his monastic home. While this exiling of the country's spiritual leader has been among the most painful chapters of Tibetan history, the teachings of the Dalai Lama and many other gifted teachers have entered and influenced the world's spiritual communities. The Divine Light was released into the lives of countless "mystics without monasteries"—laypeople who embrace extraordinary spiritual teachings within the privacy of their personal lives.

This shift from religion to spirituality is not simply a cultural trend. It is an archetypal reorganization of our planetary community, which now has access to the universal truths available through symbolic sight. Symbolic sight includes a sixth sense of intuition, which senses the connections among all living energy systems.

In one of my workshops, a woman spoke about her connection to nature. "Each day, as I prepare to work in my garden, I say a prayer to invoke the assistance of spirits that are the guardians of nature, and I sense immediately that these energetic beings are next to me. Had someone told me years ago that I would be saying things like this, I would have said they were crazy. But eight years ago, after I witnessed an environmental disaster, I became over-whelmed with grief, unlike any I had known in my life. I couldn't release it. Then one afternoon, as I was walking through the woods, I heard a voice that sounded as if it were knee-high. It said, 'Help us.' I wept because I understood down to my soul that the nature kingdom itself was talking to me. That evening I contacted my boss and turned in my resignation as a store manager. I never even gave a thought as to how I would support myself. I simply had to follow that voice. I then said a prayer asking to be shown a path to help nature. Within two weeks a person I knew only casually at that time asked me if I had any interest in starting a business growing and selling herbs. That was the beginning of my life, as far as I'm concerned."

This intuitive sense of connection is moving us as a planet toward a *holistic* understanding of health and disease, of the environment and its biodiversity, and of social priorities for service and charity. This movement toward working as "one world" is an extension of the release of the Divine Light into the world. It seems as though humanity is "under orders" to mature spiritually to a level of holistic sight and service, and any number of paths of service to fulfill those orders have opened up to us.

One mystic who is working at a global political level to bring peo-ple and countries together and make the world a better place is Jim Garrison, forty-four, president of the Gorbachev Foundation, presi-dent of the International Foreign Policy Association, and chairman and CEO of the Diomedes Corporation. Jim is also a theologian who earned his doctorate in theology from Cambridge University. His accomplishments include inspiring Mikhail Gorbachev to start the Gorbachev Foundation, creating a space-bridge for American astro-nauts and (formerly) Soviet cosmonauts, and originating the First Global Forum, a gathering where numerous world leaders—such as

George Bush, Margaret Thatcher, and Mikhail Gorbachev—meet with powerful voices of the spirit, such as Deepak Chopra and Thich Nhat Hanh, to discuss a new vision for our global society. Jim is a man fueled by vision and the power of the human spirit.

Born in China, the child of American missionary parents, Jim describes his first spiritual experience this way: "At age five I wandered into a Buddhist temple in a small village in Taiwan, where for the first time I saw a monk meditating. As I watched him, I noticed a fly crawling over his face, and it captivated me because the monk did not twitch a muscle. The fly flew off his face and then returned, and still the monk never moved. I realized that this man was in a different place. I sat in the temple and continued to watch him, and all I could think was, 'Where is he?'

"That next Sunday, as my father was preaching during the service, I realized that I didn't believe in what my father was preaching. I suddenly knew that the Orient was a treasure trove of truth and that the East was a culture that should be honored, not converted. I was eventually sent to a Protestant boarding school, and at age seven I was beaten severely because I would not agree with what the missionaries were teaching about God. During that experience the image of that monk returned to my mind, reminding me of a place that we can go that is beyond time and space. That image helped me survive boarding school.

"When I was nine, I became argumentative about theological issues. I remember coming to the defense of a Catholic girl named Jackie who was also a student at my boarding school. The other students told her that she was going to hell because she was Catholic, and I said that no one who believes in God goes to hell. I said that it didn't matter that she was a Catholic. Because of that I was put in solitary confinement for two weeks. Shortly afterward one of the dorm mothers gathered all the other children together in a room to give them candy. From the next room I heard her tell the children that they could have more candy if they would agree not to play with me until I accepted Christ. Again the image of the monk came into my mind, reminding me that there is a place beyond circumstance where you can go to survive the outside world.

"Once I began to go to that place, I began to learn the virtues: that when confronted by small-mindedness, your task is to be part of the Light—to protect others, to stand up to others whose ideas are negative. Out of that insight came the notion of social justice that is now my life. I believe we are vessels through which Spirit is working to accomplish tasks for the furthering of human development. That's the only thing I've ever done with my life. I believe my spiritual life and work began because I refused to release the authenticity of the experience with that monk. Somehow, on the day that I saw him, I must have gone with him to that inner place. Since that time I have never returned to ordinary consciousness. I believe that sometimes we need to meditate, sometimes we need to pray, and sometimes we need to face our challenges on the street, so to speak. Other times we have to adore creation and the multiplicity of Divinity. This is the task of the human spirit."

Jim lives as a contemporary mystic. As he gathered world leaders together at the First Global Forum, to "thoughtfully consider the next phase of human development," he was a model of the full potential of the human spirit and the capacity of one person armed with faith to make a difference in healing this planet.

Spiritual Crisis and the Need for Devotion

The "symptomology" of a spiritual crisis is almost identical to that of a psychological crisis. In fact, since a spiritual crisis naturally involves the psyche, a "beginning mystic" may be unaware that the crisis is spiritual in nature and may describe his or her dilemma as psychological. The symptoms of a spiritual crisis are distinct, however, and threefold.

The crisis usually begins with an awareness of an *absence of meaning and purpose* that cannot be remedied merely by shuffling the external components of one's life. One feels a much deeper longing, one that cannot be satisfied by the prospect of a raise or promotion, marriage or new relationship. Ordinary solutions hold no attraction. Of course, some people have never found meaning and purpose in life, but these people are probably wrongly expecting life to deliver "meaning" to their doorstep. Chronic complainers and people who lack ambition are not suffering from a spiritual crisis. Those who are in a spiritual crisis, however, have a feeling that something is trying to wake up inside them. They just don't know how to see it.

Strange new fears are the second symptom of a spiritual crisis. These fears are not ordinary, such as fears of abandonment and aging; rather, they make a person feel as if he or she is losing touch with a sense of *self* or *identity*. "I am no longer sure of who I am and of what I want out of life" is a standard report from a person saturated with the energy of the seventh chakra.

The third symptom is the need to experience *devotion* to something greater than oneself. The many psychological texts available today that describe human needs rarely mention our fundamental need for devotion, yet we all biologically and energetically need to be in contact with a source of power that transcends human limitations and turmoil. We need to be in touch with a source of miracles and hope. Devotion commits a part of our conscious minds to our unconscious eternal self, which in turn connects us directly to a Divine presence. Even brief and fleeting encounters with this presence and its infinite power help our conscious mind release its fears of life, and human power ceases to command our attention.

Our need to be devoted to a higher power has found numerous inappropriate surrogates: devotion to a corporation, a political party, an athletic team, a personal exercise program, even a street gang. All these earthbound surrogates will eventually fail the devotee. No matter how much you exercise, you will age. You may remain healthy in the process, but you will still get older. And much of the anguish people suffer when they are let go from companies they have served loyally for years undoubtedly occurs because their loyalty contained an unconscious devotion. We expect our devotions to earthly things and people to return to us a quality of power that can take care of all our woes, but no human being or organization commands such power. No guru, minister, or priest can manage the energy of devotees for long without some form of scandal. We are not meant to be devoted to a human being; devotion is meant to be directed upward and to take us with it.

The absence of meaning, the loss of self-identity, and the need for devotion are the three strongest symptoms indicating a person has entered into the "dark night." Certainly these characteristics are similar to common psychological dilemmas that people experience. Yet when their root is spiritual, the person *lacks the motivation to blame other people* for causing the crisis. Rather, he or she realizes that the cause of the crisis is within. The inadequacy of the external components of the person's life is a *consequence* of the spiritual crisis, not the *cause*.

A skilled spiritual director can help a person get through the "dark night," many of whose challenges involve facing intense psychological issues. Standard psychological counseling would seek the cause by looking into the negative patterns in his or her relationships, from childhood onward. While identifying these negative patterns is certainly helpful in spiritual counseling as well, a spiritual director investigates, as a priority, the content of a person's inner dialogue related to matters of the spirit, such as:

What questions have you asked that seek insight into
    your life's purpose?
What fears do you have related to your understanding
    of God?
Have you judged your life as meaningless when you eval-
    uate it within a spiritual context?

What spiritual fantasies do you have? Do you, for example, believe that seeking a spiritual path makes you
superior to other people, or that it makes God
more aware of you than of others who are not as
involved in a spiritual path as you are?

Have you asked, in the privacy of your prayers or
thoughts, for insights into the reasons you find it
difficult to have faith in God?

Do you feel that you have, in some way, failed in the
choices that you have made for yourself?

Are you conscious of ever having violated your own spiritual rules?

Have you ever desired to be healed?

Have you ever desired to know God in a deeper way than
you presently do?

These are not ordinary psychological questions. One can become
more open to receiving the answers to them by reorganizing one's
life in ways that remove mental and emotional blockages. That reorganization will at first make one feel worse as one experiences the
"dark night of the soul," through which one comes to know the content of his or her mind and heart, confronts fears and beliefs, consciously pursues the shadow side and challenges false gods who do
not give up their hold upon the human psyche without a fight.

Illness is often a catalyst of spiritual transformation and the "dark
night." Per, now forty-nine, designs ocean liners—a career that has
brought him great financial success. For years, Per traveled the
world, dealing with powerful businesspeople and enjoying a glitter-
ing social life. Then at forty-three, Per was diagnosed as HIV positive. Within a year of his diagnosis, his mother, to whom he had been
very close, passed away. The combination of these two traumatic
events sent Per into despair and depression.

Prior to that tragic year, Per had had no spiritual life to speak of.

As he would say, that dimension served no purpose in his life. After his mother died, however, he sought the assistance of a minister but drew little comfort from his family's religious background.

Simultaneously Per continued to work, telling no one of his physical and spiritual condition. He became more withdrawn and more frightened that people might find out about his illness. The combination of fear and loneliness drove Per to a near breakdown. He cut back on his work commitments and decided that he had to get away from the city for a while. So he returned to his mother's country home, which was located in a fairly isolated spot in the mountains. To keep himself busy, Per renovated the house. During the evening the only thing he could do to fill in the time was read, so one morning he headed into the nearest city to find a bookstore. That was his introduction to alternative health and spiritual literature.

Per returned to his mother's place loaded with reading material and for months did nothing but educate himself on alternative health care, including the healing benefits of meditation and visualization. Inspired, Per began to meditate. At the same time he changed his eating habits to a strict healing diet. With his isolation, meditation, and dedication to macrobiotics, he adopted a lifestyle similar to that of a monk.

As the months went by, Per felt growing optimism and hope. He practiced keeping his spirit "in the present moment" and consciously did all that he could to rid himself of his unfinished business. During his meditations he began to experience a transcendent state of consciousness. At first he had no idea what was happening to him, only that the sensations were wonderful.

Per began to read books on mysticism and discovered descriptions of mystical experiences that came close to his transcendent state. Then, during a meditation in which Per says he "visited heaven," he felt his spirit separate from his body and enter into a dimension of "ecstasy beyond human consciousness." In that state, all Per's fear disintegrated, and he felt "eternally alive."

Afterward Per decided to return to work. With each passing day, he felt physically stronger and stronger. He returned to his physician for another blood test, and although his blood still contained the AIDS virus, his immune system had returned to a maximum state of health. Per now describes himself as "more fully alive, now that I have faced death," than he ever had been before. His entire life is centered around his spiritual practice, he says, and even his creativity has reached a new level.

"I don't know how long I will live," Per told me, "but the truth is, even if I didn't have this virus, I wouldn't know. I believe, ironically, that this virus has made me spiritually healthy. I live more fully alive each day than I ever did before, and I feel a connection to a place that is more real to me than this earth and this life. If someone offered me all that I now know and experience and then said that the only way I could get to this place was by becoming HIV positive, I believe I would agree because this inner place is so much more real than anything I ever experienced before."

Per's spiritual journey not only embodies the "dark night," it radiates the power of the spirit to become stronger than the body. His is the saga of a man who found a spiritual avenue for what he had long been missing: a devotion to something greater than himself.

Enduring the "Dark Night"

Enduring the "dark night" requires faith, prayer, and if at all possible, a spiritual director. If finding a spiritual director is impossible, you can turn to spiritual literature for support. (See the bibliography on page 295.) Finding a person who understands the nature of the journey can feel like finding a life raft. Keep a journal, record your thoughts and your prayers, and above all, hold on to the truth that all dark nights end with a light illuminating a new path.

Become devoted to a daily form of prayer with which you feel comfortable. Devotion—not obsession, but devotion—is an extremely healing and comforting force. Pray at specific times each day: upon rising, perhaps at midday, and prior to going to sleep. The quality of the prayer is measured not in time but in intention. Even five minutes each morning and evening is sufficient. If certain prayers bring you a sense of tranquillity, then make those prayers a part of your daily devotion.

Ron, fifty-seven, is a former Catholic priest who earned a national reputation because he had the ability to heal people. He discovered he had this ability when he was a young priest. He describes his first experience as a healer this way:

"In the spring of 1976 I was asked to deliver to a group of people from various religious backgrounds a lecture on the power of God. At the time, I was involved in bridging the gap between different religious traditions. At the conclusion of my lecture, a man asked if I would 'pray for the sick who were in the audience.' I assumed he was asking me if I would pray for these people in the privacy of my home, so I assured him that I would. As soon as I answered him, he went to the podium and announced that 'Ron would be delighted to pray for the healing of those in the audience who are sick.'

"When he made that announcement, I almost had a cardiac arrest. Theologically I believed in the power of God, but the 'power of God to heal' was another matter. Approximately two hundred of the nearly four hundred people in attendance come forward for this time of prayer. Not knowing what to do, I asked for direction and was intuitively guided to simply lay my hands on people and let the power of God do whatever needed to be done.

"I clearly recall the first person standing before me. I laid one hand on her head and—out of habit—made the sign of the cross over her body with my other hand. I felt nothing but fear and moved swiftly through the crowd so that I might make a quick exit. Approximately four months later this same woman showed up on the doorstep of my church to share with me what had since transpired in her life. She had felt something like a lightning bolt pass through her body that day, accompanied by an inner voice that told her to return to her doctor for further tests. She did so, only to find she was fully healed from her cancer. I was awestruck.

"From that time, my life took a direction I had not consciously charted. Spiritual healing became my major focus. People began coming to me for help, and although I did not understand how I could provide this help, a phrase from the prayer of Saint Francis embedded itself into my consciousness: 'Make me a channel of your peace.' This prayer suggested that I needed to surrender to a force far greater than myself that I could trust to do the work. I just needed to offer that 'spiritual force' a vehicle through which to operate."

Ron's "dark night" began in 1987, when he realized he wanted to leave the priesthood. A series of events led him to believe that he could not survive the political atmosphere of the church or adhere to its teachings, which he felt were incompatible with the teachings of Jesus.

"I was literally filled with despair, depression, and feelings of inadequacy," said Ron. "Yet this was not enough to get me to leave, for fear of what others, particularly my family, would say. I was living in fear of the tribal mind, yet it turned out that when I did leave, I had my family's support.

"Then a series of events forced me to confront myself, my lone-liness, in a difficult situation that brought everything to a head. I really believed I was committed to advancing my spiritual conscious-ness, but a deep conflict developed between a particular bishop and myself. During that same time I received an invitation to appear on the Joan Rivers talk show. I was by then having an identity crisis. I had spent twenty-five years as a priest, but Joan Rivers introduced me as a spiritual healer who heals with prayer. It was as if someone had hit me with a hammer and said, 'This is your identity now.' That was when the light began to come back into my life.

"While I was flying home from New York after doing that TV show, I decided to leave the priesthood. Shortly afterward I met a deeply spiritual teacher who told me that I would be able to transcend religion and be more credible that way than as a priest—a comment that shocked me. Although I have left the institutional priesthood, I still feel that I am a priest in the deepest meaning of 'ordination.'

"Coming out of this tomb, I set out on the path of a spiritual healer. I let go of every attachment of which I knew. I kept the mystical truths that I learned while a priest, but I let go of the religious teachings. New opportunities immediately began to open to me, such as within the medical community."

Ron is now a leading voice in healing, not only for people who need his help in healing but for those who are motivated to become healers themselves. His insights into the nature of healing through prayer are of value to everyone:

"First, let me define what it means to be an ordained healer. An ordained healer is one who is open to the energy of God through prayer and utilizes that energy to heal individuals as well as the planet. Many people who refer to themselves as healers, although well-meaning, are not what I would call 'ordained' healers. The signature of the ordained healer is having gone through a 'dark night' and endured the sensation of abandonment by God. The significance of abandonment, I now realize, is that it represents a question from God: 'Are you capable of believing in Me even in the darkest night?'

"Your own spirit breaks during the abandonment, and you realize that the only way through that hell is to turn back to God and accept the terms of the Divine, regardless of what heaven asks of you from that point forward. The memory of the 'dark night' remains in your consciousness as a reference point, keeping you aligned to God, humble, and forever aware that resurrection can come at any time, no matter how dark the night.

"What type of people seek my help? People with terminal illnesses come to me—and incidentally, the vast majority of them feel abandoned by God as well as punished by God. Their attitude implies, 'If this is what God wants, I can accept it,' but they certainly don't mean it. Their conflict is obvious, but beyond their physical illness, they are terrified to learn why their spirit is in such pain. Some find the courage to say to God, while I pray over them, 'I am willing to take Your grace and use it as Jesus did, to heal my fears and forgive those I need to.' I suspect they receive the grace that destroys physical illness.

"What does healing through prayer actually mean? It means invoking the energy of God to 'grace us' in a way that allows us to feel more powerful than the illness.

"Can all illnesses be healed? Yes, of course, but that doesn't mean every illness *will* be healed. Sometimes a person has to endure the illness for reasons that help that person confront his or her own fears and negativity. And sometimes it is time for the person to die. Death is not the enemy; fear of death is. Death may well be the ultimate experience of abandonment—which is the reason we are compelled to try to contact those who have gone before, to make sure we will have a greeting party when we arrive.

"Is healing through prayer going to become increasingly credible as a consequence of this New Age of spiritual consciousness? Yes, if we understand what authentic prayer is all about. Prayer represents one's conscious connection with God. Authentic prayer does not mean to turn to God in order to get something; it means to turn to God in order to be with someone. Prayer is not so much our words to God as our life with God. When this is understood, then prayer becomes 'energy medicine.'

"Once they leave me, people need to continue their own prayer life with God. Thinking of me as the responsible one, or thinking that I have a power they lack, is a mistake that comes from thinking of priests as having a deeper connection to God than ordinary mortals. This is an error and a grave mistake. The individual must seek a personal and responsible spiritual life. I just 'jump-start' the energy, but the person must keep the vehicle operational."

Ron's work represents the reemergence of a form of healing that has always existed and was always meant to exist: being healed through faith, in the present moment.

Our goal while on this earth is to transcend our illusions and discover the innate power of our spirit. We are responsible for what we create, and we must therefore learn to act and think with love and wisdom and to live in service to others and all of life.

Questions for Self-Examination

1. What questions have you sought guidance with during meditation or moments of prayer?
2. What answers to these questions would you most fear?
3. Do you bargain with God? Do you complain to God more than you express gratitude? Do you tend to pray for specific things rather than pray in appreciation?
4. Are you devoted to a particular spiritual path? If not, do you feel a need to find one? Have you found surrogates to be devoted to? If so, list and evaluate your relationship to them.
5. Do you believe that your God is more authentic than the Divine in other spiritual traditions?
6. Are you waiting for God to send you an explanation for your painful experiences? If so, list those experiences.
7. How would your life change if God suddenly decided to answer your questions? And how would it change if the answer you received was "I have no intention of giving you insight into your questions at this point in your life"? What would you be prepared to do then?

8. Have you started and stopped a meditation practice? If so, what are the reasons that you failed to maintain it?
9. What spiritual truths are you aware of that you do not live by? List them.
10. Are you afraid of a closer spiritual connection to the Divine because of the changes that it might trigger in your life?

A Guide for the Contemporary Mystic

I know that I'm not the first to announce that this is a most exciting time to be alive. We are living in a time unlike any that have come before. We are living between two paradigms of power, or two paradigms of reality—internal and external, energetic and physical. We are restructuring ourselves and our relationships to personal and spiritual authority. Inevitably, that restructuring will reshape every aspect of our world culture in accordance with the sacred truth *All Is One*.

The fact that our global society is now saturated with crises that touch every nation, every organ, and every system in our global "body" has symbolic significance. Nuclear poisoning, the shortage of fresh water, environmental concerns, and the thinning of the ozone layer are just the first of many issues that are no longer national in scope but global. At the macrocosmic level the threat of global disasters is forcing us to create a politics of unity, much as an individual faced with a serious illness must unite all the powers of his body and his life in order to survive. We have reached the end of the "divide and conquer" system of power, and that system is being replaced by an attempt to unite the powers of the different nations in order to survive and move safely into the next millennium. Our interconnected "information age" is the symbol of a global consciousness.

Information technology is a physical representation of our energy interactions. We have created on the outside what already exists in our energy fields. Energy information is used everywhere: in holistic models of health; in corporate "health and development" programs and seminars for teaching positive attitudes; in athletic training where mental attitudes and visualization skills are considered as important as players' physical skills. Whether motivated by money, a desire to win a sports event, or the need to heal an illness, pioneers in every field are turning to energy solutions to maximize physical results.

Seen from our first chakras, the energy age of civilization is an "information age," supported by the computerization of businesses, classrooms, and households. From our seventh chakra, however, we can see it as an age of consciousness that requires the energy management skills of the mystic: prayer, meditation, continual self-examination, and unity of all people. Ironically, both eras are the same; we are all on the same path.

Guidance for the Contemporary Mystic

Think in a vocabulary of oneness.

Look through the lens of symbolic sight. Remind yourself that all physical and emotional obstacles are illusions. Always seek the energy meaning of a situation, and follow it.

Evaluate your daily choices and the consequences of those choices for your energy system. This will help you sense when you are losing energy to fear or negative thinking.

Look at the sacred text of your biological energy system (see figure 6) for daily guidance. Keep in mind the seven sacred truths of the body and spirit:

1. All Is One
2. Honor One Another
3. Honor Oneself
4. Love Is Divine Power
5. Surrender Personal Will to Divine Will
6. Seek Only the Truth
7. Live in the Present Moment

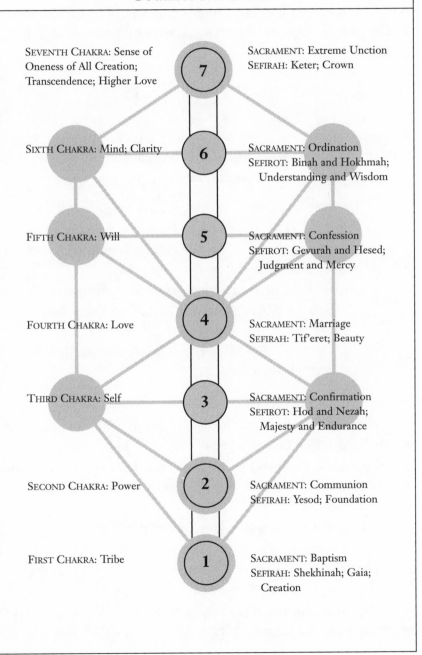

FIGURE 6: THE HUMAN ENERGY SYSTEM:
CORRESPONDENCES

SEVENTH CHAKRA: Sense of
Oneness of All Creation;
Transcendence; Higher Love

SACRAMENT: Extreme Unction
SEFIRAH: Keter; Crown

SIXTH CHAKRA: Mind; Clarity

SACRAMENT: Ordination
SEFIROT: Binah and Hokhmah;
Understanding and Wisdom

FIFTH CHAKRA: Will

SACRAMENT: Confession
SEFIROT: Gevurah and Hesed;
Judgment and Mercy

FOURTH CHAKRA: Love

SACRAMENT: Marriage
SEFIRAH: Tif'eret; Beauty

THIRD CHAKRA: Self

SACRAMENT: Confirmation
SEFIROT: Hod and Nezah;
Majesty and Endurance

SECOND CHAKRA: Power

SACRAMENT: Communion
SEFIRAH: Yesod; Foundation

FIRST CHAKRA: Tribe

SACRAMENT: Baptism
SEFIRAH: Shekhinah; Gaia;
Creation

Simple and powerful, these truths help focus the mind, body, and spirit back to a contact point with Divine awareness. So long as you use these truths as reference points, you can evaluate any loss of power and retrieve your spirit by consciously recognizing which truth you are not honoring.

A Daily Meditation

Finally, as a daily act of meditation, draw your attention consciously into each of your chakras, beginning with the first and working your way up. As you focus your attention:

1. Ask yourself the following questions: "Am I losing energy? If so, what fear is drawing power from this part of my body?" Take a deep breath and consciously disconnect your energy from that fear.
2. Invoke the protective energies of the spiritual guardians, the sefirot or sacrament, of that particular chakra.
3. Enter consciously into the energy of that chakra and sense the quality of energy activity increasing in that part of your body.

Proceed through the chakras, focusing in the following ways:

For chakra one, focus on the energy of the sefirah of Shekhinah, and feel yourself connected to all of life. Then focus on the symbolic meaning of the sacrament of Baptism, and bless the life you have agreed to live, and the family, both personal and extended, that makes up your life.

For chakra two, focus on the energy of the sefirah of Yesod, and sense the energy you have released from this area of your body into acts of creation. If your energy is contaminated—filled with negativity and fear—reexamine your intention. Bring into your mind the energy of the sacrament of Communion: see each person in your life as having a Divine purpose. Wherever you cannot see that Divinity clearly, ask for the energy to see through the illusions that are controlling you.

For chakra three, focus on the energy of the sefirot of Nezah and Hod, integrity and endurance. Evaluate your own code of behavior and whether you have compromised your honor in any way. If so, meditate on the significance of honor, and ask for assistance in maintaining your personal standards. Then bring into your mind the energy of the sacrament of Confirmation, a commitment to yourself to honor your own dignity.

For chakra four, focus on the energy of the sefirah of Tif'eret and the energy of love and compassion. Evaluate how well you extend love to others as well as to yourself, including the loving energy contained within acts of forgiveness. Then focus on the care you give yourself and how well you honor your symbolic vow of the sacrament of Marriage to yourself.

For chakra five, focus on the energy of the sefirot of Hesed and Gevurah, mercy and judgment, and evaluate the quality of the thoughts you are holding about other people, as well as yourself. Evaluate the words you have shared with others, and if you have expressed harmful words, send positive energy to those people. If you have expressed false words, consciously acknowledge that you have acted to deceive others, and examine the fear that exists within you, from which deceitful actions emerge. This is utilizing the energy of the sacrament of Confession. Ask the Light to enter that fear and give you the courage not to act in that negative pattern again.

For chakra six, focus on the energy of the sefirot of Hokhmah and Binah, Divine wisdom and understanding, and continue to evaluate your daily life. Request wisdom and insight for the situations in which you feel confused or frightened. And remind yourself of the promise of the sacrament of Ordination: that each of us has a special gift to give to this life and that each of us is inevitably led to that path. It is impossible to miss our life's purpose.

For chakra seven, focus on the energy of the sefirah of Keter,

your contact with the Divine, and the sacrament of Extreme Unction, consciously completing and releasing your unfinished business.
Allow the energy of God to enter into your mind, body, and spirit,
and breathe that energy into your being.

In this daily meditation practice, you will evaluate the health of
your body, your mind, and your spirit. Working with this meditation
will let you feel the health of your spirit and your body. With it you
can work to increase your awareness of the balance of power within
your energy system.

In addition, remind yourself on a regular basis of the archetype of
the Promised Land. This archetype is not meant to inspire us to seek
out a "one-time" physical solution to all our problems. It is meant to
draw us into ourselves to discover the power behind our eyes. We can
transcend every dilemma through the power of our spirits; that is a
Divine promise.

Through this self-evaluation you will develop the skill of reading
energy and sensing intuitive guidance. Developing this skill requires
daily practice—in times of crisis, even hourly. This simple act of
awareness, coupled with a conscious commitment to learn from
your experiences, will weaken your fears and strengthen your spirit.

Above all else, as you learn the language of your spirit, establish
a code of honor for yourself that reflects the spiritual content of your
biology. This age of consciousness is not pushing us merely to
indulge in new spiritual theories or play thought games that unite
physics with Zen Buddhism. We are meant to move toward self-
discovery and spiritual maturity, to be ready and able to live a life that
matters to us and those around us.

We contain the scripture. We contain Divinity. We are Divinity.
We are the church, the synagogue, the ashram. We need but close
our eyes and feel the energy of the sacraments, the sefirot, the
chakras, as the origin of our own power—as the energy that fuels our
biology. Ironically, once we realize the stuff of which we are made,
we have no choice but to live a spiritual life.

Acknowledgments

I am grateful to so many people who have been part of writing this book and supporting my work. To my agent, Ned Leavitt, I extend my deepest gratitude for leading the way into this project and for being a person of such fine integrity and skill. To my editor, Leslie Meredith, I will be forever grateful for so very much—her endless optimism, her refined talent, her warm and caring spirit. But mostly I will always hold a special place for her in my heart because of her capacity to understand the vision I needed to give birth to in this book, especially since I redirected the manuscript in midstream, and she was able to embrace the idea. I admire her scholarly nature enormously and her genuine dedication to bringing the work of her authors to the public, my own included. My thanks also to Karin Wood, assistant editor, for her many kind words and her tremendous efficiency. I am also deeply indebted to Janet Biehl for her extraordinary copyediting skills. And to my personal editor, Dorothy Mills, I extend a heart full of love and gratitude, both for her professional support and for her friendship. Dorothy has become a resource of strength and optimism for me, and I will forever be grateful to fate for introducing the two of us so many years ago.

C. Norman Shealy, M.D., Ph.D., has been my research colleague for more than ten years. He is also one of my dearest friends, a confidant, a counselor, a guide. I do not believe I would be doing this work today if he had not become a part of my life. Thanks are not enough for what I feel for all he has given to me. To his wonderful wife, Mary-Charlotte, who has become a dear friend and an integral part of our work, I extend my warmest appreciation. And to Roberta Howard, our Virgo-skilled secretary, my sincere gratitude for all that you do to assist our work.

My life is filled with friends I both love and admire and whose lives and work have been a constant source of inspiration for me. Christiane Northrup, M.D., a gifted physician and author, asked me to work with her five years ago. Since that time we have continued to learn together, and I have found in her a source of great humor and energy, as well as dedication to holistic medicine.

Joan Borysenko, Ph.D., has touched my heart deeply with her constant words of support for my work, a sentiment that is mutual. Mona Lisa Schulz, M.D., Ph.D., a visionary and brilliant woman, has given me personal courage when I needed it most and taught me so much about the path of healing. Ron Roth, a gifted healer, and Paul Fundson, a dear friend, have been the backbone of my spiritual support, and I will always appreciate their presence in my life, especially during the darker times, which were many these last two years.

I met Clarissa Pinkola Estés, Ph.D., shortly before beginning this book. I have found in her a lifetime friend, and I am ever so thankful for her wit, wisdom, genius, and depth of spirit, as well as the bond of faith we share in our spiritual heritage. And to Tami Simon, the founder of Sounds True Recording, I extend an endless stream of gratitude and love for her support of my work, for her friendship, for her honorable spirit, and for her generous nature.

I also wish to extend my gratitude to Elmer Green, Ph.D., the "father" of the biofeedback movement, who has served as a faculty adviser during this project. Dr. Green is world renowned for his contributions to the human consciousness field, and I consider it an honor to have his support all these many years for my work.

Nancy W. Bartlett, a computer wizard, came to my rescue continually during the creation of this book. I thank her from the bottom of my heart for her many trips to my home and for her patience with my lack of skill and my inability to learn the simplest of computer instructions. And I thank the wonderful team at Danny's Deli for supplying me with my daily allotment of cappuccino—with no cinnamon. You'll never know how much your warmth and hospitality helped to make me feel at home again in the neighborhood I grew up in.

To M. A. Bjorkman, Rhea Baskin, Carol Simmons, Kathalin Walker, and the rest of the team of The Conference Works, all my love. I have found in your organization a quality of care that has touched me more than I can say. Working with you is more than a pleasure, not just because of your genuine concern for my well-being but because of your honor and integrity as business associates. You are a blessing in my life.

And to so many of my dear friends, who have only and always been treasures in my life, treasures I have especially appreciated during the writing of this book, I am forever grateful: Eileen Kee, Susie Marco, Kathy Musker, Reverend Suzanne Fageol, David Luce, Jim Garrison, Penny Tompkins, Lynn Bell, Carole Dean, Carol Hasler, Ron Roth, Paul Fundsen, Tom Williams, Peter Brey, Kaare Sorenson, Kevin Todeshi, John May, Sabine Kurjo, Siska Pothoff, Judy Buttner, Paula Daleo, Fred Matzer, DeLacy Sarantos, and the many others who make my life a rich tapestry of friendship.

Also, I extend an endless stream of gratitude to the many people who support my work by attending my workshops and lectures. No words can communicate the appreciation I feel toward all of you, who have played such a significant role in helping me to refine my work. Without your enthusiasm and your feedback, I would not have had the inspiration to continue to develop and teach this material.

And to the many people I have neglected during these past two years due to a schedule that has kept me from answering letters and phone calls, my deepest apologies.

Mostly, however, I want to acknowledge the love and support that

I have always received from my family, especially my dear mother. I consider my mother to be one of God's direct blessings in my life. Her care, love, strength of character, bottomless heart, and limitless energy have helped me not only to write this book but to heal myself. She has always opened her heart to my ideas, no matter how radical they were. I recall with such warmth the many times we would discuss new ideas about God I had as a graduate student, sometimes into the middle of the night. Never did she discourage my pursuit of truth. And her role model as a woman who knows the intimate power of faith inspires me still. My brother Edward, his wife, Amy, and their children, Rachel, Sarah, and Eddie Jr., fill my life with so much joy as do my nieces Angela and Allison, my nephew Joey, my sister-in-law, Mary Pat, and my brother Joseph. These wonderful people have helped me through very difficult times and knowing all of you are a forever part of my life makes me grateful to be alive. All of you are "home" to me.

And to my dear cousins, whom I love so very much, I thank you for always supporting and encouraging me, even though I realize that half the time you had no idea what I was doing. It just felt good to know you believed in me unconditionally. And so to Marilyn and Mitch, Chrissy and Ritchie, Pam and Andy, Wanda, Mitchie, Father Len, Aunt Virginia, to all the rest, and to my wonderful Aunt Gen who recently left us for heaven, all my love. I am so grateful we have each other.

Selected Bibliography

Achterberg, Jeanne. *Imagery in Healing: Shamanism and Modern Medicine*. Boston: Shambhala Publications, 1985.

Assagioli, Roberto. *Psychosynthesis: A Manual of Principles and Techniques*. New York: Viking Press, 1971.

Atwater, P. M. H. *Coming Back to Life: The After-Effects of the Near-Death Experience*. New York: Dodd, Mead, & Co., 1988.

Bailey, Alice A. *Esoteric Healing*. New York: Lucis Publishing, 1953.

Becker, Robert O., and Gary Sheldon. *The Body Electric: Electromagnatism and the Foundation of Life*. New York: William Morrow, 1985.

Bennet, Hal Zina. *The Doctor Within*. New York: Clarkson N. Potter, 1981.

Benson, Herbert, and William Proctor. *Beyond the Relaxation Response*. New York: Berkeley, 1985.

Berkow, Robert, editor in chief. *The Merck Manual of Diagnosis and Therapy*, 14th ed. West Point, Penn.: Merck, Sharp & Dohme, 1982.

Borysenko, Joan. *Fire in the Soul: A New Psychology of Spiritual Optimism*. New York: Warner Books, 1993.

———. *Guilt Is the Teacher, Love Is the Lesson*. New York: Warner Books, 1988.

———. *Mind the Body, Mending the Mind*. Massachusetts: Addison-Wesley, 1987.

Brennan, Barbara Ann. *Hands of Light: A Guide to Healing Through the Human Energy Field.* New York: Bantam, 1987.

———. *Light Emerging: The Journal of Personal Healing.* New York: Bantam, 1993.

Bruyere, Rosalyn L. *Wheels of Light: A Study of the Chakras.* Arcadia, Calif.: Bon Productions, 1989.

Campbell, Joseph. *The Mythic Image.* Princeton, N.J.: Princeton University Press, 1974.

Cerminara, Gina. *Many Mansions.* New York: New American Library, 1978.

Chopra, Deepak. *Ageless Body, Timeless Mind: The Quantum Alternative to Growing Old.* New York: Harmony Books, 1993.

A Course in Miracles. 2nd rev. ed. Set of 3 vols., including text, teacher's manual, workbook. Found Inner Peace, 1992.

Diamond, Harvey and Marilyn. *Fit for Life.* New York: Warner Books, 1985.

Dossey, Larry. *Healing Words.* San Francisco: HarperCollins, 1993.

———. *Meaning and Medicine: A Doctor's Tales of Breakthrough and Healing.* San Francisco: HarperCollins, 1992.

———. *Space, Time, and Medicine.* Boston: Shambhala Publications, 1982.

Epstein, Gerald. *Healing Visualizations: Creating Health Through Imagery.* New York: Bantam Books, 1989.

Feldenkrais, M. *Body and Mature Behavior.* New York: International Universities Press, 1970.

Gawain, Shakti. *Living in the Light.* San Rafael, Calif.: New World Library, 1986.

Grof, Christina and Stanislav. *The Stormy Search for the Self.* Los Angeles: J. P. Tarcher, 1990.

Harman, Willis. *Global Mind Change.* Indianapolis: Knowledge Systems, 1988.

Hay, Louise L. *You Can Heal Your Life.* Santa Monica, Calif.: Hay House, 1982.

Jaffee, Dennis. *Healing from Within: Psychological Techniques to Help the Mind Heal the Body.* New York: Simon & Schuster, 1980.

James, William. *The Varieties of Religious Experience.* New York: New American Library, 1958.

Joy, W. Brugh, M.D. *A Map for the Transformational Journey.* New York: Tarcher/Putnam, 1979.

Krieger, Dolores. *The Therapeutic Touch: How to Use Your Hands to Help or Heal.* Englewood Cliffs, N.J.: Prentice-Hall, 1979.

Kuhlman, Kathryn. *I Believe in Miracles.* New York: Pyramid Books, 1969.

Kunz, Dora. *The Personal Aura.* Wheaton, Ill.: Theosophical Publishing House, 1991.

Leadbetter, C. W. *The Chakras.* Wheaton, Ill.: Theosophical Publishing House, 1974.

Liberman, Jacob. *Light: Medicine of the Future.* Santa Fe: Bear & Co., 1991.

Masters, Roy. *How Your Mind Can Keep You Well.* Los Angeles: Foundation Books, 1972.

McGarey, William A. *The Edgar Cayce Remedies.* New York: Bantam Books, 1983.

Meek, George W. *Healers and the Healing Process.* Wheaton, Ill.: Theosophical Publishing House, 1977.

Merton, Thomas. *The Asian Journal of Thomas Merton.* Naomi B. Stone et al., eds. New York: New Directions, 1973.

Moody, Raymond A., with Paul Perry. *Coming Back: A Psychiatrist Explores Past-Life Journeys.* New York: Bantam Books, 1991.

The New Holistic Health Handbook, ed. Bill Sheperd. Lexington, Mass.: Penguin Books, 1985.

Orstein, Robert, and Cionis Swen. *The Healing Brain.* New York: Guildford Press, 1990.

Peck, M. Scott. *People of the Lie: The Hope for Healing Human Evil.* New York: Touchstone/Simon & Schuster, 1985.

Pelletier, Kenneth. *Mind as Healer, Mind as Slayer*. New York: Delacorte Press, 1980.

Psyche & Symbol: A Selection from the Writings of C. G. Jung, ed. Violet S. de Laszlo. New York: Doubleday & Co., 1958.

Reilly, Harold J., and Ruth H. Brod. *The Edgar Cayce Handbook for Health Through Drugless Therapy*. New York: Berkeley, 1988.

Reincarnation in World Thought, eds. Joseph Head and S. L. Cranston. New York: Julian Press, 1967.

Sagan, Leonard A. *The Health of Nations*. New York: Basic Books, 1987.

Schwarz, Jack. *Voluntary Controls: Exercises for Creative Meditation and for Activating the Potential of the Chakras*. New York: Dutton, 1978.

Selye, Hans. *The Physiology and Pathology of Exposure to Stress*. Montreal: Acta, 1950.

Shealy, C. Norman. *The Self-Healing Workbook: Your Personal Plan for Stress-Free Living*. Rockport, Mass.: Element Books, 1993.

Shealy, C. Norman, and Caroline M. Myss. *The Creation of Health*. Walpole, N.H.: Stillpoint Publishing, 1993.

Sheldrake, Rupert. *A New Science of Life*. Los Angeles: J. P. Tarcher, 1981.

Siegel, Bernie S. *Love, Medicine, and Miracles*. New York: HarperCollins, 1991.

Simonton, O. Carl, and Reid Henson, with Brenda Hampton. *The Healing Journey*. New York: Bantam Books, 1992.

Smith, Huston. *The Religions of Man*. New York: Harper & Row, 1965.

Stearn, Jess. *The Sleeping Prophet*. New York: Doubleday & Co., 1967.

Weil, Andrew. *Health and Healing: Understanding Conventional and Alternative Medicine*. Boston: Houghton Mifflin, 1983.

Weiss, Brian. *Through Time into Healing*. New York: Simon & Schuster, 1992.

Index

About the Author

Caroline Myss, Ph.D., is the author of the best-selling *Anatomy of the Spirit* and *Why People Don't Heal and How They Can* and a pioneer and international lecturer in the fields of energy medicine and human consciousness. Since 1982 she has worked as a medical intuitive: one who "sees" illness in a patient's body by intuitive means. She specializes in assisting people in understanding the emotional, psychological, and physical reasons why their bodies develop illness. She has also worked with Dr. C. Norman Shealy, M.D., Ph.D., founder of the American Holistic Medical Association, in teaching intuitive diagnosis. Together they wrote *The Creation of Health: The Emotional, Psychological, and Spiritual Responses That Promote Health and Healing.* She lives in Oak Park, Illinois.

For information about Caroline Myss's other books, audiotapes and videotapes, and her workshops, please visit her Web site: http://www.myss.com

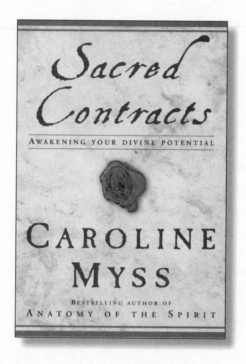